C0-CEU-407

CHICAGO PUBLIC LIBRARY
HAROLD WASHINGTON LIBRARY CENTER

R0017255218

APPLIED SCIENCE &
TECHNOLOGY DEPARTMENT

FORM 125 M

VK549
.M38
Cop. 1

The Chicago Public Library

Received August 27, 1973

A History of Marine Navigation

A History of
Marine Navigation

By

Commander W. E. May
Royal Navy, F.R.Inst.Nav.

With a Chapter on
Modern Developments

by

Captain Leonard Holder
Extra Master, M.R.Inst. Nav.

W. W. Norton & Company, Inc.
New York, New York

First Impression April 1973

© W. E. May pages 1 to 221 and
L. Holder pages 222 to 266 1973.

First American Edition, 1973

VK549
.M38
Cop. 1

ISBN 0-393-03140-3
Printed in Great Britain

THE CHICAGO PUBLIC LIBRARY

APP AUG 27 1973   B

To Commander A. V. Thomas, O.B.E., C.St.J., J.P., D.L., Royal Navy, who has remained my firm friend although we shared an office for many years.
He read this book in type and made many valuable suggestions for its improvement.

Contents

Illustrations

Introduction
The Art of Navigation

Navigation is the art of conducting a ship successfully from one place on the earth's surface to another. I say ship because this book is mainly concerned with the navigation of ships, but navigation is just as much concerned with the conduct of aircraft or even space craft. The technique is different but the basis is the same.

There is often an argument as to whether navigation is an art or a science. I prefer to call it an art, for though modern improvements make the practice of navigation ever more easy, automatic and scientific, for its perfect performance the human element is always a vital factor. Even on the occasion of the first moon landing the captain of the lunar module took over from his instruments and exercised his art in selecting the actual landing place, which was not where science would have placed him.

Art must always have some place in efficient navigation. The exact path that a ship has made through the water can be determined with tolerable accuracy by some instrument, but knowledge and experience are necessary in forecasting what way she will pursue.

The distance travelled by a screw steamship in a given time will be the pitch of her propellor blades multiplied by the number of rotations made, less a percentage amount which may be called the slip. Experience shows that for a given ship the percentage slip will always be the same, provided that all the conditions remain the same and so for a given number of revolutions per minute her speed should be the same. The slip however will be changed by the lading of the ship which will increase her draft and may change her trim so that the ship is deeper in the water forward than aft or vice versa, by the length of time out of dock which will increase marine growth on her bottom and cause increased skin friction, by a head sea which by physical impact may slow her down, and the aftermath of a prolonged gale may well be a surface drift of the sea. All such things the expert navigator will take into account in making his plans and so will exercise his art.

A navigator may utilise his own experience in estimating the effect of these various circumstances upon his ship, or he may make use of the experience of others, but in the end it is a matter of his own judgement. Many years ago I was in a small ship which was ordered to tow a target from Malta to Platea, in Greece, a distance of about 350 miles. My captain said that we would sail at 8.00 on Monday morning and steaming at our usual ten knots would arrive on Tuesday evening. I told him that from some notes left by a predecessor I had ascertained that towing this type of target would reduce the speed of the ship by three knots so that we should not arrive until Wednesday morning. I also mentioned to him that according to the sailing directions we might encounter a southerly set while crossing the mouth of the Adriatic. He knew better. The target could not possibly reduce our speed by more than half a knot and there was never a southerly set. My sights on Tuesday morning showed that we were making exactly seven knots and that if we did not alter course slightly to counter the southerly set we should pass south of the island of Zante instead of north, so adding about another twenty miles to our voyage. The author claims no particular virtue on this occasion; he merely exercised the art of the navigator by taking into account the best information available to him.

There are some who seem to have an extra sense when navigating. A friend of mine had to take a sloop from Malta to Plymouth towing a lighter. Between Malta and Gibraltar he took care to ascertain the effect of the tow upon the speed and handling of his ship. Thereafter the weather was bad and he could get no sights. Off Ushant the tow parted and the wire fouled the sloop's propellor. Good seamanship cleared it and got the lighter in tow again. In the mouth of the Channel the wind dropped and was replaced by a thick fog. My friend told his captain that if land had not been sighted by a certain time they should anchor. This was done and when some hours later the fog lifted there was Plymouth breakwater a cable's length away. He was a true artist!

In the Royal Navy navigation is divided into two kinds — pilotage when in sight of land and true navigation when out of sight. Others may use the expressions coastal and blue water navigation. It makes no difference. The point is that in the first the position of the ship may be fixed with reference to the land while in the latter she can only be fixed by reference to heavenly bodies or by reckoning of the course and distance made good since the last fix. Nowadays the last statement is no longer strictly true since electronic aids are available.

This book can only be considered as a short history of navigation, for to write a complete history would require several large volumes.

What has been done here is to give just an outline of this immense subject. I recommend the reader who wishes to go further to study some of the more detailed works which deal with particular aspects in depth. A list of some of these will be found on page 267.

In my first chapter I will endeavour to give a reasonably consecutive history of the development of navigation, showing how new methods and new instruments have become successively available and how, sometimes after long delays, the practice of navigation gradually improved. In this part I will try to avoid going too deeply into any particular branch of the subject, as to do so would break up the overall picture. Instead, I will use a separate chapter to deal more thoroughly with each aspect.

These specialised chapters naturally vary considerably in length and it will be found that the one entitled 'Direction', which is the one which deals with compasses, is by far the longest. It may be thought that this requires some comment. About sixty years ago when I read *Westward Ho*, that great book of Elizabethan adventure by Charles Kingsley, I was struck by a remark put into the mouth of Salvation Yeo, the old gunner, who said on one occasion: 'It may be that being a gunner I overprize guns.' I have never forgotten it and have sometimes thought that it may be that being an old compass officer I overprize compasses. I am unrepentant. I still feel that this chapter is not too long for its subject.

One other chapter requires some explanation. I personally swallowed the anchor some forty years ago. During that period great strides have been made in the instruments and methods available to the navigator and I have not had practical experience in the use of these at sea. I have, therefore, been extremely lucky in persuading Captain Leonard Holder to undertake the writing of a final chapter on these modern developments. He has the cognizance of present day conditions at sea which I lack and being a lecturer in Navigation at the Liverpool Polytechnic is exceptionally well fitted for the task. I should perhaps make it clear that neither of us has had any responsibility for the work of the other.

I must explain one convention which I always like to use. I find it convenient to print the names of ships of the Royal Navy in capitals while using italics for all others. This avoids the necessity of distinguishing war-ships, in which practices might differ from those of merchant vessels, by any such device as using the expression H.M.S., which if one is pedantic is strictly only correct usage since about 1790.

One
The Practice of Navigation

Navigation must have had its origin in man's desire to avoid having to walk more than need be and to be able to transport heavy loads over considerable distances. First he would wish to travel about, either in search of food or to obtain some substance which he desired and could only obtain by going to the place where it was to be found. It might be that someone else could be forced to give up this desirable commodity or would be willing to exchange it for something else. So trade began. After a while man domesticated animals to carry for him, but where a river flowed through the land he was traversing, what easier than a log to carry him. Originally this would only help him to go down stream but the desire to get to the other side of the river would produce the need of something more manageable and so would come the beginnings of a boat, made by hollowing a log or by tying branches or bundles of reeds together. Next it would be realised that this more manageable craft could be towed or poled up stream so that the movement became two-way. Then someone watching wind blowing across water would notice its effect on floating leaves and so would come the first idea for a sail. And so we come gradually to larger and larger boats, but their handling was still governed by the use of eyes and there was no need for navigational aids.

After a while, however, came boat-handlers who were particularly skilled in this river traffic. They were the men who first noticed that a spit often built up on the inside of a river bend while the swirl of the water scoured out the bottom under the outer bank and gave greater depths. The tyro might try to lessen the distance by cutting close to the inner bank and so would go aground. The experienced man would keep well out to get the advantage of the current and deeper water. But when poling up-stream the case was different. Now the craft needed to keep in water as shallow as possible to make it easier to pole and to avoid the strength of the current. Yet if the water was too shallow the vessel might ground. And so came the first need for a navigational instrument — some means of finding the depth of water.

1

The obvious implement for sounding would be a light rod. There would be no need to graduate it. It was only necessary to judge the length that was wet, or the length above the surface, for it to be possible to tell by eye whether or not one was getting into dangerously shallow water. The use of such a rod would make the handling of a boat in a big river much easier, especially among the mud banks and channels of a delta.

So far we have only considered boat handling in a river. In an archipelago the same needs for water transport would have arisen to enable the inhabitants to reach other visible islands. On the sea it might well be desirable to know the depth of water at depths where a sounding rod of sufficient length would be unwieldy. It is much easier to forestall running aground if one can find the water gradually shoaling before danger is actually reached. The obvious way was to sound with a length of cord attached at first to a stone and much later to a sounding lead.*

The purpose of sea-voyaging would at first only be to reach another island which could be seen, or to save trouble when travelling along a coast, this latter being merely the development of the use of a river. Even in the time of St. Paul it was customary only to make coasting voyages under ordinary circumstances. Sooner or later however someone would get out of sight of land. There are many ways in which this might occur. Of course there are the obvious accidents, such as a boat blown to sea by a sudden storm or one steered in the wrong direction when overtaken by fog or by thick weather at night. Apart from these accidents someone could mistake a cloud for the outline of a land usually hidden and set out to see if living conditions might possibly be better there. There would be the adventurous individual who would leave his island for the next one, see another beyond and go thither and so on until at the last island when there was nothing but an empty horizon he might be tempted to see if there was not something more just beyond. Again it would be noticed that clouds often form over islands, and then that there was often a cloud in a particular direction and a man would come to the conclusion that there must be land below it just beyond the horizon.

So voyages gradually became extended further and further and the next navigational aid came into being. This was the compilation of

---

* "And sounded, and found it twenty fathoms: and when they had gone a little further, they sounded again, and found it fifteen fathoms." St. Paul off Malta, in 62 A.D. *The Acts of the Apostles*, Ch. xxvii, v. 28.

Sailing Directions, the collecting together of the experience of those who had been there before for the benefit of those who wished to follow in their wake. These sailing directions were compiled at least as early as the sixth century B.C. and may well have been earlier. They were constantly being revised and added to. At first they gave little more than the distances from place to place and there were no courses. Thus they were only suited to coastal navigation.

It has been stated categorically by some authors that navigation of the oceans would have been impossible before the introduction of the mariner's compass. This is not true. When propulsion was by sail the course steered by the ship was necessarily governed by the direction of the wind. A sailing ship cannot sail directly against the wind though she may, if well rigged and handled, make a course slightly to windward of that at right-angles to the wind's direction. When on passage the master set his sails to the best advantage for the course he wished to pursue and the ship was then so steered as to keep her sails full. The wind might shift a little but this would not matter as the ship would only be sailing in an approximate direction. It was only if there were a major shift in the wind that there would be any difficulty. In the Indian Ocean, subject to the monsoons, such shifts would not occur. An Arabian ship wishing to go to India merely sailed there with the South-West Monsoon during the months of May to September and returned in October to April when the North-East Monsoon blew. In the Mediterranean, winds were by no means so accommodating and the direction might change while the ship was on her voyage. Here, however, clear weather is never far away during the sailing season of summer. It is then possible to use astronomical means to check the direction of the wind and if necessary to shape a new course. The direction of the sun at sunrise and sunset was known and so the direction of the wind could be checked at these times. At other times during the day the direction of the sun could be obtained very roughly by taking into account the time estimated from the sun's height above the horizon. At night the direction of north could be obtained very approximately from the position of the Pole Star. I say approximately because the earth's axis is gradually tilting and the Pole Star was 11° from the actual pole of the heavens in the year 1 A.D. and 14° from it in 500 B.C. It is believed that the Phoenicians used Kochab (Ursa Minoris) to show them the north as this was the nearest bright star to the pole in their time, being 7° away in 500 B.C. and moving slowly further.

There were times, and this was specially so in northern seas, when the wind might change while the sky remained obscured. Then the navigator was liable to be lost, though he still had some tricks up his sleeve. One was to carry ravens, for if one of these were released it would usually fly towards the nearest land, but still it was a rather hit or miss business.

A suggestion has been made that the Norsemen used the 'sunstone', a crystal which would indicate the direction of the sun even through cloud, a scheme which has recently been revived, but nothing has yet been proved.*

The Compass

The advent of the magnetic compass must have been a great boon, though when at first it came into use, probably towards the end of the twelfth century, the compass was not used directly for steering but only as a means of checking the direction of the wind. The navigator almost certainly kept his compass out of sight and used it in private. By this procedure he scored two great advantages. He kept his methods secret and preserved his reputation as a skilled navigator, and he avoided the possibility of being accused of witchcraft. No doubt the use of the mysterious property of magnetism must have stank in the nostrils of the superstitious.

It has been claimed that even as late as 1260 A.D., when the compass had been in use for more than half a century, Brunetto Latini wrote: "No master mariner dares to use it, lest he should fall under the supposition of being a magician; nor would even the sailors venture themselves to sea under his command if he took with him an instrument which carries so great an appearance of being constructed under the influence of some infernal spirit." This oft-quoted passage was not, however, written by Brunetto Latini but by a man called Dupré as late as 1802 (see note on page 106). It does, nonetheless, describe what may well have been the state of affairs in the twelfth century.

I suggest that there is a very strong pointer to confirm the theory that at first, and for some time, the compass was kept out of sight. This is, that the receptacle in which the compass is kept is called the *habitacle* in France and the binnacle (originally the bittacle) in England. Both these words are derived from the Latin *habitatio*

---

* *Lodestone and Sunstone in Medieval Iceland,* by Bruce E. Gelsinger (Mariner's Mirror, Vol. 56 (1970), pp. 219-226.)

meaning a dwelling. Now why should the receptacle for a compass be called a house if it started as something like a cupboard? If however it was originally kept in some larger structure, such as the navigator's cabin or a sort of forerunner of a charthouse, this becomes quite understandable. If the compass had started in a cupboard some word based on the Latin *armarium* would have been more likely, in fact a French dictionary describes the *habitacle* thus:

"Petit logement à deux étages, en façon d'armoire."

We have no evidence how quickly the use of the compass spread, but it may have done so more quickly than is generally supposed. One writer suggests that as the compass is not mentioned in a Spanish galley inventory of 1364 but does appear in one of 1409 it indicates that the compass could not have been in use in Spanish ships at the former date. I would challenge this view. In inventories of ordnance stores returned from or supplied to His Majesty's Ships before about the year 1610 one does not find swords mentioned, although other weapons such as muskets, halberds and billhooks invariably appear. Surely no one would suggest that this means that swords were not used at sea before this date? There must be some other explanation for the omission of swords from these inventories, so there well may be for the omission of compasses from the galley inventories. Perhaps the reason is that the compass was at first the property of the navigator and the sword of the seaman and neither was a ship's store. After all, compasses are mentioned among the effects of John Aborough, master of the *Michael of Barnstaple,* in 1533*, and it was not until the 1920s that officers of the Royal Navy ceased to be expected to provide their own sextants.

It cannot be stated with any certainty when maps were first drawn. For a very long time those that existed were far from accurate and were only freehand drawings intended to illustrate descriptions of various journeys. Towards the end of the thirteenth century the so-called portolan maps began to appear in the Mediterranean. At first they were very definitely intended merely to illustrate and elucidate the sailing directions. At this period a book of sailing directions was sometimes referred to as a compass, in the sense of a circuit of the sea. What we now call dividers, for measuring distances on a chart, were also called compasses. This is liable to cause confusion when ancient records are being read, for unless

---

* *English Merchant Shipping 1460-1540*, by Dorothy Burwash, 1947.

forewarned the reader may take the word erroneously to refer to the directive instrument when something else is intended.

The new maps carried a distinctive feature. They were crossed by a network of loxodromic lines. From a number of points on the chart were drawn thirty-two radiating lines. With the aid of these lines the course from port to port could be determined with comparative ease. From about 1375, when the Atlas Catalan was produced, a single wind-rose was drawn on the chart at one of these intersections and following Cantino's map of the world of 1502 these wind-roses multiplied, each being the centre of a system of radiating loxodromes.

A feature of these wind-roses was that, while the representation of the directions seems to follow the points on a compass card with which we are familiar, these drawings cannot actually represent compass cards, for the north point, and usually the east point as well, is invariably drawn outside the circle which encloses the other points. Thus the drawing can hardly represent a compass card and since they considerably pre-date true drawings of compass cards they cannot be accused of being artistic degenerations from them. It is not until the sixteenth century after the wind-rose had become duplicated on a chart that we find two types of drawings appearing together. We still have the wind-roses, usually large and very ornate, but we also have among them true representations of compass cards where the north and east points are within the bordering circle. It is significant that from this time the compass-roses, as they are called, are almost invariably coloured in the accepted style for compass cards, while some of the wind-roses, which before were painted at the cartographer's whim, now tended to follow the same scheme.

Nevertheless it has frequently been suggested that the existence of these wind-roses on charts proves that the compass card must have been placed on the needle before their production, even in the mid-thirteenth century at latest. I do not think that this is an acceptable argument. The distinction between wind-roses and compass-roses on charts, which I have described, would seem to invalidate the claim, even though the introduction of the wind-roses is by no means so early as some would suggest.

Tides

A navigational hazard which bothered the north European sailor but not his Mediterranean brother was the existence of the considerable rise and fall of the tide and the consequent tidal streams. The mass of water flowing in with a flood tide to raise the level and flowing out with the ebb to drain it away inevitably causes considerable currents.

The alternation of high and low water is caused by the attraction of the moon and sun, the former having by far the greater effect. A tidal wave passing around the earth is caused below the moon, with a balancing one on the other side of the earth. That due to the sun modifies the moon's wave causing exceptionally high and low tides, called springs, when the two are working together at the times of new and full moon, and less high and less low tides, called neaps, when the two bodies are acting at right-angles to one another. There is actually a lag in the tidal wave and this is accentuated in narrow waters, which not only cause a delay in the time at which high and low water reach them but also accentuate the amount of the rise and fall.

By the fourteenth century the main features of the tides were understood by our sailors and tidal information was beginning to become available to them.

Latitude

Latitude and longitude as a means of describing positions on the earth's surface owe their origin to a conception of Eratosthenes about 150 B.C. For a very long time they were of no practical value to the navigator. To the Mediterranean sailor the narrowness of that sea made the latitude of no great importance, while no methods of determining the longitude, other than by keeping a reckoning, were available to him. What was of more value was the distance between ports and this was given by his sailing directions, while his progress towards his destination was derived from his estimation of the distance made good. Should he make the land to one side or other of his port and be uncertain of his position he could usually land in what was always a civilised country and ask the way!

When in the fifteenth century the Portuguese started their series of explorations down the coast of Africa a new factor was introduced. It now became most valuable to be able to measure the distance one had sailed north or south from the point of departure. It will be noted that what was of most importance was to be able to measure difference of latitude rather than actual latitude.

The first instrument produced for the purpose was the quadrant which is known to have been in use by 1460. This instrument was not originally graduated in degrees but the names, or symbols, of important ports or headlands were marked upon its arc. By observing the Pole Star it was thus possible to discover when one had reached the latitude of one's destination. In thus using the Pole Star there was a complication. The Pole Star was at that period some 3½° from the position of the North Pole, so the navigator had to be told that he must always make his observations when it was in a certain position, indicated by other stars called the Guards, so that the Pole Star was level with the pole, or at any rate always in the same position.

In 1481 the Portuguese crossed the equator, and shortly before this event had become faced with the loss of the Pole Star as it dipped below the horizon. Two courses were now open to them; to find a southern star which would be as useful as the Pole Star or to use the sun. The complication with the sun was that in summer it is to the north of the equator, in winter to the south, by an amount known as the declination and this declination has to be added or subtracted from the altitude when calculating the latitude from an altitude of the sun. Tables for the declination of the sun throughout the year were first calculated by an Englishman called Robert at Montpellier in 1292-1295 but did not become available to seamen generally until about 1485.

Of course the use of the sun made it necessary to have an instrument, for observing its altitude, which was graduated in degrees. By this time the graduation of the arc of the quadrant was already coming into vogue and the astrolabe was also available.

The calculation to obtain the latitude from the altitude of the sun presented some problems for the mariner who was not very mathematically inclined. While an observation of the altitude of the Pole Star gave the latitude direct, the latter could only be calculated from the altitude of the sun at midday by means of the formula:

Latitude = Zenith Distance $\mp$ Declination

where the Zenith Distance is 90° − Altitude. The calculation is complicated by the question of whether the sun and observer are on the same side or not of the equator, and if on the same side which is the closer. If the latitude and declination are of the same name then the declination is added, but if they are of contrary names then it is the difference between the Zenith Distance and Declination which must be taken.

One measure adopted in the seventeenth century to simplify the calculation was to graduate the instrument to read zenith distance instead of altitude, thus saving one subtraction. Some instruments were graduated for both altitude and zenith distance and this must have caused some errors through the observer carelessly reading from the wrong scale.

The Regiment for the Southern Cross was provided about 1505. It happens that when the constellation called the Southern Cross stands vertically in the heavens above the pole, an instant that could be determined by viewing the top and bottom stars of the cross against a plumb line, the stars are in the meridian and have their maximum altitudes. The bottom star ($\propto$ Crucis) was then said to be 30° from the south pole of the heavens and it followed that if 30° were subtracted from its observed altitude one obtained the altitude of the pole and therefore the latitude direct. This constellation is visible for some distance to the north of the equator and so the north latitude would be obtained by subtracting the altitude from 30°. Actually the star was found to be rather closer to the pole than 30°. In 1669 Sturmy gave the distance as 28° and at the present date it is about 27° 5'.

The Southern Cross was only observed by navigators bound for India or the East Indies and even then does not seem to have been used very often, for the meridian altitude of the sun was much more convenient and quite sufficient for ordinary purposes. The author of one account of James Lancaster's voyage of 1591-1594 complains that after they had rounded Ceylon and were bound for the Nicobar Islands they had six days of bad weather. The master lost an opportunity to check his latitude by the Southern Cross and in consequence missed the Nicobars and made Gomez Pulo (Klapa) off Sumatra instead. This island is about a degree further south than the Nicobars*. I wonder whether the master did not make another error. The account implies that they took their departure from Cape Comorin, the most southerly point of India, but it is clear that they must have passed around Ceylon. Cape Comorin is in latitude 8° 5' N. while Dondra Head, the southernmost point of Ceylon, is in 5° 55' N. Now if the master had steered east true from Dondra Head he would have arrived near Gomez Pulo, while if he had forgotten Ceylon and thought that he was steering east from Cape Comorin he would have expected to reach the centre of the Nicobars, which stretch from 7° to 9° N.

One recorded observation of the Southern Cross was in January

---

* *The Voyages of Sir James Lancaster to the East Indies.* Hakluyt Society 1877. p. 10.

1612 when Nathaniel Marten, master's mate of the *Globe*, used it in a comparison with the latitude of Petepoly obtained from a meridian altitude of the sun*. Others I have come across were by Rand Pye, master of the PHOENIX, on 24th February 1687 (see page 23), by Daniel Kelley, master of the SCARBOROUGH, on four occasions in 1704 and 1705† and by Captain Charles Gough in the East Indiaman *Richmond* on 10th February 1732‡. (Captain Gough's observation was made because on that day the sun was vertically overhead. Two of Kelley's observations were checked by altitudes of the Pole Star, the two resulting latitudes being meaned.)

For accuracy both the quadrant and the astrolabe depended upon gravity. If the ship were subject to any movement the plumb bob of the quadrant would swing about and it was just as difficult to keep the astrolabe hanging vertically. The first solution was the cross-staff which appeared about 1514 (page 123). With this instrument one was measuring the angle between the heavenly body and the horizontal, represented by the sea horizon, instead of between it and the vertical.

Traverse Table.

When a ship is steering a course other than on one of the four cardinal points her distance run can be resolved into change of latitude north or south and departure east or west. This is known as working a traverse. To help the seaman a table was introduced in about 1390 and was followed by a diagram (Fig. 1). This was usually a drawing of a wind-rose with figures marked around the circumference showing the number of leagues it was necessary to steer on each point to make a change of latitude of one degree. It will be observed that at this time there was no question of using the diagram to work out a difference of longitude. By the seventeenth century this diagram was being replaced by tables showing the differences of latitude and of departure for any course and distance.

The Log.

To obtain the distance made good by a ship it was necessary to be able to make an estimate of her speed and until late in the sixteenth

---

*   *Purchas His Pilgrimes.*   Hayluyt Society.   1905.   Vol. III   p. 309
†   Public Record Office.   ADM.52/280
‡   India Office Library.   L/MAR/B.329a

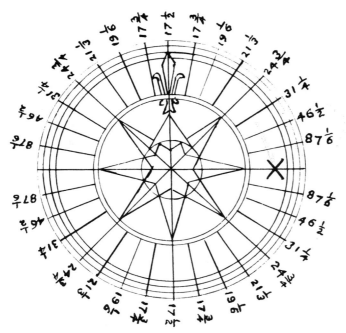

Figure 1　　Diagram showing the number of leagues to sail on any course in order to change the latitude one degree.

century this was entirely a matter of experience and judgement by the pilot. It was not until a little before 1574, in which year we first hear from Bourne of the use of the log-ship, that any instrument for measuring the speed appeared (page 109). There is no doubt that this was an English invention. Several writers condemned it as being inaccurate but it must have been better than nothing, and in any case it was extensively used. Writing in 1637 Richard Norwood censured the old methods in these words: 'Some have thought that the way which the ship maketh, may be known to an old Sea-man by experience (as they say) that is by conjecture; which opinion makes some neglect the use of the *Log*, lest they should be accounted Young Sea-men.'

Variation of the Compass.

Another complication had appeared in the fifteenth century when it was first discovered that the magnetic compass needle did not point

to true north and later that it did not even point in the same
direction in all parts of the world (page 80). The angle by which the
indication of the compass differed from the true north was at first
known as the north-easting, or north-westing, of the needle and later
as the variation. It has often been suggested that the existence of the
variation was discovered by Columbus during his first voyage, but
this is not true although it is possible that he was not himself aware
of it when he sailed. Even when the knowledge of the variation had
been firmly established there were some writers, such as Pedro de
Medina, who stoutly denied its existence. Of course the
determination of whether or not variation existed was complicated
by the inaccuracy of compasses. On the other hand neglect of the
variation might well lead to quite considerable errors of course and it
is extraordinary that many navigators ignored it. Harrison, as late as
1696, tells us that about two years earlier the commodore taking a
squadron across the Bay of Biscay omitted to allow for the variation,
with the result that the ships got uncomfortably close to the Burlings
in the night and some even had to go inside the islands. He goes on to
say: 'I have belong'd this War to Six several Rates in the Navy, and
never saw an Azimuth Compass Aboard any of them.' Even in 1845
Maury wrote of American usage: 'The azimuth compass is falling into
disuse very much in the merchant service; but is of vast importance
in navigation, and is just beginning to be properly appreciated in the
navy.'

The variation could be measured if the bearing of the Pole Star
were taken with the compass and compared with true north. It was
of course necessary to consult the diagram (Fig. 2) to make sure that
the star really did bear north at the time of observation and that an
error of up to $3\frac{1}{2}°$ was not being introduced. This was apparently the
method adopted by Columbus after he had come to realise that there
was such a thing as variation.

The sun provided another means for the determination of the
variation, and its use soon replaced that of the Pole Star. An
amplitude is the angle between the point at which the sun rises or
sets and the east or west point of the horizon. In 1535 Faleiro*
suggested that the morning and evening amplitudes should be
observed and the difference of either of these from the mean would
give the variation of the compass. A slightly more difficult method,
but one which could be completed more rapidly, was to take an

---

* Francisco Faleiro, *Tractado de esphera y del arte del marear.* 1535.

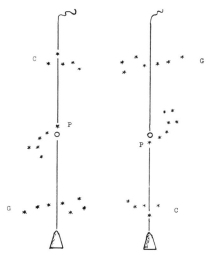

Figure 2   Diagram showing the use of the lead-line to determine when the Pole Star is exactly above or below the pole, and hence the correction to be applied to an altitude when determining the latitude. C, Casseopeia: P, Pole Star: G, Great Bear.

azimuth (bearing) of the sun in the morning and at the same time to observe its altitude. In the afternoon the navigator waited until the sun was once more at the same altitude and then took the azimuth again. The mean of the two azimuths would be the magnetic bearing of the sun at midday and if different from south would give the amount of the variation.

The actual amplitude could be calculated from the latitude and declination and in 1595 Thomas Hariot* produced a table of amplitudes already worked out to save the navigator's labour: the variation could then be obtained from a single amplitude. An error, nevertheless, could arise from this. Owing to refraction, when the sun is low (page 151) it still appears to be above the horizon when it has already set, while in the morning it appears in sight before it has actually risen. In the tropics the sun appears to rise out of the sea, or to plunge into it almost vertically, so that there is little or no error of bearing if the amplitude is observed when the sun's centre is upon the horizon, but in high latitudes where the sun crosses the horizon at a small angle the error can be very considerable. In modern times

* The table of amplitudes may have appeared in his manuscript *Articon* (1584) which is now lost. It is in the introduction to the *Instructions for Raleigh's Voyage to Guiana* (1595) (British Museum Add. M.S. 6708) which is believed to be a copy of that work.

the observer is told to take his amplitude when the sun's lower limb is half its diameter above the horizon, allowing for refraction equal to the diameter of the sun. This necessity must have been known to a few in quite early times but though it was mentioned rather vaguely by Harrison in 1696 and very definitely by Harris in 1730 the earliest mention I have found of it in any of the usual writers is in the 1807 edition of Hamilton Moore. It must, therefore, have been generally ignored with the consequent introduction of errors.

No doubt, because of the convenience of the Tables of Amplitudes the amplitude was a very favourite method of obtaining the variation. It would, though, have been more accurate to observe a single magnetic azimuth and calculate the true azimuth from the latitude, declination and altitude.

The calculation of azimuths and amplitudes was described by most writers from at least the middle of the seventeenth century.

Progress in England.

In the fifteenth and early sixteenth centuries all the progress in the art of navigation had been made by the Spaniards and Portuguese, who trained their pilots well. Such books on the subject as existed were in manuscript and it was not until near the middle of the sixteenth century that famous books appeared in print. The most important of these were *Regimento de Navegacion* (1543) and *Arte de Navegar* (1545) which being both by Pedro de Medina are often confused with one another, and *Breve Compendio de la Sphera y de la arte de navegar* (1551) by Martin Cortes.

It has sometimes been said that navigation in northern Europe was still in the primitive coastal stage before this time, but this is not true. Since the ninth century the Norsemen had made voyages to Iceland, Greenland and even America. It is evident from their records that they indulged in sailing along a parallel of their latitude until they reached their destination. How they kept to their latitude, however, or regained it if they drifted away, is by no means clear.

In the *Libell of English Policie,* said to have been written about 1437, though it may be a little later, we find:

> "Of Island to write is little nede,
> Save of Stock-fish: Yet forsooth in deed
> Out of Bristowe, and costes many one,
> Men have practised by nedle and by stone

Thider wardes within a little while,
Within twelve yere, and without perill
Gon and come, as men were wont of old
Of Scarborough unto the costes cold."

This makes it clear that the English were making quite long voyages. In 1497 John Cabot in a Bristol ship made the first recorded English voyage to Newfoundland and with others began to establish the great era of the Elizabethan sailor who in a short time appeared in most of the seas of the world. At first these adventurers had often to employ Spanish or Portuguese trained pilots, but they soon began to learn and were helped by those who translated Spanish books on the subject into English. The first of these to appear, in 1561, was a translation by Richard Eden of Cortes' book, and this was followed twenty years later by a translation of Medina's *Arte de Navegar* which John Frampton produced in 1581. The latter never had anything like the success which attended the former.

Already, however, the English were putting out their own books, the first being *An Almanack and Prognostication for iij Yeres with Serten Rules of Nauigation* (1567) and *A Regiment for the Sea* (1574), both by William Bourne, while of books on the more limited subject of the compass and its use we have *The Newe Attractive,* by Robert Norman, and *A Discourse of the Variation,* by William Borough, both of which appeared in 1581.

An idea of the conservatism of some English seamen in the field of navigation at this time is given by Bourne in the Second Address to the Reader with which he prefaced his third (1580) edition of *A Regiment for the Sea.* He wrote:

"And who doubteth but a simple Fisher-man of Barking knoweth Barking Creeke, better then the best Nauigator or Master in this lande: so who doubteth but these simple men doth know their owne places at home. But if they should come out of the *Ocean* sea to seek our chanel to come vnto ye riuer of *Thames,* I am of that opinion, that a number of them, doth but grope as a blinde man doth, & if that they doe hit wel, that it is but by chaunce, and not by any cunning that is in him.

But I doe hope that in these dayes, that the knowledge of the Masters of shippes is very well mended, for I haue knowen within this .20. yeeres that them that were auncient masters of ships hath derided and mocked thē that haue occupied their Cards and Plats, and also the obseruatiō of the altitude of the Pole, saying that they care not for their Sheepes skins, for hee could keepe a better account vpon a boord.

And wen that they did take the latitude, they would cal them starre shooters and Sunne shooters, and would aske if they had striken it. Wherefore now iudge of their skilles, considering that these two poyntes is the principal matters in Nauigation. And yet these simple people will make no small brags of themselues, saying: that he hath ben Master this .20. yeeres, and neuer had no misfortune, and also if that they could heare of any that did vse Plats and Instruments that had any misfortune, then they woulde not a little bragge of themselues what notable fellowes they themselues were."

Bourne describes the use of the compass, log and cross-staff, the declination of the sun and stars and how to obtain a latitude from a meridian altitude. He also shows how to convert course and distance run into difference of latitude and what is now called departure, and how according to the latitude that the ship is in, so the length in miles of a. degree of longtitude will change. He gives rules for discovering the distance off shore from the difference of bearing of two points of land whose distance apart is known.

The English were also making their own practical contributions to the art. In 1594, in *The Sea-man's Secrets*, John Davis described his back-staff which in a modified form was to be the best instrument available for observing altitudes for more than a century (page 127).

Existing instruments for observing altitudes were most unsatisfactory. As we have seen, the astrolabe and quadrant suffered in a seaway because of their dependance on gravity. The cross-staff on the other hand limited the observer in practice to altitudes between 20° and 60°. Since the sun had to be looked at directly the observer was liable to be dazzled, if not blinded, even though he might use smoked glass. With Davis's instrument the observer stood with his back to the sun and could measure angles up to 90°.

Measurement of the Earth.

The first measurement of the earth was made in Egypt in the third century B.C. by Eratosthenes who from his observations calculated that one degree of latitude equalled 700 stadia which, as the stadium is usually taken as 600 feet, equalled 420,000 feet. A smaller measurement was made by Poseidonius in the first century B.C. which worked out at 500 stadia or 300,000 feet for a degree.* This

* These early measurements are a little doubtful for it is difficult to reconcile different standards of length. According to Richard Norwood an Alexandrian foot was 6/5 times as long as an English foot so that the degree of Poseidonius would have been 360,000 English feet, equivalent to a 6000 foot mile.

latter measurement was adopted by the English who thus reckoned 5000 feet to the mile, three miles to a league and twenty leagues to a degree. The Spaniards and Portuguese also reckoned 5000 feet to the mile but four miles to the league and 17½ leagues (350,000 feet) to the degree.

Between 1633 and 1635 Richard Norwood measured the distance from London to York and from this calculated that the length of a degree was 367,200 feet. From this he laid down that a mile ought to be taken as 6120 feet instead of 5000. The modern estimate of a degree is 364,800 feet or 6080 to a mile, which was made by French Astronomers in 1756.

In his *Sea-man's Practice,* published in 1637, Norwood drew attention to the large errors in reckoning resulting from the inaccurate measurement of the log-line through using the old 5000-foot mile.

Mathematics.

When ocean navigation first reached the stage of finding the latitude from a meridian altitude of the sun the only arithmetical rules required were addition and subtraction, but after a while this was not enough. By the end of the sixteenth century arguments were beginning between the rule of thumb navigators and the more theoretical mathematical practitioners. One result of this was that for the next two centuries most of the works on navigation were clogged with much mathematical material, of no real value to the seaman, and by frightening him with a mass of unnecessary rules must actually have delayed his progress. What useful rules were given when they could be found among the unnecessary matter, were usually so clumsily stated that to this day it is difficult to follow them.

Some mathematical knowledge was, however, becoming necessary. Spherical triangles needed to be solved for calculating the azimuth of the sun so that the variation could be determined, and for problems in mercator sailing.

Knowledge of the trigonometrical functions, or ratios, had existed since pre-Christian times and the first table of sines was published in 1533, followed a few years later by tables of the other functions. But it was not until 1583 that tables became available in a convenient form for use at sea. In England, Blundevile in 1594 published the first tables seen there, together with an explanation of their use.

For all calculations a great deal of cumbersome multiplication and division was required, considerably simplified, however, in 1614 by the introduction of John Napier's logarithms. The instructions for the use of these were at first given in Latin, but it was not many years before an explanation in English appeared. Attempts were also made to design instruments by which problems could be solved by geometrical means without the use of any calculation. In the 1590s Thomas Hood designed a sector, principally for the use of surveyors. In 1606 Gunter adapted the sector to the needs of navigation, writing a description in Latin which was only circulated in manuscript. Nevertheless many of the Sectors were made for and used by seamen. In 1623 he published a description in English and a year later introduced his famous Gunter's Scale, which was to remain in service for at least 250 years.*

The Sector consisted of two arms, hinged like a carpenter's rule, graduated with lines of sines, tangents &c., and with this instrument and a pair of dividers any problem involving right-angled triangles or proportion could be solved. The Gunter's Scale was a straight rule, engraved with logarithmic scales of numbers and trigonometrical functions and since all that was involved when using logarithms was to add or subtract, the same process could be achieved by measuring with dividers.

Gunter's first scale was embodied in a cross-staff and variations of both sector and scale appeared from time to time.

Plane and Mercator Charts.

Sixteenth century charts were Plane charts, made on the assumption that the earth was flat although this was known not to be the case. They showed the meridians as being parallel to each other instead of converging towards the pole, thus causing grave errors. Pedro Nunez, in 1537, was the first man to draw attention to these. In 1569 the first Mercator chart of the world appeared and in this the difficulty of the meridians becoming closer together was overcome by making them parallel but stretching the latitude scales as one receded from the equator. The mathematical principles behind such a projection were demonstrated by Edward Wright in 1599. Within a few years the method of Mercator sailing was explained to all who would

* The Gunter's Scale is still described in the *Complete Epitome of Practical Navigation*, By J. W. Norie, 21st edition revised by A. B. Martin, 1877.

listen. It was a long time, however, before its use became universal. Teachers of navigation taught both Plane and Mercator sailing, some only the former. Plane was often incorrectly written as Plain and so has come into the English language the expression 'Plain Sailing' for something that is easy and straight forward. This rather emphasises the difficulty which seventeenth century navigators had in understanding Mercator sailing. The reason why they had to multiply their departure (the distance run in an east-west direction) by the secant of the latitude to get their change of longitude was quite beyond many a seaman. The more knowledgeable might have done as Richard Swan, master of the *Roebuck*, did during her voyage to the East Indies in 1620-1622. In his log-book it shows that he used both Mercator and Plane sailing, for he records both longitudes. Most navigators would however have confined themselves to the latter method.

Halley told Pepys* in 1696 that most masters used Plane sailing. Those who traded to the West Indies went south on their outward voyage to get into the region of the north-east trade winds, but on returning home they first went north into the region of the westerlies. In this way their departure as measured by the log was greater when steering west than when coming east, and this they explained by claiming that there was a constant easterly current in the Atlantic.

Isaac Pike, purser of the East Indiaman *Rochester*, who sailed from England for the east in 1704, tells us that Plane sailing was usually used on long voyages, but that in men-of-war Mercator sailing was considered to be more accurate.† Strangely enough however his captain, Francis Stanes, used Mercator sailing, though even as late as 1750 examples will be found of East Indiaman who still clung to the old methods and kept their reckoning by Plane sailing.

It is difficult to discover for certain how ships were actually navigated at any particular date. The manuals of navigation were usually written by mathematicians who tended to write of what *could* be done under ideal conditions rather than what it would have been convenient to do in practice. It is true that there were some writers who had at one time followed the sea, but even these often tried to compete with the mathematicians in order to show their own erudition.

---

*   British Museum. Add. M.S. 30221.
†   British Museum. Add. M.S. 24931, page 353.

At sea, navigators have always kept their reckoning on slates, boards, or in work-books which were ultimately cleaned off or destroyed. Then they entered in their log-books only the more important results of their observations and principal occurrences. Few log-books have survived and those that have are of warships or of ships of the great East India Company. Even then it is difficult to find anyone who has permitted himself to produce a record which is both legible and intelligible to the reader.

The Log of the PHOENIX.

One example of a helpful log-book is that of the PHOENIX, sent out to India by Charles II in the years 1684-1687. Here is her log entry for 10 April 1687, a few days after the ship had sighted the Cape of Good Hope on her homeward voyage:

"Latt Obser^d 32° 16'S^o SUNDAY ye 10^h faire weath^r & very little
Mer Dis^t 02°55'W^t wind at SE & ESE & sometimes Callme. our
Morning Varia p^r Cors by Comp^s hath been NW runn by logg 24
Ampl^d 08°00'W^t miles wch dist^s I alow to be 30 miles because of
                                a great swell out of ye S^o ward bord & what we
                                have gale^d away when o^r sailes have been hale^d
                                up wch upon or Cors steer^d gives 18 miles
                                N^{o}ing but by Observa^t we 6 miles more to y^e
                                N^{o}ward which I impute to somewhat of a
                                streame we have had these 4 days although in
                                trying to day we finde none I alow ye true Cors
                                to be made NW¼W dis^t 36 miles diff^r latt^d 24
                                dep^e 27"

The first item in the margin is the latitude observed by a meridian altitude of the sun. Next comes the estimated meridian distance at noon, i.e. the difference of longitude from the last point of departure. Instead of measuring longitude from some prime meridian, such as that of Greenwich, longitude was measured from the last port visited. Occasionally during a long voyage a fresh reckoning was started from some conspicuous point passed, in this case the Cape of Good Hope. Lastly comes the variation of the compass, in this case obtained from an amplitude of the sun at sunrise, but sometimes obtained from an azimuth. The master of the PHOENIX did not observe the variation until after passing the Cape Verde Islands on the outward voyage, but thereafter he seldom missed an opportunity.

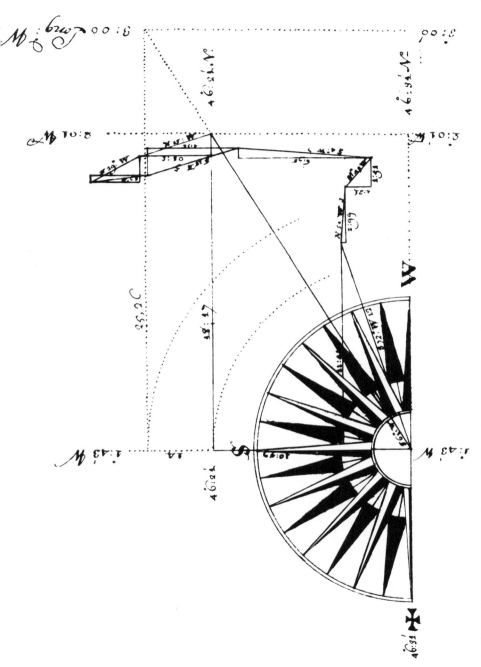

Figure 3   An example of a Day's Work being plotted in a log book instead of being worked out by Traverse Table. (Copyright: British Museum)

In the main column of the log-book there are remarks on the weather followed by the course steered by compass and the distance run by log during the last twenty-four hours. These had been recorded on the traverse board (see below) and taken off it after each watch by the master and worked up to give the total run entered here. He then had to correct the course for variation and leeway and on this occasion decided that he must allow more than the log indicated for the distance run because of a swell from the south. He was confirmed in his opinion by his sight which showed that he was six miles still further to the northward. This he thought might be due to an ocean current, but he tried for this and found none. The method of trying the current was to hoist out a boat and to 'anchor' her by lowering a large pot or kettle deep down into the sea. Then the log-ship was put over and the speed at which it was carried away measured by the log-line and log-glass. This was supposed to give the surface current but of course only did this if there were no deep current.

The next entry in the log-book tells us the master's final conclusion of the true course and distance made good after taking everything into account, and finally this is resolved into the change of latitude and departure, these being applied to the position of the previous day to give that in the margin. Here we see how the master has confined himself to Plane sailing and has assumed that the departure for the day is the same as the difference of longitude, adding it to the Meridian Distance for the previous day to obtain 2° 55′. The departure of twenty-seven miles is really equivalent to a difference of longitude of thirty-six minutes. It may be mentioned here that for this voyage the PHOENIX had two masters, John Saphier who took her to India and there died, and Rand Pye who brought her back. It is the latter's log-book from which we have the extract given here. Saphier called his Departure the Meridian Distance but navigated by Plane sailing in the same way.

Although the taking of stars on the meridian to obtain the latitude was explained in the manuals, the masters of the PHOENIX never took them and I do not believe that the taking of star sights was practised by the ordinary navigator for at least another century. On 17 February 1696 Edmond Halley wrote to Samuel Pepys on deficiencies in the practice of navigation. He stated that if masters were unable to get their meridian altitude of the sun they did not ever remedy the lack by taking a star sight but preferred to rely upon their dead reckoning. "Any clear star in the Night time would suffice to give them their Latitude with even greater certainty than the Sun at Noon, which vulgarly is esteemed the only moment when the Latitude can be taken.* The earliest reference which I have been able to find of the use of a star, other than the Southern Cross, is in the log-book of James Gray, master of the ASTRAEA, who found his latitude to be 57° 20′ N. from a meridian altitude of Aldebaran observed at midnight on 29 November 1793†. The only occasion in the PHOENIX on which a star was used occurred when she was crossing the Indian Ocean on her way home. After three days without a noon sight the weather cleared during the night and at 2 a.m. the master observed the latitude by the Southern Cross in the approved fashion (see page 9). This sight gave him a latitude of 8°0′S. In fact, the weather remained clear and he was able to get a meridian altitude of the sun, giving him a latitude of 8° 17′S., showing a very fair agreement as the difference of latitude in the ten hours at the speed they were sailing might have been expected to be about 20 miles.

As in the extract quoted above, the masters often noted a discrepancy between the observed latitude and the 'Latitude by accompt'. They sometimes tried to account for this; on one occasion suggesting that it was due to the log-glasses running for too long, causing an over-estimate of the speed, and on another, the error was put down to bad steerage. On one or two occasions the discrepancy was in opposite directions on consecutive days, although the runs had been small. It does not seem to have struck them that their sights might have been in error, except on one occasion when the horizon was said to have been hazy. It was generally considered that even the Davis back-staff was not accurate within six minutes.‡ Comparison of log-books of officers in the same ship often shows differences of opinion as to the latitude of at least that amount, and I have detected a case where the master of one ship always recorded latitudes about ten miles different to the other officers, suggesting that either he had a personal error or that his quadrant had an index error.

When shaping his course to the next port the master usually aimed to get into the latitude of his port several degrees of longitude away and then to steer east or west until he sighted land. He may have

---

*   British Museum. Add. M.S. 30221, page 169.
†   Public Record Office, ADM.52/2703
‡   Walter Maitland, in *An Essay towards the Improvement of Navigation* (c.1750), says twelve minutes.

been hampered by not really knowing the difference of longitude between the ports of departure and destination. For example the difference of longitude between St. Jago in the Cape Verde Islands and the Cape of Good Hope, which is about 42°, was given by Sturmy in his *Mariner's Magazine,* 1669, as 47° 16', by Seller in his *Practical Navigation* of the same date as 45° 40' and by Seller in his *Oriental Navigation,* 1675, as 45° 24'. The master of the PHOENIX'S reckoning made it about 38½° but he was gravely in error by practising Plane sailing and allowing his departure as difference of longitude. If he had calculated correctly he would have made the meridian distance something like 46°. This shows the difficulties of Plane sailing. In this case he had reached the latitude of the Cape of Good Hope when almost due south of St. Jago before turning East.

It must not be assumed however that no navigator of this period in the Royal Navy used Mercator sailing. In the log of the DRAGON, returning from Newfoundland in 1693, it is clear that Captain William Vickers knew how to convert his departure into difference of longitude, for he gives the figures for both. On this passage his reckoning proved to be about two degrees ahead of the ship when she neared the Channel and started to take soundings. An interesting point from this log is that the captain speaks of 'protracting' his courses, so it would appear that each day he plotted his courses and distances to find the day's run, instead of calculating it from a traverse table.

The Traverse Board.

The Traverse Board to which I referred consisted of a board of which the upper part was painted to look like a compass card and had eight holes arranged radially for each of the thirty-two points (Fig. 4). The lower part had four or eight horizontal rows of holes. Attached to the board were a number of pegs. The use of the traverse board was thus: when the watch-glass was turned at the end of each half-hour the quartermaster put in a peg opposite to the course on which he had been steering for most of the time. When the log was hove the offficer responsible put one or two pegs into the appropriate row of holes at the bottom of the board to indicate the speed in knots and fathoms.* At the end of the watch the master transferred to his slate

---

* Warships and East Indiamen hove the log every hour, other ships every two hours.

Figure 4   Traverse Board. (Copyright: National Maritime Museum)

the information derived from the traverse board and pulled out all the pegs so that the board was ready for the next watch.

Great Circle Sailing.

If one lays a thread on a globe joining two ports which are far apart, it will be seen that this thread does not cut all the intermediate meridians at the same angle. This thread will indicate a great circle on the surface of the earth and will be the shortest distance between the two ports. If one joins the same ports on a Mercator chart the line joining them will cut all meridians at the same angle and the distance along it will be considerably greater than the great circle distance. Thus it will be seen that on long voyages there will be much advantage to be gained by taking the great circle track, in spite of the fact that frequent alterations of course will have to be made.

In modern air navigation great circle routes can be turned to great advantage, for it matters little to an aircraft whether it crosses sea or land and if desirable even the polar regions can be crossed. The navigation of sailing ships was a very different matter. The advantage of great circle navigation was first pointed out by Pedro Nunez in

1537 and subsequent writers gave it lip service. In 1656 Benjamin Hubbard wrote an entire book on the subject*. It was not, however, a practical possibility at that time. Positions of ports were not known with sufficient accuracy and it was no use trying to save distance if you did not know where you were going. With a sailing ship one was also limited by the wind. If the great circle track took you out of the area of favouring winds it was of little value. An example of this was the crossing of the Atlantic westward where the great circle track would have taken the ship out of the area of the favourable trade winds into that of the anti-trades. It was no doubt for these reasons that no one really considered the question of how to work out great circle courses.

Printed Charts.

The portolan charts and their immediate successors were manuscript charts, usually drawn on sheep skins, and must have been much treasured by their lucky possessors. They were in common use until about three-quarters of the way through the seventeenth century, when printed charts were becoming easy to obtain. For the first atlas of printed charts sailors were indebted to the Dutchman, Lucas Janszoon Wagenhaer. The initial part of his *Spieghel der Zeevaerdt* appeared in 1584 and a year later was followed by the second part. Besides charts, this work contained sailing directions and some notes upon navigation. An English translation by Anthony Ashley was commissioned in this country and was printed in 1588. During the following century several Dutch cartographers followed in the footsteps of their countryman, many of them going so far as to bring out English editions. It was felt to be rather a slur on the English that they had to rely on the Dutch for their charts, even for those of their own coasts, and in 1675 John Seller published his first volume of a set of five which would ultimately cover most of the known world. It has been said however that Seller's work was based on that of the Dutch and that he even bought up, amended and used, some of their out-of-date copper plates.

As an auxiliary to charts, most books on navigation printed lists of places with their latitudes and longitudes. It was possibly the exception for a navigator to lay off a course on a chart as we would

---

* Benjamin Hubbard: *Orthodoxal Navigation, or the Admirable and Excellent Art of Arithmeticall Great Circle-Sailing.*

today. It would have done much too much damage to a valuable object. He probably calculated his courses direct from the latitude of his dead reckoning position and those of his destination.

The practice of listing geographical positions in books of navigation has been continued in some publications until the present day, notable exceptions being the *Admiralty Manuals of Navigation*. The Admiralty chart organisation is so good that none of Her Majesty's Ships should ever find themselves at sea without adequate chart coverage. During the last war, however, occasions arose when ships had to be detached suddenly to distant seas without having any chance to amend their normal chart sets. In one case destroyers from the Mediterranean, which had been sent to escort a damaged vessel to Freetown en route for the United States, had suddenly to be sent to Trinidad to fetch some oil tankers. The destroyers had no charts on board to take them beyond 30° W. and so navigated by the wardroom atlas. A table of geographical positions might well have been useful!

Sir Clowdisley Shovel.

In 1707 there occurred a disaster which has become renowned, partly through the recent discovery by divers of one of the wrecks of the vessels involved.

Sir Clowdisley Shovel with a fleet of twenty-one ships departed from Cape Spartel on the 30th September 1707, and sailed for home. Soon after dark on 22nd October the ASSOCIATION, EAGLE and ROMNEY went ashore on the rocks of Scilly with the loss of practically all hands. The ST. GEORGE, PHOENIX and FIREBRAND also went ashore but managed to get off, though the FIREBRAND was so holed that she sank immediately.

I have examined the forty-four log-books which have survived from this fleet. Four of the officers copied from their friends, leaving forty log-books worth considering. Stories that the weather had been thick throughout the voyage so that no sights could be taken, or that the officers all thought that they were close into Ushant when they were actually nearing Scilly, can be discounted, as can the tale recently advanced to me that all these forty-four log-books were deliberately cooked by mutual agreement after their return home to hide their negligence, an idea too fantastic to be seriously contemplated!

If we first consider the longitude, though there were some officers who were as much as three degrees in error, the majority were something less than a degree to the westward of their reckoning. Even if lunars had been available to them, as to their descendants a century later, they could not have been expected to be much more accurate, especially when it is realised that in 1707 estimates of the difference of longitude between Spartel and Scilly varied considerably. In fact with a reckoning based on a departure from Cape Spartel, which was usually located too far to the westward, it is a wonder that more ships did not place themselves in that direction.

When we come to consider the latitude, we find that while most ships thought that they were about thirty miles to the southward of the Scillies three gave their positions in the correct latitude. But even these must have thought themselves quite safe as most of the tables showed the islands fourteen to twenty miles too far to the north. It is true that Samuel Pepys and probably many others had known that the islands were ten miles or more to the southward of their recorded positions. This was given as one of the reasons for employing Greenville Collins on his resurvey of the British Islands, but when his charts appeared he still placed them about nine miles too far to the north.

I am convinced that this failure to know the correct latitude of the Scillies was the primary cause of the catastrophe. It made the officers think that they had much more sea-room than was the case. Their errors in longitude were not a contributory cause. It was known that longitudes were bound to be unreliable and no one trusted them. The intention was to get into the latitude of the mouth of the Channel and then to turn east. They trusted to their latitude and on this occasion their trust was misplaced.

The Board of Longitude.

In 1714 the British Government offered prizes of up to £20,000 to anyone who should disclose a method of finding the longitude at sea within half a degree, with smaller sums for lesser standards of accuracy. This absence of any means of finding how far one had progressed to the eastward or the westward had been the bugbear of navigators for a very long time, though it must be stressed that in an age when the world was not yet properly charted the fact that one did not know the longitude of one's destination meant that the longitude of one's position was less important than it would be today. Flamsteed, writing to Pepys on 21st April 1697, put it thus: "Tis in vain to talk of the Use of finding the Longitude at Sea, except you know the true Longitude and Latitude of the Port for which you are designed."*

The dire results of a lack of means of observing the longitude have been overstressed by many writers. In 1691 the CORONATION was lost off Rame Head and the HARWICH went ashore under Mount Edgecumbe while entering the Hamoaze at Plymouth. It has been said that failure to be able to observe their longitude caused the fleet to mistake the Dodman for Berry Head, about a hundred miles to the eastward. But the fleet had just reached across from Ushant in thick weather and there would have been no possibility of taking a sight during the last thirty-six hours. The first thing that they saw (and identified) was the Eddystone and they were nowhere near the Dodman. More accurate knowledge of the longitude would not have prevented these wrecks.

I have already referred to the case of Sir Clowdisley Shovel. Another case which is mentioned was the wreck of the ROYAL ANNE on the Lizard in 1721, a few hours after sailing from Plymouth. Here again no longitude sight would have saved her from what must have been the result of bad navigation. Her pilot had already put the ship ashore when leaving the Thames!

Of all the cases usually quoted of embarrassment due to lack of being able to discover the longitude, the one which stands up best to an examination is that of Anson's squadron in 1741. On 8th March his ships passed through the Straits of Le Maire and the master of the GLOUCESTER, Robert Lambert, took his departure from Cape Good Success (Cabo Buen Suceso in 54° 49' S., 65° 13' W.). Furthest south was reached on 17th March in 60° 3' S., 8° 9' W. from Cape Good Success and thereafter the ships edged to the northwards and westwards as the winds would allow. On 3rd April the master observed his latitude as 55° 3' S. and reckoned his longitude to be 19° 11' W. of the Cape (84° 24' W. of Greenwich). The officers of the squadron were confident that they now had plenty of sea-room to steer north-westwards clear of the coast of Chile, but for the next ten days adverse winds kept them more or less in the same area. On the 13th April the master put the ship in 55° 0' S., 19° 24' W. (84° 37' W.), standing to the N.N.E., when land was

* British Museum, Add. M.S. 30221, page 187

unexpectedly sighted. This was probably the high south-west extremity of Stewart Island, which is just north of 55° S. in about 72° W.

The Commodore in the CENTURION kept his reckoning for longitude from Greenwich. When passing through the Straits of Le Maire he already made his longitude about four and a half degrees too far to the westward, but of course at this time no one really knew what the longitudes should be. Those estimated were about eight degrees too far west for Le Maire and twelve degrees for Cape Horn*. On 13th April when land was sighted the Commodore made his longitude 87° 51′ W., considering that he had made 17° 57′ westing since the 8th March. Two of his Lieutenants, Peter Denis and Piercy Brett, made it 17° 28′ and 18° 14′ respectively. These figures compare with 19° 17′ recorded by Lambert. The reckonings of these four officers were therefore all from ten to twelve degrees in excess during what should have been only seven degrees in a voyage of thirty-six days!

The Commodore corrected his longitude, reducing it by about ten degrees, his two lieutenants took new departures from the land seen, and Lambert carried on his reckonings from Cape Good Success as though no land had been sighted.

The squadron steered away to the S.S.W. again and got still further to the west before again trying to work to the northward. During this period the GLOUCESTER became separated. On 18th May she once more made the coast, this time in St. Stephen's Bay in 46° S. Her master made the bay to be in 23° 45′ W. from Cape Good Success (88° 58′ W.) whereas it is in about 75° W. so he had overestimated his westing by another two degrees. On his passage thence to Juan Fernandez, where he rejoined the Commodore, he overestimated by another two or three degrees.

Meanwhile the CENTURION had steered direct, as Anson thought, for Juan Fernandez and had reached the neighourhood of 34° S. on the 28th May. His estimation of the longitude was 83° 58′ W. from Greenwich, reckoning he had made five and a half degrees of westing since the 14th April. I have not been able to discover what he thought the longitude of Juan Fernandez to be, but it had been given a few years earlier as 86° 48′ W.†, its true longitude being 78°

---

* Andrew Wakeley, *The Mariner's Compass Rectified*, 1761. This book also puts the latitude of Cape Horn about one and a half degrees too far south.
† Joshua Kelly, *The Modern Navigator's Complete Tutor*, 1733.

50' W. It is therefore rather surprising that Anson thought that he must be west of the island and turned east, discovering his error two days later when he sighted the main land of South America in 33° 52' S., 81° 22' W. by his reckoning. Actually the coast in this latitude is in about 72° W. Anson then turned west again but did not anchor at Juan Fernandez until the 10th June when he reckoned it to be in about 87° 20' W. During his search for the island about seventy men had died of scurvy, victims to the uncertainty concerning the longitude.

A study of this incident brings to light not only the difficulties experienced by navigators who could not determine their longitude, but those caused by the fact that surveyors could not determine their longitude either, so that the geographical positions of places were grossly inaccurate. The navigator in fact faced a double problem — where was he and where was the place that he hoped to reach.

Other governments had offered rewards for the discovery of the longitude. One had been offered by Philip III of Spain in 1598. Holland was popularly supposed to have offered one but no trace of it has ever been found. France followed England with an offer made two years afterwards.

The chance by which the British government came to offer its prize and to set up the Board of Longitude to administer it, is somewhat diverting. Two men, William Whiston and Humphrey Ditton, formulated a plan by which they proposed to anchor lightships permanently at intervals along all the principal trade routes. These lightships would fire star-shell to a height of 6440 feet at regular intervals and any ship seeing one would be able to fix her position relative to the lightship by timing the interval between the flash and the sound of the explosion. The absolute impracticability of such a plan will be manifest to all, but its authors managed to get considerable publicity for it, and to extend this still further had a petition submitted to parliament. A committee was set up to examine this petition and it was on its subsequent recommendation that the Board of Longitude was established. A number of small sums were paid out but it was not until 1772 that the full amount was honoured.

Reflecting Octant.

In 1732 an invention was disclosed which was to have tremendous impact upon the art of navigation. In that year John Hadley showed his reflecting octant, often erroneously called a quadrant (page 141). By its aid, altitudes and horizontal angles could be observed with far greater accuracy than with any previous instrument, and when it had been perfected by improved methods of graduating the arc, by its expansion to a sextant and by the addition of a telescope there was no difficulty in observing angles to an accuracy of one minute of arc, or even less. This instrument was not only suitable for observing altitudes so that latitude sights and, later in the century, chronometer sights for longitude could be observed with accuracy, but since the instrument could be used for observing angles in any plane it was adapted to the observation of lunar distances, when these became useful, and for surveying.

Hadley's octant did not immediately replace the Davis quadrant. As an example Robert Lambert, master of the GLOUCESTER during Anson's voyage of 1740-1744, may be quoted. This officer recorded in his log-book that he had with him both Hadley's and Davis's instruments. When he arrived at any harbour he always recorded the latitude by the Hadley and sometimes by the Davis as well. These records would seem to indicate that his Davis quadrant had an index error and over-read by from five to ten minutes. Unfortunately we do not know which instrument he used at sea for ordinary navigation. He may have reserved his Hadley octant for fixing latitudes of harbours.

Longitude.

During the period of about thirty-five years that followed Hadley's invention the 'Discovery of the Longitude' at last became possible, or at least available to some navigators. In 1735 John Harrison (page 168) completed his first timekeeper and trials were made at sea during the following year. It was not until 1764, however, that he was finally successful. The provision of an accurate timekeeper which would keep the time of the prime meridian while at sea and would enable the longitude to be determined had been proposed by Gemma Frisius as early as 1530,* but no one before Harrison had succeeded in making one which would maintain a steady rate in a ship at sea under the varying conditions of motion, temperature and so on that might be experienced.

---

* *Structura Radii Astronomici et Geometrici.*

Harrison's first timekeeper gave considerable promise when it was tried at sea in 1736 on a voyage to Lisbon in the CENTURION, and back in the ORFORD.

Meanwhile in 1755 Tobias Mayer completed his tables for forecasting the motions of the moon and at last made it possible to use her as a clock. He proposed to expand Hadley's octant into a circle and, after trials with this, the less unwieldy alternative of a sextant was evolved. These trials in 1757-1759 showed the possibility of the lunar distance method of finding Greenwich time and hence the longitude. Experiments made by Nevil Maskelyne during a voyage to St. Helena in 1761 confirmed this view. The result of these was the publication of the first *Nautical Almanac* for 1767 and thereafter it became an annual publication.

These two methods of finding the longitude, the one by the aid of the chronometer (timekeeper) and the other by lunar distance, were introduced to the navigator at about the same time. The chronometer method proved to be the more accurate in the early part of a voyage, but might progressively deteriorate as the voyage continued. It could however be given a new lease of life if a new error of the chronometer were found at some place where the longitude was accurately known. The lunar distance method required less initial expense and though its accuracy was at first inferior this did not get any worse. In the end both methods came to be used, some navigators preferring one, some the other. There were always some who used both methods in conjunction, employing the lunar distance as a warning device to advise them of any serious deterioration in the running of the timekeeper.

Use of Chronometers and Lunars.

It would appear that the East India Company was in advance of the Royal Navy in the introduction of chronometers. Around the year 1790 it issued its ships with new printed log-books.* Among other things these provided spaces for the daily noon recording of three longitudes, those by account, by lunar and by chronometer. Whereas in 1786 we find the *Royal Bishop* and her consorts (page 201) using lunars frequently and exclusively, the *Osterley* in 1793 was recording chronometer sights almost daily with an occasional lunar as well.

---

* According to D. W. Waters the first East India Company log-book on a printed form was used for the voyage of 1702-3, but they do not seem to have come into general use before the 1760s.

These ships did not correct their longitude by account when a longitude by observation had been obtained, but carried on the account until a new departure could be obtained from some definite point of land.

On her voyage to China in 1793 (page 201) between the 1st and 10th October while sailing off the coast of Indo-China the *Osterley's* reckoning was always about a degree to the eastward of the longitude by chronometer. Then when she turned eastward the difference gradually increased until on the 26th October when nearing the Balabac Strait it was about four degrees. During the last few days lunars were also observed, giving a position about three quarters of a degree nearer to the longitude by account than that by chronometer. While the *Osterley* corrected her account by taking a new departure when passing through the Balabac Strait, one of her consorts did not. This was the *Glatton,* whose difference between account and chronometer had been very similar.

In 1797 the *Arniston* passed through the Celebes Sea out into the Pacific on her way to Whampoa. During the first five days after entering the ocean the difference between the longitudes by reckoning and by chronometer increased steadily to about four degrees, that by the chronometer being to the eastward. The accuracy of the chronometer was confirmed when land was sighted near Macao.

The voyage of four battleships in 1802 is interesting because it shows something of navigational practice in the Royal Navy at that period.

On 15th January the ST. GEORGE (98), SPENCER, POWERFUL and VANGUARD (74s), left Ceuta for the West Indies. The ships did not keep station as one would know it today, being often four or five miles apart. The master of the SPENCER began observing lunars on 26th January and continued daily until 2nd February. His reckoning would appear to have been pretty accurate for on 26th January it put him in 41° 33′ W. and his lunar in 41° 10′ W. His change of position since the previous day is what one would expect and shows no break in continuity, such as would have occurred if he had corrected his reckoning by the observation. On this same day the POWERFUL recorded 44° 43′ W., the ST. GEORGE 45° 2′ and the VANGUARD 47° 26′.

The next day the master of the ST. GEORGE observed a lunar and found his reckoning five and a half degrees too far to the westward. He continued to take lunars daily from 30th January until 3rd

February and by a 'watch', which in those days was the name usually used for a timekeeper, on the 1st, 2nd and 3rd February. The longitudes by the watch showed his reckoning on those days to be 7° 14', 7° 34' and 5° 27' too far to the west. The longitude by lunars was very consistent being always between 5° 57' and 6° 1' to the eastward of that by account.

On 31st January the SPENCER signalled that her longitude was now 54° W. That of the previous noon must have been intended when she recorded 53° 35', the POWERFUL 55° 21', the ST. GEORGE 58° 9' (and by lunar 52° 16') and the VANGUARD 61° 36'. None of the other ships appears to have taken any notice of the SPENCER's signal at that time.

At dawn on 3rd February the island of Deseada (now known as Désirade, 18° 20' N., 61° 6' W.) was sighted S.W. by W. seven or eight leagues. This would have put the ships at noon in about 16½° N., 61° W. If we work forward from the noon positions recorded on the previous day we shall find that on the 3rd they would have expected to be in:

ST. GEORGE	16° 40' N., 66° 17' W.
SPENCER	16° 36' N., 61° 44' W.
POWERFUL	16° 39' N., 64° 6' W.
VANGUARD	16° 32' N., 69° 21' W.

Thereafter all ships corrected their longitudes, taking fresh departures from Deseada. The reason why they had carried on with their original reckonings so long, though the ST. GEORGE since the 27th January and the others since the 31st at least had known that they were far astern of their calculations, was probably due to the predilection of seamen at this time and for some time afterwards for *expecting* to make the land much earlier than they were certain would be the case. One is reminded of Columbus who worked the other way round, keeping his reckoning behind the ship so as to make his crew imagine they were not so far from home as was really the truth!

An interesting disclosure found from the log-books of these ships is that in some the captains navigated independently of their masters. The captain of the SPENCER did not always agree with the master as regards the latitude, showing that he was taking his own sights, and the captain of the ST. GEORGE sometimes differed in the results of his observations of the variation. The differences in both cases are too small to be material, but they do prove independence.

Another example of the use of a lunar distance is shown in the log kept by the master of H.M. Schooner RACER in 1814. This vessel was on passage to North America. After steering W.N.W. across the Atlantic she altered to the S.W. expecting to find the island of Bermuda when she reached the correct latitude, but she failed to make her expected landfall. The master then observed a lunar and found that his ship was still two degrees to the eastward of his reckoning. It is evident that no other lunars were taken during this voyage and none would have been taken if the master had found Bermuda as he expected.

Iron Ships.

In the early years of the nineteenth century a new hazard assailed the navigator. This was the increased use of iron for ship's fittings, followed very quickly by the introduction of the material for shipbuilding. It began to be realised that the magnetic quality of all this iron was responsible for causing compass errors and these in turn for wrecks or near strandings. Many of these passed unnoticed, an 'unknown current' usually getting the blame, but some did not and examples of these are of interest.

In 1803 the APOLLO, followed by forty vessels out of a convoy of seventy, ran ashore on the north coast of Portugal due to the errors of her compass. The thirty ships who escaped realised in time that the convoy was being led into danger.

In 1812 the COURAGEUX (74), ran ashore near Anholt but was refloated. It was subsequently proved that the compass needle had been deflected through no less than one and a half points due to small arms, belonging to the marines, being placed below it.

In 1842 the *Reliance* was sailing up the Channel and through getting too far to the southward of her course ran ashore near Boulogne. It was subsequently established that the wreck was almost certainly due to her compass being deflected by a large iron tank, forty-six feet long, placed about eighteen feet from the compass.

Many cases were noted where ships steering reciprocal courses by their compasses did not make good reciprocal courses over the ground, and these were usually attributed to currents or to indraughts into bays. Thus warships, going to and from the Baltic during the French wars, often found themselves too close to the Dutch coast, and some twenty or thirty years later the packets which carried the mails across the Irish Sea usually found that they appeared to be set off course, always in the same direction.

The problem was recognised by a few navigators, and earnest endeavours were made to elucidate the rules behind these compass errors and to discover how the errors could be eliminated. In particular, the practical work of Flinders, Barlow, Airy, Johnson and Evans must be mentioned, and the theoretical work of Poisson and Smith. There were also many inventors who tried to develop improved compasses, for bad compasses made the errors more difficult to assess. In 1837 the Admiralty appointed a Compass Committee to consider the whole problem and in 1855 the ship-owners of Liverpool set up another committee for the same purpose (page 98).

The Double Altitude Problem.

Through the past two centuries navigation, or rather the processes which were suggested to navigators, continued to be improved by attempts to expand astronomical aids. Men sought to make more frequent the occasions on which the position of the ship could be fixed, to increase the accuracy of fixes, to simplify the calculations. The last was particularly imperative, for without simplicity many navigators would necessarily be confined to the old ways.

The meridian altitude sight for latitude had always put a great limitation on navigation. It so often happened that the sun might be obscured at the instant of its meridian passage though during much of the rest of the day the sky would be clear and the sun would shine when it was of no use to the navigator with no other latitude sight at his disposal.

As early as 1537 Pedro Nunez showed that if two altitudes and azimuths of the sun were obtained at two different times during the day it was possible to discover the latitude by manipulating a globe. In 1733, J. Kelly showed how the same problem could be solved by calculation. Reliance upon the difference of two azimuths could never give an accurate result and it is extremely doubtful whether this scheme was ever more than of academic interest.

Difference of time between two sights rather than difference of azimuth should be a little more accurate, even in the days of rudimentary clocks, and in 1594 Hues showed how to solve this problem, also on a globe. Personally I am extremely doubtful whether globes ever were carried to sea, except possibly by a few enthusiasts.

In 1728 a solution was published by Nicholas Facio Duillier* which involved the calculation of the latitude from two altitudes of the sun and the elapsed time between them and this was followed in 1754 with another solution by Cornelis Douwes†. The latter method is said to have been very popular in England, possibly because special tables to aid the calculation were published in the *Nautical Almanac* for 1771. Even then the calculation was very cumbersome until the appearance of further tables in the *Nautical Almanac* for 1794.

The double-altitude could be used for a single star, or even for two different stars observed at the same time. In 1836 C.F.A. Shadwell published tables giving the latitude from altitudes of two stars.

Other solutions of this problem were numerous and are given by most writers on navigation, but I am unable to quote any actual example of one of them being used.

Ex-Meridian Altitude.

This was a method by which an altitude of the sun could be observed shortly before or after the meridian passage and corrected to give the altitude and consequently the latitude, at noon. In 1800, Joseph de Mendoza y Rios published tables by which the necessary correction could be obtained for a sight taken anything up to eleven minutes from noon. Other tables published at a later date had the advantage of extending the time from noon at which the sight could be taken. In later days the ex-meridian was very popular among those who wished to observe their latitude at noon, ship's time, when this was some time before the actual meridian passage. Sights were finished earlier and one could get away to lunch.

The Sumner Method of Navigation.

There is no doubt that the first great stride made in astronomical navigation in the nineteenth century was the introduction of the Sumner method in 1843 (page 172). It greatly improved the accuracy

---

* *Navigation Improved*, 1728.
† *Actes de l'Academie de Haarlem*, 1754.
  Dr. H. Pemberton in *Philosophical Transaction of the Royal Society*, 1760, Vol. LI, pp. 910-929.

by which the position of the ship could be obtained and like the double-altitude and ex-meridian methods avoided the tyranny of the noon sight.

In the Sumner method the navigator observed the altitude of the sun and worked out the longitude by chronometer using two different assumed latitudes. This gave two different positions which were plotted on the chart and joined by what was called a position line. The ship had necessarily to be on that straight line or its extension. In conjunction with a second Sumner position line observed later, or even a noon latitude, a fix could be obtained, subject of course to the allowance made for the run between sights.

The great advantage of the Sumner method was that sights could be taken at any time of the day, or any two convenient stars could be observed at twilight.

The Marcq St. Hilaire Method.

In 1875 Captain Marcq St. Hilaire showed a new way of obtaining a position line which was simpler than that of Sumner (page 174). It was taken up gradually by navigators and by the beginning of the present century was generally taught in the Royal Navy. In the merchant service the Sumner method was required by Board of Trade examinations from 1898 and was consequently the one usually practiced. About the time of the outbreak of the First Great War it ceased to be compulsory but it was still extensively used by officers of the Royal Navy Reserve with whom I served at that period. In fact in battleships of the Grand Fleet it was customary for midshipmen of the Royal Navy and of the Royal Naval Reserve to receive separate instruction in navigation. Younger officers of the merchant service seem to have reverted to the straight longitude by chronometer sight used in conjunction with the traditional noon sight, either a meridian altitude of the sun or an ex-meridian altitude using the appropriate tables. This was less dangerous than it would at first appear for dead reckoning had become so much more accurate that there was considerably less likelihood of the latitude being so far in error as had been the case a century before. Since about 1930, candidates taking Board of Trade examinations have been permitted to use any suitable method and the St. Hilaire position line is now almost universally used although there are still some who cling to the longitude sight. In the British merchant service the use of tables to shorten computation has never made serious progress.

The End of Lunars.

Lecky, writing in 1881, foretold the end of the lunar distance as a means of finding longitude. By that date the use of steam had made voyages much shorter and chronometers had come down in price to £25 or £30. The only vessels to whom lunars were likely to be of use were small ill-found vessels with only one chronometer, or none, and these were unlikely to carry the expensive sextant necessary for the accurate observation of a lunar.

In 1896 the master of the four-masted *Port Jackson* found his two chronometers differing by thirty-nine seconds and so used lunars, finding that the longitudes from these were nearer correct than those by either chronometer. He subsequently wrote: "These observations are a grand check on chronometers, and their practice at sea would, at the same time, be a pleasant pastime for young shipmasters and officers who prefer sail to steam."*

Nevertheless the days of the lunar observation were drawing to a close. In 1909 the *Nautical Almanac* ceased to publish the necessary tables and so the sight passed into history, lamented apparently only by the mathematicians and instructors in navigation.

The Thomson Compass.

In 1876 Sir William Thomson patented a compass and binnacle which were to revolutionise thought on the subject (page 99). Hitherto magnets and masses of soft iron had been placed around the compass in somewhat haphazard fashion in order to correct it. Now, instead of the correctors having to be attached in the vicinity of the compass by whatever means the compass adjuster could devise, provision was made for correctors of standard sizes to be inserted in suitable racks or brackets on the binnacle at varying distances from the compass.† Thomson also designed a new compass, following rules set down by the best thought on the subject, and this was received with far greater acclamation than it really deserved. Though undoubtedly an excellent well-made and well-designed compass it is doubtful whether it would have triumphed so decisively in a fair competitive trial. Thomson's system was always tried, at any rate in

* *Nautical Magazine*, 1902, p. 457.
† Other binnacles with correctors fitted in them had been designed earlier, but none seems to have been adopted.

the Royal Navy, as a complete unit against other types of compass which were either not corrected or only partially corrected.

Since compass correction not only eliminated, or at any rate reduced, deviations but also made the compass steadier and easier to navigate by, a closely corrected compass must always be the best.

The Thomson compass was still a dry-card compass, a type that was already giving ground to the liquid-filled compasses which were constantly being improved at this time (page 77). It delayed their introduction, which the vibration of steam vessels was already making inevitable. They were used abroad, however, and extensively began to be adopted by the Royal Navy in 1906. Since the Second Great War the Thomson has almost dropped out of use everywhere.

Magnetic Mines.

During the Second Great War a new problem forced itself upon navigators. The Germans adopted the magnetic mine which was fired by the near proximity of the magnetic hull of a ship. Two methods of countering this came into use and became known as De-gaussing. In one the hull was 'wiped', that is to say was partially demagnetized by having electro-magentic coils passed over it. In the second method a coil was wound around the ship and, being energised electrically, formed a great corrector magnet whose effect was equal and opposite to the magnetic field of the ship.

Both schemes affected the compasses of ships and introduced new deviations. At first sight the wiping method would seem to create less difficulty, since all that was needed on completion of the operation was to recorrect the compasses. But the effect of wiping was not permanent, it wore off in time and this might well have been hastened if the ship were subjected to violent shocks, such as the explosion of nearby bombs or mines. This resulted in the need for constant vigilance and further recorrection as the deviations of the compass continually changed.

With the coil method it was necessary to fit each binnacle with a system of coils supplied electrically from the same source. The usual arrangement was to fit each binnacle with three coils, whose axes were fore-and-aft, athwartship and vertical, each coil being connected in series with an adjustable resistance to regulate the current passing through it. It was then necessary to adjust every compass twice, once in the ordinary way with the current in the de-gaussing coil switched off, and once by means of the corrector coils with the current switched on.

One result of de-gaussing was to increase the adoption of the gyro-compass which, since 1911, had been gradually fitted by warships and the better-found merchant vessels. It remains usual, however, for ships fitted with gyro-compasses to carry additionally one or more magnetic compasses for use in the event of a gyro-compass failure. It must be pointed out that it is quite useless to fit a magnetic compass, even as a stand-by, unless it is placed in a reasonable position and adequately corrected. Otherwise, when it is needed, the magnetic compass may be found to be pointing always to the same spot in the ship, whatever course is steered. It has been argued that gyro-compasses are now so reliable that it is a waste of time to adjust the magnetic compass after it has been fitted as a stand-by. One of His Majesty's ships was once fitted with *three* gyro-compasses and no magnetic. It was quite impossible one would have thought for all three compasses to fail at one time. They did. Fortunately the ship was out of sight of land and for an hour or so, while one gyro-compass was being repaired, the ship was steered by the stars!

Of recent years there have been several great improvements in methods of navigation and these have been made the subject of a separate chapter (page 222).

Two
Direction

The first instrument of direction which was adopted by navigators was the magnetic compass, but before it came into use there were four milestones in the history of magnetism which had to be passed — first, the discovery that there existed a certain ore, named lodestone, which had the property of attracting to it pieces of ferrous metals; second, the discovery that this power of attraction, known as magnetism, could be transmitted to such pieces of ferrous metal; third, the discovery that there was some curious property by which certain magnetic objects appeared to repel instead of to attract each other; and, finally, the discovery that a piece of magnetized metal of suitable shape would, if freely suspended, point towards the north.

The history of all this development is very obscure, for it took place long before there were any accurate records. There are, nevertheless, plenty of legends. For example, the poet Nicander, who lived in about the second century B.C., tells how a neatherd in Crete was walking on the slopes of Mount Ida when he found that he had become anchored in his tracks by the iron nails in his sandals and the iron tip of his staff adhering to the rock. There is reason to believe that even in Nicander's time the legend was by no means new. At least two centuries earlier we hear of the Samothracian Rings — rings of iron which when touched adhered to and supported one another to form a chain although they were not linked together.

The whole history of magnetism before the invention of the compass is far too extensive and complicated to be discussed here. It is complicated by the difficulties of translation and of realising exactly what an author intended to convey. It is further complicated by the whole history of ancient records. One is never sure what exactly was the state of knowledge when an author wrote. Since his time errors of copying may well have crept in, either through carelessness or ignorance on the part of the copyist, the attempt of a later copier to rectify the errors of a predecessor, or the introduction of deliberate glosses on the original text. In some cases it is probable that there have been attempts, deliberate or merely misguided, to claim knowledge for an ancient people who lived long before. There is for example, the legend of the hanging statue. One version is that Ptolemy II, King of Egypt, who died in 247 B.C., wanted to commemorate Arsinoë his sister-queen by placing an iron statue of her in a lodestone-lined vault, where it would hang in the air suspended between equal and opposite attractions. We are told that king and architect both died before the plan could be put into execution; perhaps just as well for the attempt would have been doomed, but it would have been quite possible in the then state of knowledge for such an attempt to have been contemplated. The legend grew to embrace versions in which the attempt was actually successful and its narrators included Rabbi Mosheh ben Mainon, writing in the late twelfth century, who averred that Jereboam in the tenth century B.C. suspended in this way the golden calves which he ordered Israel to worship, and it has been suggested, though never by Muslim authorities, that the coffin of Mahomet was similarly suspended.

All these tales and suppositions are only the forerunners of the magnetic compass and this is the matter in which we are really interested here.

In considering the early history of the compass we must take into account the circumstances in which it first appeared. The handling of ships was a craft entirely in the hands of the close section of the community which had little communication with the outside world. In a period of general illiteracy few, if any, could read or write. Professional knowledge was obtained by sons from their fathers, by apprentices from their masters, by all men from their own experience, and though some might be obtained by conversation with old friends the tendency was to keep knowledge a close secret.

We can imagine how the compass needle came to be invented. Some scientific experimenter, who must have been a landsman possibly with maritime interests through trade, may have been experimenting with a lodestone and a suspended magnetized needle. Then one day he would realise that after he had removed the lodestone to some other room the needle always turned towards the same direction and that this direction was not that of the storeroom where the lodestone was kept. A search for what was attracting the needle would be unsuccessful and at last the truth would dawn upon him that a suspended magnetic needle would always point towards the north. There was frequent correspondence between learned men and between them and the universities and so the knowledge would spread.

The First Mariner's Compass.

It is shortly before the year 1200 A.D. that we know definitely that the compass was in use in some ships in European waters, for references to it begin to appear in the writings of scholars. The first of these was Alexander Neckam, a man of whose life we know an unusual amount for this period of history. One reason for this is that he happened to have been born in St. Albans on the same day in September 1157 that the future king, Richard I, was born at Windsor and Alexander's mother was employed to nurse the royal infant. We are told rather picturesquely that she suckled the prince from her right breast and her own son from the left. I have always wondered why it was necessary to send so far as St. Albans for a wet-nurse!

In 1180 Neckam was at the University of Paris and there is no doubt that it was here he heard of the compass which was already in use in some ships at sea. Shortly after his return to England he compiled two works which were evidently known before the end of the century and were probably written about the year 1187. The more important of these is an encyclopaedia called *De Naturis Rerum**, the second a less important work called *De Utensilibus*. Taken together we get a clear view of the occasional use of the compass needle and of the need to magnetize it every time it was used, but its actual construction is still rather obscure.

Our next authority is Guyot de Provins, a minstrel turned monk, who wrote a long satyrical poem between the years 1203 and 1208. In it he castigates the pope and regrets that the holy father is not as constant as the Pole Star, and this gives him an opportunity to describe the use of the compass needle and how it was floated on the surface of water in a bowl by means of a straw which it transfixed. Other rather similar references appear in the works of thirteenth century writers†.

In 1269 a noted scholar, Petrus Peregrinus, whiled away the tedium of the siege of Lucera, in Italy, by writing a celebrated letter to his friend and neighbour in Normandy, Sigerius de Faucoucourt. In this he describes at considerable length two compasses. The first is merely a lump of lodestone floated in water on a piece of board on

---

* As an example of the difficulties of a historian who cannot be always consulting original sources on every point, it may be related that three distinguished authors on the subject have variously described this book as *De Naturis Rerum* *De Natura Rerum* and *De Rerum Naturis*.

† For example Cardinal Jacques de Vitry, 1218; Baïlak of Kibdjak, 1242; Krolowiz, 1252-1255. Vague references also appear in the works of such poets as Guido Guinicelli and Dante.

which the north-south line was drawn by the aid of astronomical means. This would be a very crude instrument but could have been used for checking wind direction. He then describes a magnetized needle mounted horizontally in a vertical axle which could turn between upper and lower pivots. It is unlikely that Peregrinus could every have seen either form used at sea. It is likely that he knew of the usual needle floated by a straw and thought that he could improve it. How often does one find some landlubber, who has never been to sea, advising the sailor on how to improve his equipment without having any idea of the practical conditions to be encountered.

Although an attempt was made in the mid-nineteenth century to use a double-pivoted compass needle as suggested by Peregrinus it had no practical use at sea. As soon as the axis is deviated even slightly from the vertical in any other than the north-south plane the needle must inevitably be subjected to the influence of the vertical component of the earth's magnetic field as well as to the horizontal and this will pull the end of the needle downwards, forcing it to deviate from its proper direction.

The next improvement to the compass may have been the placing of the needle on a single pivot instead of floating it,* thus enabling the water to be eliminated, and the attachment of the needle to a card on which the directions were marked. Let us consider the second. It has often been suggested that as charts of the portolan type had appeared in the Mediterranean by 1290 and that as these had on them representations of a compass card, it follows that the compass, more or less in the form we now know, must already have been in use when these charts were made. But this is to jump to conclusions and to overlook most of the facts.

Points of the Compass.

What we now call compass points were originally wind directions. In very early times in places where winds blew chiefly from particular directions it would be natural to give them names. By the time of Homer in about 900 B.C. the Greeks already used four names for winds. These were *Boreas*, the north wind; *Euros*, the east wind; *Notos*, the south wind; and *Zephuros*, the west wind. It must not be assumed, however, that these were very definite directions. They

* *See* Note on page 104.

indicated at first merely arcs of the horizon from which the winds blew and these might well differ in different parts of Greece and even at different times of the year.

With the increase in navigation and particularly with the introduction of sailing directions it became necessary to detail more exact directions, and these four wind directions became more standardized and were later increased to eight or twelve.

The twelve-wind system seems to have come about in the Mediterranean in the following way. At the summer solstice the sun rises and sets at directions to the north of east and west and at the winter solstice to the south of those points. These four positions provided four other directions, or daughter winds, one on each side of east and west. For the sake of tidiness, perhaps someone added daughter winds on each side of north and south. Thus there appeared four groups each of three winds with sizeable gaps between them. This would be inconvenient. The spaces between the daughter and main winds would be opened out to provide twelve equally spaced winds. Later these could be increased to twenty-four by bisecting each space. This arrangement suited the tidy minds of astronomers and tied in with their notion of a twenty-four hour day.

The eight-wind system was derived more simply by adding an additional wind midway between each adjacent pair and when need arose bisection to sixteen and then to thirty-two points occurred. It was claimed by Bartolomeo Crescentio* that the men of Amalfi first expanded the system to thirty-two winds. It may well be so, for Amalfi had a great reputation as a cradle of seamen.

At about the beginning of the Christian era both systems were in use in the Mediterranean, but the one based on eight winds was more popular with seamen and gradually squeezed out the other.

As to the names of wind directions the first eight winds acquired their own names in Greece. In about 100 B.C. the celebrated Tower of the Winds was erected in Athens by Andronicus Cyrrhestes and was embellished with emblematic figures in relief representing eight named winds: *Boreas*, north; *Kaikias*, north-east; *Apeliotes*, east; *Euros*, south-east; *Notos*, south; *Lips*, south-west; *Zephuros*, west; and *Skiros*, north-west. The way in which *Euros* has apparently shifted since the time of Homer from east to south-east will be noted. It confirms my previous remarks about the very approximate nature of early wind directions.

---

* Bartolomeo Crescentio, *Nautica Mediterranea*, 1607, p. 157.

There were Latin names for the wind directions but owing to the multiplication of names for some directions, and the use of the same names for different directions in both the eight- and twelve-wind competing systems, there is some confusion among authorities.

By about the twelfth century, the Italian eight-wind system had become established in the Mediterranean, but writing in about the middle of the following century Brunetto Latini tells us that the actual names varied in different localities, while sailors used their own names for some of the winds*.

The most usual names were variations of the following:-

Tramontana	North	Across the mountains.
Greco	North-east	From the direction of Greece.
Levante	East	Sunrise.
Scirocco	South-east	Said to be derived from the Arabic.
Ostro	South	Dati† gives *Mezodi* or *Affricone* the latter being apparently an exchange of names with the next wind.
Garbino	South-west	Said to be derived from the Arabic. Dati gives *Austro* or *Libeccio*. (see below)
Ponente	West	Sunset.
Maestro	North-west	Apparently the master, the strongest wind, but Latini says it takes its name from that of the seven stars.

When the number of winds increased beyond eight the others received combination names, such as *Tramontana-Greco* for north-north-east, taking its name from the wind on each side of it.

Sailors had two alternatives for *Garbino* which they called *Libeccio* or *Africus*. Both Latini and Dati gave the former of these, but it is noteworthy that while I have seen A for Africus used on the wind-roses of portolan maps from the fourteenth to the sixteenth centuries I have not seen an L before the fifteenth and in the latter part of the sixteenth it replaced *Africus* entirely.

It has been suggested that sailors discarded *Garbino* because with *Greco* this would have meant two Gs on the compass card, which might have led to confusion. I do not think that this theory is a tenable one, particularly as *Libeccio* and *Levante* both begin with an L. Of course it might be said that, as the east was usually marked by a cross instead of an initial, there would be no confusion. Incidentally, I have never seen G for *Garbino* on a wind-rose.

---

*   Brunetto Latini, *Li Livres dou Tresor*, Livre I, Part III, Chap. cvii.
†   Gregorio Dati, *La Sfera*. Book III.

The system adopted in northern Europe for naming directions was based upon four monosyllabic names, in English north, east, south and west with very similar words in the other languages. No special names were ever adopted for the second four (half-cardinal) winds, but these were given compound names, such as north-east. Other combinations followed as the number of winds increased to sixteen and then to thirty-two. The comparative simplicity of the North-European system led to its adoption in the Iberian countries. In the seventeenth and early eighteenth centuries French ships were using either system, according to whether they came from Mediterranean ports or from those outside. This must have been very inconvenient. In Italy their system lingered on and only gave place to the North-European system late in the last century.

The Finnish Compass

Yet another system of naming winds originated in Finland*. Here they started with six named directions, those of north and south and for sunrise and sunset at the summer and winter solstices, taken as being 60° from north and south. Thus there were six evenly spaced winds. The original six were expanded to twelve in the normal way by the use of compound names. It will be noted that the names used for east and west were therefore compound names — *Itä-Kaako* and *Luodet-Länsi*. By about the beginning of the last century contact with the Germanic peoples to the west increased and it became inconvenient for sailors who had served in foreign ships to find a compass very different to that to which they were accustomed. The Finnish compass card was therefore changed to a basic eight-point one by moving the names for N.60°E., S.60°E., S.60°W., and N.60°W. to East, S.45°E., West and N.45°W. respectively with compound names for north-east and south-west. Later the inconvenient inconsistency of having compound names for north-east and south-west was overcome by introducing new names for these two points and thereafter a reasonable thirty-two point system evolved.

---

* *Mnemosyne*, April 1822. A translation of this article appears in W. E. May, *The Finnish Compass Card. Journal of the Institute of Navigation*, VI (1953) p. 248-254.

Figure 5   Wind-rose from a Portolan Chart.
(Copyright: National Maritime Museum)

Charts and Compass Points.

After this digression let us return to the early chart and wind-rose. The first portolan charts did not in fact exhibit any wind-roses: the first of these did not appear until 1375 when a single one is to be found in the Atlas Catalan. It is most significant that the early representations on charts are usually not compass cards but wind-roses, for while the wind directions are marked very much as on a compass card, the north and east points are marked outside the containing circle and could not possibly have formed part of a compass card. It is not until 1502 that Cantino's map of the world set the fashion for having more than one wind-rose on a chart. Then came another development. Some of the roses on a chart were now true compass cards and with their introduction came a significant development. While the compass cards followed the standard system of colours to which we shall refer later, the wind-roses, with their external north and east points, were painted in such colours as the chart-maker saw fit, as had always been the custom.

From the above I am satisfied that since no illustration of a true compass card appears until 1568 it is impossible to agree that the wind-roses necessarily prove any connection between the introduction of the compass card and the chart.

We are left with the two improvements to the compass, the pivot and the card, with absolutely no evidence as to when either took place, though they were probably associated. It was at one time stated that a gentleman named Flavio Gioia of Amalfi invented the compass in 1302. When it was pointed out that the compass needle was in use at least a century earlier, some historians of the compass promptly asserted that Flavio Gioia must have introduced the two improvements. Now, however, the whole development of the story has been traced and it has been proved that no such man existed and the whole tale has no other foundation than the reputation of the men of Amalfi as sailors and a vague statement that they perfected the compass.

The first reference we have to a compass card is by Francesco da Buti in 1380 in his commentaries on the works of Dante showing that it was well established by that date, while the first illustration that we have is a few years later as a marginal illustration in a manuscript by Gregorio Dati entitled *La Sfera* (Fig. 6). (*See* note on page 53).

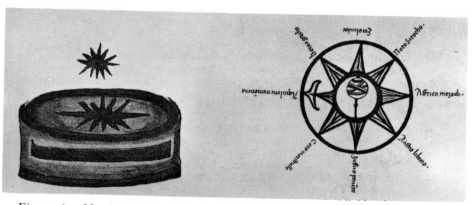

Figure 6   Marginal illustration from some manuscripts of *La Sfera* showing compass and card.

The Chinese.

It is popularly upheld that we are indebted to the Chinese for the invention of the compass. Such tales usually start with the legend of Huang-ti who reigned over China in 2634 B.C. and whose authority was challenged by Ch'ih-yu. The two armies met on the plains of Cho Lu and finding himself in danger of defeat Ch'ih-yu called down a cloud from heaven behind which he withdrew his forces. This was probably the first use of a smoke screen in history! Huang-ti had with him a south-pointing chariot and this led his troops on a steady course through the cloud and on the other side of it they fell upon the unfortunate rebels and slew them.

There are other accounts of such chariots in China and how their secret was lost and regained several times. Led by the early Jesuit missionaries to China, many assumed that such a chariot must have had a concealed magnetic compass to provide its directive system, but recent research has shown that there is little doubt there was a pointer, worked off the two wheels through a differential gear.

The first authentic mention in China of a magnetic needle pointing in a fixed direction is in about 1088 A.D. by Shen Kua in the *Mĕng Chhi Pi Than*. He speaks of a magnetized needle floating on water, pivoting on a hard surface, or suspended by a thread, pointing to the south rather than to the north, but does not make any suggestions as to its practical use. He was followed in about 1116 by Khou Tsung-Shih in the *Pen Tsao Yen I* who largely supports the earlier work but describes the needle being thrust crosswise through a rush and floated on water as in the European compass of a little later.

In about 1100 and 1126 there are references to the use of compass needles in ships. Both these dates are earlier than any recorded in Europe and on this ground it may be claimed that the compass was invented in China and taught to Europe by the Chinese. The contact between the Chinese and Europeans at this period was very tenuous and mostly through the Arabs. If, therefore, the compass had been transmitted from the East through the Arabs, one would have expected some record of the instrument to have remained with them, yet no mention of the compass has been traced in Arabic records and what knowledge the Arabs had of magnetism seems to have been derived from the Greeks. I am inclined to think that we have a case of two completely independent inventions.

It is not until the sixteenth century that one really begins to know anything of the compasses used in the Chinese seas and then it is a strange glimpse. Sir Thomas Cavendish returning from his voyage of circumnavigation of 1586 brought back two men, one from Japan and the other from the Philippines. Of all the men who must have talked to them in England, William Barlowe, Archdeacon of Salisbury, was the only one who took the trouble to ask what sort of compasses were used in their countries. They told him that they used a long needle, about six inches in length, pivoted in a bowl of water, and instead of a card they made do with two lines painted at right-angles to each other in the bottom of the bowl. From these they estimated the course steered. I have been unable to find any information about the compasses used in Chinese vessels during the next three hundred years, but in later times they apparently used a much smaller compass with a bare needle only two inches long, pivoted in a dry wooden bowl with the points marked around the verge. It is of considerable interest that they divided their horizon into twenty-four points.

Compass Cards.

Apart from the sketch which appears in the margin of some manuscripts of Gregorio Dati's *La Sfera** the earliest known illustration of a compass card is that in Martin Cortes' *Breve Compendio de la Sphera*, 1551, (Fig. 8), unless we accept the compass roses which appear on charts. It was necessary, when ordering a course to be steered, to be able to differentiate easily between the different points on the compass card. For this reason the four cardinal points were painted blue and the four half-cardinal points red. Since this system is used on the compass roses of some charts it evidently dates from as early as the fifteenth century. The system, while useful, was not sufficient and the east point was marked by a cross, an obvious development in a Christian world. Other points were marked by initial letters, the north sometimes with some sort of arrow. It was not until about 1500 that the *fleur-de-lys* came into use as a symbol for north. Many suggestions have been put forward to provide a reason for the almost universal adoption of this device, once introduced. One suggestion was that it was out of compliment to the French, who invented the compass. I do not think that this idea can possibly hold water, since there is no

* A number of manuscripts of this work exist. Some show a compass (Fig. 6) and some only a diagram of winds (Fig. 7). Their respective dates have not been determined.

Figure 7   Page from manuscript of *La Sfera* by Gregorio Dati showing the simple diagram of wind names which on some manuscripts is replaced by a drawing of a compass and card. (Copyright: British Museum)

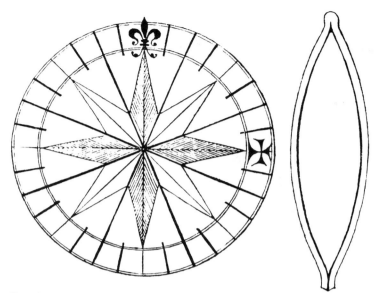

Figure 8   Compass card and needle, from *Breue Compendio de al Sphera y de la arte de Nauegar*, by Martin Cortes, 1551.

evidence that anyone in the fifteenth century gave France credit for the discovery of the compass. Another suggestion is that the design really represents the lotus and shows the eastern origin of the compass, but this also can be dismissed. I think it far more likely that in one of the schools of chart makers, probably Spanish or Portuguese, it became customary to mark the north with a T for *Tramontana,* reinforced with an arrow-head to make it stand out more than the other letters. Then someone in embellishing the design would have seen the resemblance to a *fleur-de-lys* and having perfected the design would have adopted it. In a wind-rose on a chart of 1492 (Fig. 9), the north is marked by a T with very drooping serifs. This is intended to be viewed from the edge of the card, but if looked at upsidedown from across the card it certainly suggests a very primitive *fleur-de-lys*. However the draughtsman produced his design, once it was evolved he would have taken it into regular use, it would have been adopted by his companions and before long the use of the *fleur-de-lys* would have become widespread.

Not all compass cards were coloured. Some were black and white.

Figure 9   Wind-rose from a chart of about 1492. Note the form of the T of Tramontana at North with its drooping serifs. Viewed upsidedown this may well have suggested the *fleur-de lys* mark of a few years later.

In badly-lit binnacles it was found that it was easier to steer by the so-called dark card. In this the points were shown white on a black ground (Fig. 10), instead of the usual opposite arrangement.

    In the late seventeenth century a vogue came in which lasted until late in the eighteenth century, especially among Danish compass makers. This was to replace the solid white, black or colour of the seven principal points, other than north, by triangular frames enclosing little engraved pictures. These pictures usually formed a set. A favourite was a set of human figures representing the sun, moon and five plants (Fig. 11), but I have met Faith, Hope and Charity interspersed with four ships, and animal, bird, fish and reptile with three (Fig. 12). One of the most decorated that I have seen showed seven pictures representing academic disciplines, such as logic, arithmetic and rhetoric, while the eight intermediate points represent four queens and four seamen (Fig. 13). In many of these cards the frames of the sketches retained the appropriate red and blue colours, but these were going out of fashion. Another thing that had largely disappeared by the end of the seventeenth century was the cross at east. It was generally replaced by a design consisting of a couple of scrolls or something that looked very like the ornamental head of a double boat-hook. These east marks persisted into the present century (Fig. 14).

By the end of the eighteenth century the plainer cards, sometimes with an ornamental trade mark in the centre, were in general use, the points being either white on black or black on white. The two seem to have been equally popular. In the Royal Navy during the Second World War it was found that with compasses now universally lit from below the use of black cards cut down the amount of undesirable light emerging. Only the external circle with its degree graduations

Figure 10   Dark Compass Card c. 1820. Note the ornamental mark at East.

Figure 11   Eighteenth century ornamental compass card from Denmark, showing figures representing the sun, moon, and planets.

and the points remained translucent. Since the use of compass points had gone out of fashion these were reduced to the *fleur-de-lys*, shaded triangles enclosing the letters E, S and W, and the simple letters for the four half-cardinal points (Fig. 15).

As soon as azimuth compasses came into use, their cards had degree scales as well as points. These ran from zero at north and south to 90° at east and west. On the other hand compasses particularly intended for observing amplitudes were graduated from zero at east and west to 90° at north and south. This led to a curious result. Many navigators, when giving courses or bearings in degrees measured them indiscriminately from north and south or from east and west. Perhaps it was convenient to measure from the nearest cardinal point; thus though N. 44° E. would have been used, E. 44° N. would have been preferred to N.46°E., but some navigators were

Figure 12 Eighteenth century ornamental compass card from Denmark, showing figures representing Faith, Hope and Charity.

quite indiscriminate in their phraseology and you can find, for example, N.80°E. and E.10°N. used on the same page.

The conversion of points into degrees and vice versa with 11¼° equalling one point was very inconvenient. About the year 1790, compass cards were produced in which the right-angle was divided into 96°, thus making 12° to a point, but the idea was not popular. (Fig. 16). In more recent times there have been attempts to introduce a right-angle of 100° and Adolf Hitler is said to have been anxious for this to be adopted, but there are too many difficulties. Suggestions were made from time to time that compass cards should be marked all the way round from 0° to 359°, but though adopted in some countries* in Britain they never had much impact until about the time of the First World War. Then it became the custom to mark the

* 360° cards were first proposed for the United States Navy in 1901 and were adopted for it a few years later.

Figure 13 **Eighteenth** century ornamental compass card from Denmark, showing animal, fish, reptile and bird. This card is intended for an overhead compass and, being viewed from below, the East mark appears on the left.

cards of gyro-compass repeaters in this way and the advantages were evident immediately to those who used them. When converting magnetic courses and bearings to true, easterly variations and deviations are invariably additive and westerly variations and deviations invariably negative. With the old 90° system of marking cards, however, this was only true when the courses and bearings to be corrected were in the north-east or south-west quadrants. There was still greater confusion when the correction to be applied took the course or bearing from one quadrant into the next. When the first gyro-compass repeaters appeared in the Royal Navy, an advantage for keeping the 90° system for magnetic compass cards became apparent. By using the 360° notation for true courses and bearings and the 90° notation for magnetic no confusion was possible in realising which was intended. Officers had been brought up with magnetic compasses and so had little difficulty with the 90° system. By the time of the Second World War conditions had rather changed. Gyro-compasses were much more generally used and with officers far less accustomed to magnetic compasses there was a greater risk of their applying corrections the wrong way than of mistaking magnetic for true and vice versa. Consequently the Royal

Figure 14   Seventeenth century ornamental compass card from England, showing figures representing academic disciplines.

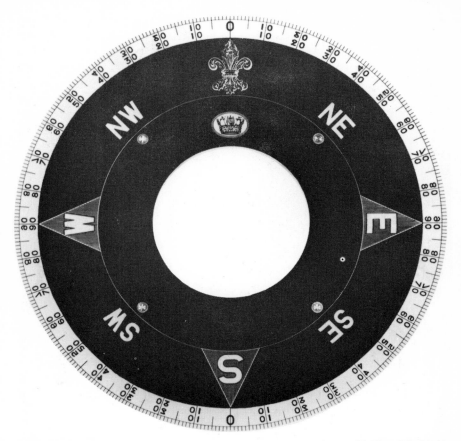

Figure 15   Compass card used in the Royal Navy about 1940, with black central portion to reduce glare. This type of card is still used, but with the graduations clockwise to 360° instead of by 90° quadrants.

Navy went over to 360° magnetic compass cards and the system has now become almost universal.*

It is interesting to learn how the Royal Navy came to adopt the 360° card. During the Second World War the rapidly expanding

*   An interesting case of card confusion occurred during the Second World War. A trawler, which had been taken up for naval service and fitted out accordingly, ran ashore. It was discovered that her skipper, who had always been accustomed to the compasses of fishing trawlers which were marked in points only, had thought that her naval compass being marked in degrees must show true. He had therefore omitted to allow the variation when shaping his course.

Royal Canadian Navy was supplied with compasses from Royal Naval sources and these had the 90° cards then in use. Many Canadian officers had served in merchant vessels on the other side of the Atlantic where 360° cards were common, following the practice of the United States Navy, and they found inconvenience in the use of 90° cards. Some of them therefore opened up their compasses and endeavoured to re-mark their cards in ink. Inevitably they failed to make the joints of the bowl tight afterwards and the leaking compasses were returned to store where they were noticed by the officer surveying stores. The facts were reported to the Director of the Compass Department, and compasses with 360° cards were offered to the Royal Canadian Navy and accepted. The Director then took up the question with navigating officers of the Royal Navy and this resulted in the decision that the Royal Navy would also adopt 360° cards.

Figure 16   Compass card marked in 96° quadrants, c. 1790.

Compass Needles.

The first compass needles, which were thrust through straws to float them, were often simple lengths of wire, but when it was proposed to put the needle upon a pivot a problem arose. The needle obviously would not balance on a pivot by itself and needed a central recess, now known as the cap. If the needle were on the top of the cap it would be unstable. To offset the needle on the card would require something to balance it on the other side of the pivot. The solution finally adopted was to use two needles, slightly curved, so that their ends were together and the centre portions curved away to leave room between them for the cap, which would rest on the pivot (Fig. 3).

The earliest illustration of one of these needles appears in Martin Cortes' *Breve Compendio de la Sphera*, 1551, and shows this oval shape very clearly. Here the needle is made from a single piece of wire, bent double at the north end and then opened out into the oval form with the two ends touching again at the southern extremity.

During the next century a number of shapes of needles were tried. In one the wire was bent double so that the two parts lay side by side for a quarter of their length and then the two parts were opened out at 45° each. Thus when the needle was fixed under the card the double part ran from the centre towards the north with the two arms pointing to south-east and south-west respectively (Fig. 17). In another the needle was made in two halves, each secured into a ring which was fastened to the card so that it encircled the cap.

The type of needle which became most popular in this country was in the form of a lozenge, made from either one or two wires

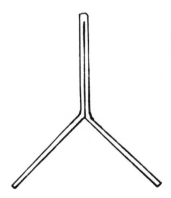

Figure 17   Y-shaped compass needle, seventeenth century.

(Fig. 20). This shape of needle had the advantage that it balanced the card, a point to which I shall return on page 69. Its disadvantage was that it did not point accurately if the two sides were unequally magnetized, or were shaped unsymetrically, or if one rusted badly or broke. In spite of many warnings about this shape it remained popular into the early years of the nineteenth century.

Figure 18   V-shaped compass needle (Fournier).

Figure 19   Shapes of compass needles recommended by William Barlowe in *Magnetical Advertisements*, 1616. Two oval sheet steel needles and a ring crossed by a pointer.

Figure 20   Back of compass card by William Farmer, c. 1750, showing diamond-shaped needles. (Copyright: National Maritime Museum)

Other needles were cut from thin sheet steel. Some of these were cut into an open oval or lozenge, sometimes with the sides connected at the midpoint by a bridge to which the cap was attached (Fig. 19).

When Sir Clowdisley Shovel's fleet came to grief in 1707 the disaster drew attention to the poor state of the compasses supplied to the Royal Navy. One result was that John England, a compass maker, proposed a flat bar needle of which the central part was split and opened out into an oval form (Fig. 21). It is not known to what extent this was actually adopted.

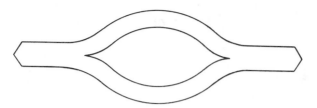

Figure 21   England's compass needle, 1710.

Magnetizing Compass Needles.

All the early compass needles had to be made of a rather soft iron which, though it could be magnetized, did not retain its magnetism for any length of time. It was the custom for ships on long voyages to carry a lodestone for the purpose of remagnetizing their compass needles, and this practice continued well into the eighteenth century. The earliest instructions for magnetizing compass needles stated that there was to be no contact. The lodestone was brought close to the outside of the compass bowl and was carried round and round with the needle following it and the motion getting faster and faster. Then the lodestone was snatched away and the needle would be sufficiently magnetized to seek the north. It does not sound as though it would be a very satisfactory method but a few years ago the late Professor E. G. R. Taylor and I prepared an experiment. We must have looked rather like a pair of witches as we crouched over a bowl of water twirling our lodestone reciting the instructions of long ago and almost uttering spells, but it worked!

The next method to be recommended was merely to rub the north-seeking end of the compass needle on the lodestone. Later the navigator was told to stroke the needle from the centre to the north-seeking end with the lodestone, and finally the needle was stroked several times throughout its length from south- to north-seeking end.

In about 1745 Dr Gowin Knight discovered a method of making artificial magnets of much greater strength than the best of lodestones. His method was to obtain a number of steel bars and to magnetize them very feebly by holding each in turn in the line of the earth's magnetic field while hammering it. He then secured several bars together, the bundle forming a stronger magnet than a single bar, though having less strength than that of a single bar multiplied by the number of bars in the bundle. With the bundle he

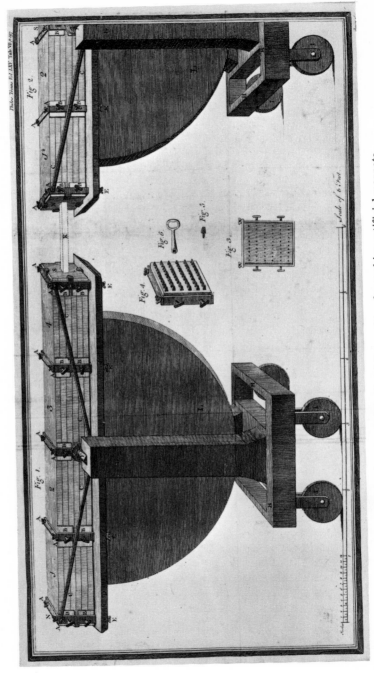

Figure 22   Dr Gowin Knight's machine for making artificial magnets.

stroked each of the other bars several times, thus increasing their magnetic strength. Then separating the bundle he stroked each of these bars with a second bundle made from some of the strengthened bars. This procedure was repeated again and again, always stroking the weaker bars with bundles of the stronger until all were as strong as he could make them. Finally he built all his bars into two great magnets of very considerable strength (Fig. 22). Now he was able to make and sell permanent magnets of much greater strength and at a much lower price than any lodestone. He hoped to make his fortune but others discovered the secret and he lost his monopoly.

The introduction of these artificial magnets revolutionised the design of compass needles. Hitherto, as we have seen, compass needles could only be made of relatively soft material. Now it was possible to magnetize harder steel and subsequently larger needles could be made which held their magnetism better and no longer required frequent remagnetization.

Improvements in Compass Needles.

Dr. Knight designed his own compass with a needle made from a flat bar of steel which originally rested on the top of the cap, the card being made bottom heavy by means of a circumferential brass ring so that it would balance. Later a hole was made in the centre of the needle for the cap. These compasses had much to recommend them and they were adopted by the Royal Navy, by the East India Company, by some of the better-found merchant vessels, and by some foreign navigators. Unfortunately it was found that the compass card was not steady when the ship was subjected to considerable motion. The reason for this was not understood at the time. However if a compass card of this type with a single heavy needle, is subjected to a rolling motion the needle tends to turn into the plane of the motion. This difficulty can be overcome if the card is balanced so that its moments of inertia in the north-south and east-west directions are equal. The old lozenge-shaped needles more nearly approached this condition and so without the reason being understood a tolerably steady compass card had been introduced many years before.

When the whole matter of the design of compass cards was considered by the Admiralty Compass Committee of 1837 it was conceived that this matter of equalising the moments of inertia could

Figure 23   Needles on card of Admiralty Standard Compass, 1840.

be realised if two parallel needles were used, of such length and at
such a distance apart that the ends of the pair subtended an angle of
60° at the centre of the card. More than two needles could be used
provided they were placed at correct distances apart. The use of an
even number of needles at correct distances had another advantage: It
avoided the introduction of certain magnetic errors. A discussion
of these so-called sextantal and octantal errors is rather outside the
scope of this book. The Admiralty Standard Compass, designed by
the Committee, had four needles which were made from strips of
steel plate, but instead of the strips being placed flat they were set on
edge. Murdo Downie, a master in the Royal Navy, had pointed out in
1792* that it was possible for a flat bar needle to become

* Murdo Downie, *New Pilot for the East Coast of Scotland*, 1792.

magnetized along an axis which was at a small angle with the centre line of the needle, and might even be along a diagonal.

During the first half of the nineteenth century numbers of different forms of compass needles were advocated, but none had any real success (Fig 24). The disadvantage of all these large strong compass needles was that they made the card very heavy and this wore and blunted the pivot. There were even cases of the pivot making a hole through the cap. The weight of compass cards was made worse by their size. The card of the Admiralty Standard Compass was of 7½-inch diameter and 8-9 inch cards were quite normal. The *Great Eastern* had one compass with a single 16-inch needle, itself the cause of large sextantal and octantal errors. This seems to have started an idea that large ships required large compasses and in 1881 Lecky was stating that some Atlantic mail steamers had 20-inch compass cards.

In 1783 Christian Carl Lous, a Danish naval officer, advocated a card with four long, thin needles which he balanced by a brass cross-bar. (Fig. 25). Little notice of this card seems to have been taken outside his own country, but it was a very definite step in the right direction. When Sir William Thomson introduced his compass of 1876 he reverted to needles which were similar in appearance to large sewing needles. These were slung by threads below a very light card, usually of 10-inch diameter, to make the system pendulous (Fig. 26). With the peculiar design of this card it was possible to make the weight on the pivot extremely small. Even then there was provision for easy replacement of cap and pivot.

In liquid compasses it has become usual to fit needles which are actually round bar magnets, and these have become shorter and shorter.

Ring-shaped Compass Needles.

I must not leave this discussion of compass needles without referring to ring-shaped needles (Fig. 27), though some will think that the word 'needle' is rather a misnomer for this type. In 1620 William Barlowe was much in favour of ring-shaped needles as they were more equally balanced than any other shape, but in his view it was too difficult to magnetize them in the right direction.

In 1687 the French scientist La Hire advocated ring-shaped needles with the curious idea that the poles might be hoped to move around the ring in step with any change in the variation, so that the

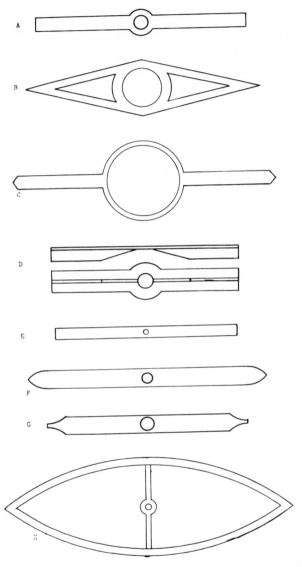

Figure 24   Forms of compass needles, early nineteenth century. *A*, maker unknown: *B*, J. Hewitson. *c*, 1830: *C*, Grant-Preston, 1844: *D*, William Walker. 1844: *E*, Thomas Jones, 1832: *F*, Thomas Jones, 1832: *G*, Dr. Smith: *H*, Captain Williams, 1825.

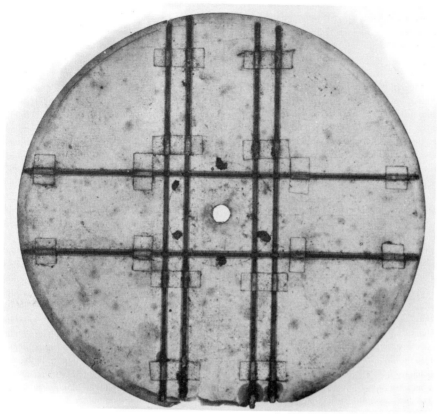

Figure 25   The light compass needles advocated by Lous.

compass would always show true north! In the 1870s Emile
Duchemin designed a compass with a ring-shaped needle and this was
adopted by the French Navy and used by them for about twenty
years. In 1944 ring-shaped needles were adopted in the Royal Navy
for the compasses of submarines. In these vessels an image of the
card had to be optically projected from the compass outside the hull
to a screen inside and it had been found that the conventional
needles threw inconvenient shadows. With modern methods of
magnetizing electro-magnetically it is easy to attach the unmag-
netized needle to the card and to place the whole unit in a solenoid,
thus ensuring that the needle is accurately magnetized across the

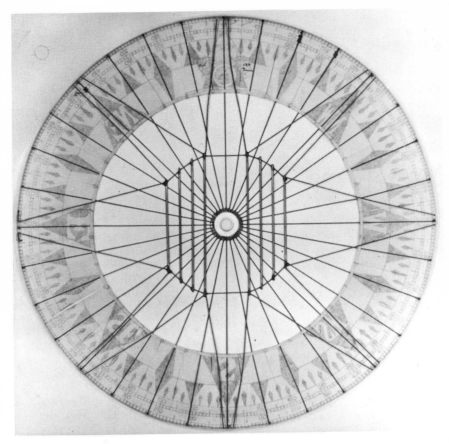

Figure 26   Needles of Sir William Thomson's compass card, 1876.

north-south diameter. Since the War these ring-shaped needles have been extensively adopted for other compasses but at the present day there is a tendency to revert to very short straight needles.

Compass Bowls.

Although in 1269 Peregrinus suggested the possibility of using brass compass bowls there is little doubt that, from the earliest compasses with needles on pivots, wood was the usual material. Cortes in 1551 gives us what is probably the earliest description of a mariner's compass of this period. There was a turned wooden bowl with a detachable bottom consisting of a disc of wood which was recessed into it. The intention behind this detachable bottom was to enable the card to be taken out for the retouching of the needle without disturbing the glass top which could be sealed in place. The disadvantage of this type of bowl was that the main body and bottom would warp unequally and the bottom would drop out, or damp would get in to the detriment of the card.

We begin to hear of brass bowls soon after 1600 but it was about the middle of the century before they started to make headway. The first type of compass with a brass bowl to be described is the azimuth compass by Seller in 1669 which will be discussed later (page 84). Soon after this date it became customary to supply a few compasses with brass bowls to ships of the Royal Navy which were going abroad or were flagships. For a while the alternative of a pewter bowl was also used.

After the wreck of Sir Clowdisley Shovel's ships in 1707 it was

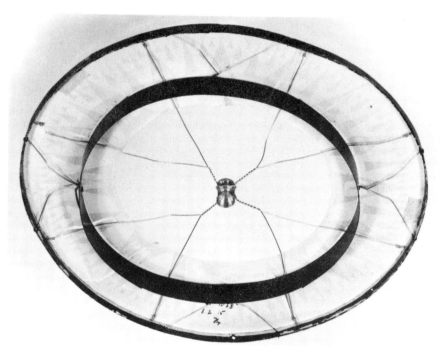

Figure 27   Compass card with a ring needle, c. 1800.

alleged by Captain Sir William Jumper of the LENOX that the disaster had been caused by the low quality of the compasses supplied to the fleet and he recommended the exclusive use of compasses with brass bowls. A resultant investigation showed a fantastic state of affairs. Compasses were ordered to be returned from the fleet for examination and of 136 wood and nine brass so returned and examined only two wood and one brass were found to be serviceable!

The Admiralty decided that for the future they would purchase only compasses with brass bowls. This did not mean that wooden bowls went completely out of use. In 1768 we find James Cook, then in command of the GRENVILLE brig surveying the coasts of Newfoundland, asking that he might be supplied with two wooden compasses as he had lost one of his own, while as late as 1811 Gibraltar Dockyard was told to stop demanding such compasses. Wooden bowls remained in use in the United States Navy until 1830, and in 1845 Maury stated that they were still common in American merchant ships.

Such was the position in the Royal Navy, but it seems probably that experience in merchant vessels would have been similar, though there was always a tendency in smaller, less well-found vessels to try to economise by using the cheaper wooden bowl.

In France brass bowls were put to use at a fairly early date and much difficulty was experienced with the quality of the brass used. It contained many impurities, some of which were of a ferrous nature and affected the accuracy of the indications of the compass needles. I am of opinion that many of the reported cases of compasses being affected by the magnetism of brass bowls may well have been due to magnetism of other fittings in the ship itself. The result of these experiences, however, was that in France brass compass bowls went out of fashion almost entirely for very many years.

The French took a new departure. Two of their seventeenth century writers on navigation, Fournier in 1643 and Dechalles in 1677, speak of bowls being either round or square. By the beginning of the eighteenth century the square wooden bowl, or perhaps it would be better to call it an inner box, had become regular French practice and remained so for nearly a century. In 1727 Radouay was noting the superiority of English compasses and by 1794 Bezout notes that the bowl was then usually round and made of copper.

The Admiralty Standard Compass of 1842 had a thick copper

bowl. It had been found that any oscillation of long strong compass needles in a copper bowl set up electric currents in the bowl itself and these tended to damp down the oscillation of the card.

Liquid Compasses.

We have seen that the first compasses were liquid compasses in the sense that the magnetic element floated on water, but I prefer to call these, which had nothing to restrain the element from drifting to the side of the bowl, floating compasses. I elect to retain the term liquid compass for those in which the element rests on a pivot which restrains it from drifting to the side, while the bowl being filled with water acts as a brake on the needle and reduces its tendency to oscillate. In addition, in most liquid compasses the card is fitted with a float which reduces the weight of the card upon the pivot without actually lifting it off. This has the great advantages of reducing the friction, enabling the card to point more freely and reducing wear of the pivot and cap. Compasses have been tried where the float had positive buoyancy and lifted the card against an inverted pivot set in the centre of the top glass.

We read of the first true liquid compass being described by two East Indian sailors to William Barlowe in 1597 (page 53), but the Archeacon does not seem to have realised the implications of this design, and the next liquid compass was described to the Royal Society by John Ingenhousz in 1779. Ingenhousz suggested three different types. The first was like the one that Barlowe had reported nearly two centuries earlier. In the second the bowl was only partially filled with water. The needle was floated by a cork as in the floating compasses of long ago, but the element was kept central in the bowl by a vertical pin which passed through a large hole in the cork. The third had the usual attributes of a liquid compass, using a cork float which just did not lift the card off the pivot.

It was Ingenhousz's experiments which probably suggested a compass which was made two years later by an instrument maker called Wright*. This had a needle pivoted in a bowl of water, with no card but the needle acting as a pointer to show the course by the compass points marked in the bottom of the bowl. It is not clear whether there was a float or whether the compass followed exactly the East Indian design. This compass was submitted by Captain Sir

* Probably Gabriel Wright of the firm of Gilbert and Wright.

William Burnaby for trial in the Royal Navy. It was found to be far steadier than the ordinary compass, especially in boats, but it was not developed, possibly because the absence of a card was unacceptable to the conservative majority of sailors. It may be interesting to record that when in the 1930s a gyro-compass repeater was designed in which the compass courses appeared on an endless horizontal tape many sailors complained that it was impossible to steer except by a circular card. When they were forced to persevere they soon found that the larger scale of the tape was a great advantage over the necessarily smaller degrees of a round card!

About 1795 a Danish naval officer whom I have already mentioned, Christian Carl Lous, made some experiments with liquid compasses, but I have been unable to find his report upon the subject.*

In 1812 Francis Crow, a silversmith and watchmaker of Faversham, developed a compass with a float in which the bowl was filled with spirits of wine, that liquid being used so that it should not freeze. The liquid was kept topped up by a reservoir which also allowed for its expansion and contraction. The needle was enclosed in a copper float, the top of which formed the compass card. The float had positive buoyancy so that it rose against an inverted pivot. Very satisfactory trials were carried out in the Royal Navy but, as so often happened at this time, we hear no more of the compass (Fig. 28).

Other inventors nevertheless took up the idea, notably Grant Preston in London about 1830 and Johan Philip Weilbach in Copenhagen some time earlier. In all these early liquid compasses, troubles were experienced with corrosion or discolouration inside the bowl and with the problem of the altering volume of the liquid under varying conditions of temperature. However, in 1845 the Admiralty issued an order that every ship of the Royal Navy was to carry one liquid compass for steering by in rough weather. These were floatless compasses.

There is a tradition that Edward Samuel Ritchie, a Boston instrument maker, visited England and saw in the Museum of the Admiralty Compass Department a liquid compass which inspired him to try to perfect the type. It was probably Crow's compass which he examined. Returning to his own country he received enthusiastic support from Captain M. Gilliss, U.S.N., Superintendent of the Naval

---

* *Einige Versuche und Vorschäge, betreffend die Theorie der Navigation.* Kiel, 1795.

Figure 28   Crow's liquid compass, 1813. (Copyright: National Maritime Museum)

Observatory. In 1862 Ritchie patented a compass with a reservoir for the liquid and an annular float, which he changed the following year to a cruciform one, enclosing the needles. This 1863 compass also had the great improvement of replacing the reservoir by an expansion chamber made from two thin flexible plates of copper, joined at the edges.

Although Ritchie experienced considerable difficulty with corrosion and discolouration he persisted and his liquid compasses were adopted by the United States Navy which, in a generation, changed from being one of the most primitive in compass design to one of the most advanced. On the other hand the Royal Navy was forced by considerations of economy to persist in the use of its floatless liquid compasses for steering in rough weather only.

In 1901 John Clark Dobbie of Glasgow patented a greatly improved liquid compass. He had noted that in all liquid compasses, as in the dry compasses, the card was made of very little smaller diameter than that of the the inside of the bowl, and the liquid would set up a swirl during a rapid turn which could carry the card round. By making his compass with a card whose diameter was at least an inch smaller than that of the bowl and reading it against a projecting lubber's point instead of a painted line, he removed the card from the area of swirl and produced a greatly improved and steadier compass.

At this time the Royal Navy was experiencing considerable trouble with the light dry-card compasses of Sir William Thomson which had been forced upon it against the technical advice of the Service. With higher speeds and greater vibration in steam-ships, to say nothing of shocks from gunfire, the dry-card compass had never been really satisfactory and in 1906 the Royal Navy went over for all purposes to a liquid compass based upon Dobbie's design. The only real improvement to this, which was introduced between the wars, was the replacement of the expansion chamber by an expanding bottom, i.e. a bottom which was attached to the main part of the bowl by a corrugated ring.

In the Merchant Navy the change to the liquid compass was rather slower but since the end of the Second World War the use of the Thomson compass has been confined to a very few vessels.

Variation.

When it was noted in the fifteenth century that the compass needle did not always point to the true north some thought that this was the fault of the lodestone with which it had been touched or of the manner in which this had been done. At one time it was even suggested that a compass needle would point differently according to the locality in which it had been touched. As late as 1574 we find William Bourne imploring sailors to experiment with compass needles which they had touched while in India or Newfoundland to see whether or not they acted in the same manner as those made in England.

Nearly a century later, in 1664, so many were convinced that the

Figure 29   Compass card with needles offset to correct for the variation.

pointing of a compass needle depended upon the lodestone used to touch it that Dr. Pell suggested that Trinity House should keep a good lodestone for use by all mariners so that all their compasses should point the same way. The matter was finally settled by John Seller who experimented with several lodestones and found that compass needles touched by any of them always pointed accurately in the same direction.*

However, by the middle of the fifteenth century it had been generally recognised that the compass needle, even if it had been carefully made and magnetized, did not point exactly to the north pole. At that time it was common to carry in the pocket a small sun-dial and before this could be used it was necessary to orientate it correctly by aligning the gnomon with a compass needle embodied in the instrument. If the compass needle varied from true north the time shown by the sun-dial would of course be incorrect, so as soon as the existence of the variation was recognised a mark was put in the compass bowl out of the true north-south line to compensate and this had to be aligned to the compass needle.

When the makers of mariner's compasses of northern Europe appreciated the matter they took to fixing the compass needles beneath the card so that they were offset by the requisite amount to make the *fleur-de-lys* indicate the true north (Fig. 29).

* *Philosophical Transactions of the Royal Society*, 1667, page 478.

The idea of doing this probably originated with the Flemish compass makers who, having seen the corrected German pocket sun-dials, offset their compass needles by a whole point (11¼°). In the time of the first voyage of Columbus the Spaniards were buying compasses in both Flanders and Italy, and as the latter had their needles set under the *fleur-de-lys* the two types of compass disagreed. By the end of the sixteenth century the Spaniards were using Flemish compasses almost exclusively and the slewing of the needles had become almost universal outside the Mediterranean. The angle of slew usually used was half a point in Spain, Portugal, the Bay of Biscay and English Channel, three quarters of a point or a point in Flanders, Denmark and the Western Baltic and a point and a half in Russia. In 1635 Henry Gellibrand reported that he had proved that the easterly variation in England did not have a fixed value but was gradually decreasing.

The Spanish writers on navigation disapproved of the use of Flemish compasses, Pedro de Medina in 1545 because he did not believe in the existence of variation and Martin Cortes in 1551 because that variation differed so much in different parts of the world.

The English were already experiencing the nuisance of the offset needle. When a compass with its needle set to correct the easterly variation was used for a Newfoundland voyage it was found that on the other side of the Atlantic it was making the error worse instead of better, for there the variation was westerly instead of easterly and amounted to no less than two points. For this reason it became common for Englishmen on long voyages to take with them not only their ordinary 'channel compasses' but also 'meridional compasses' in which the needle was not offset, and to change to using the latter when the ship was clear of the Channel. By the beginning of the eighteenth century the meridional compass was in general the only one used in English ships.

In Holland there was a different approach. Instead of reverting to meridional compasses they made their compasses with an adjustable double card (Fig. 30). This enabled the needle to be turned at will so that it could be offset from the main card by any amount desired. Coming into use shortly before 1600 these adjustable cards remained popular in Holland for more than three centuries, but though often suggested they never had any vogue in this country. Captain William Bligh reported that in Dutch East Indiamen it was the practice to readjust the card whenever the variation was observed. He thought it

Figure 30   Compass card with the central portion, to which the needles are attached, made adjustable to correct for the variation.

a most risky proceeeding as any unauthorised person could adjust the card incorrectly without it being detected. It was probably only the introduction of liquid compasses which finally ended the adjustable card.

Azimuth Compasses.

It was necessary to be able to observe the amount of the magnetic variation if accurate courses were to be steered. This could be done by observing the compass bearing of the sun or a star and comparing it with the calculated bearing, the difference being the variation. A suitable instrument for measuring the bearing was necessary and the first was described by João de Lisboa in *Livro de Marinharia* in 1514.

During the next hundred years or so several proposals were made for instruments to observe the variation. These had large scales which enabled the bearing to be read off with great accuracy, but this accuracy was nullified by the necessity of aligning the instrument to the direction of a comparatively small needle. Giovanni Battista dell Porta, in 1589, proposed a dial no less than ten feet in diameter

Figure 31   The semicircle, for measuring the variation, 1669. (From John
Seller *Practical Navigation* 1669).

which could hardly have been used in a ship. One of the last
instruments of this type was the semicircle (Fig. 31) illustrated by
Seller in 1669,* but the azimuth compass (Fig. 32) which he also
described, though more portable, suffered from the same drawback
in design.

This azimuth compass had a brass bowl on the top of which was
rotated a very broad flat brass ring. Pivoted on the outer edge of this
ring was an L-shaped index with an inclined thread. The index could
be made to traverse across a graduated scale on the opposite side of
the ring to that on which it was pivoted. To take an observation the
ring was turned on the bowl until cross-wires carried by the former
were seen to be above the north-south, east-west lines on the
compass card. Then the index was turned until the thread threw its

* Nathaniel Marten, master's mate in the *Globe* during Anthony Hippon's voyage to the
East Indies, used a semicircle to observe the variation in March 1612. *Purchas his Pilgrimes*,
Hakluyt Society edition, 1905, Vol. III, p.310

shadow on the centre of the vertical part of the index when the bearing of the sun could be read off from the edge of the horizontal part against the scale. The scale was graduated to read in minutes by the use of diagonals which gave an appearance of very great accuracy until it is remembered that the accuracy was entirely dependent upon the accurate alignment of the cross-wires, and to achieve this was impossible. These compasses were widely used and continued in service in this country at least as late as Captain Cook's first voyage of 1768, while in France they were still illustrated by Bezout in 1794.

In the variation compasses used in France in the seventeenth and greater part of the eighteenth centuries the bowl was gimballed in a high square wooden box in which two apertures were cut, opposite to each other, each fitted with a vertical wire. Here the whole box was turned until the two wires were aligned on the sun or star, when the bearing was read off by an assistant with the help of a horizontal wire above the compass card (Fig. 33).

The use of the Azimuth Compass.

Figure 32   Azimuth Compass, 1669.

86

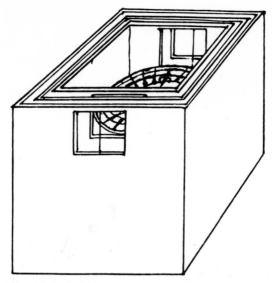

Figure 33   French Azimuth Compass, seventeenth century.

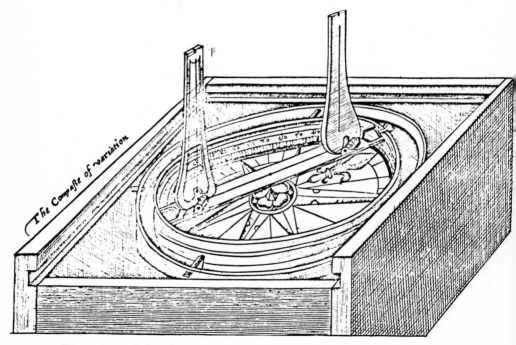

Figure 34   Azimuth Compass with sight bar and two sights, 1597. (From *The Navigators Supply* by William Barlowe, 1597)

Better than this and also parallel with the azimuth compass described earlier was a simpler type of compass, one of which was illustrated in the *Arcano del Mare* in 1546 (Fig. 34). In this type there were two vertical sights of which one usually had a slit and the other a wire, so that the latter could be aligned on the object observed. There were two varieties of this compass. In one the sights were attached to the opposite sides of the brass bowl, the whole of which had to be turned when taking a bearing which was then read off on the card against the lubber's point. Some of these compasses were gimballed in a Y which could be mounted on a tripod for easy handling. Others were gimballed in a wooden box which was carried about. In the more refined type the sights were carried by a ring rotating on the bowl top and were joined by a horozontal wire. Here the bearing had to be read off on the card as viewed under the thread. Sometimes with either type the sights could be hinged flat when not required. A disadvantage of this type of compass was that in most cases two observers were required, one to sight the object and the other to read off the bearing when told to do so.

Improvements to the azimuth compass have been suggested from time to time, usually by the introduction of lenses or prisms. In McCulloch's compass of 1788 (Fig. 35), the sights were fixed to the bowl and a lens was fitted to one so that when the instrument was properly orientated a spot of light would appear, thrown by the sun upon the other. To obviate the necessity of a second observer a card stop was fitted so that at the instant that the observation was taken the card could be locked and the bearing read off at leisure by viewing it through another lens provided for the purpose. Even a vernier was fitted to give an entirely spurious idea of accuracy. These compasses remained in use until late in the nineteenth century, if we can accept the evidence that they continued to be illustrated by Norie until 1877.

In 1793 Ralph Walker designed a compass (Fig. 36), for observing the value of the variation. It was an extremely well-made compass with a single bar needle set on edge. Above the bowl was fitted a semicircle with a latitude scale at one end so that the plane of the semicircle could be tilted one way or another through an angle with the vertical which was equivalent to the latitude. At right-angles to the diameter of the semicircle was a track graduated in degrees and this carried a slide with a small central aperture. To observe the variation the slide was set to the declination and the semicircle tilted to the latitude. The compass was then turned until the sun threw a spot of light onto the centre line around the semicircle. At that

AZIMUTH COMPASS.

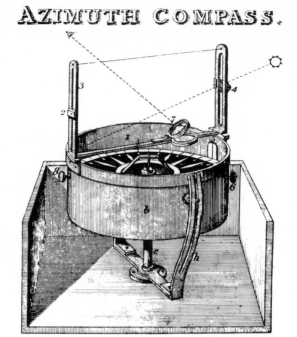

Figure 35   McCulloch's Azimuth Compass, 1788.

instant the north point of the compass card would show by its displacement from the lubber's point the amount of the variation.

Walker's compasses were intended to provide a means of ascertaining the longitude (page 167), but were found useless for the purpose because, for one reason, of the lack of knowledge of the deviation (compass error) caused by the magnetic character of the ship (page 92). His compasses were, however, so well designed and made that they became very popular in the Royal Navy and some were in use even as late as 1850.

In 1812 Schmalcalder revolutionised the azimuth compass by fitting a prism to the near sight when, provided that the card carried a second set of graduations 180° out of phase with the normal ones, the bearing could be viewed and read off simultaneously with the same eye as that by which the sights were being aligned on the object observed (Fig. 37). Some time later it was realised that there were great advantages to be gained if the prism was fitted to the far sight,

Figure 36   Walker's Meridional Compass, 1793.

and later that if a magnifying prism were used whose focal length, its height above the card, and the radius of the card were all the same, one had an instrument which gave a reading unaffected by small errors of alignment (Fig. 38). With this, both vertical sights could be eliminated and all that was necessary was a V in the top of the prism. In all these prismatic, and indeed with some azimuth instruments of the earlier type, a black glass mirror is usually fitted to enable an image of the sun to be reflected down to the horizontal.

Figure 37   Crow's Compass
fitted with Schmalcalder's prism.

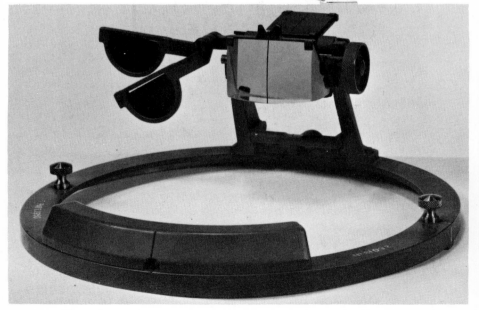

Figure 38   An azimuth instrument as used in the Royal Navy. The magnifying
prism is the only sight required.

Figure 39   An azimuth instrument of Sir William Thomson's pattern, fitted to a French naval compass.

Two special instruments of use for observing the sun only have also been employed. In one of these a horizontal glass tube is fittted to the far sight at right-angles to the line of sight. This has the peculiar property of reflecting a spot of light to the eye, whatever the altitude of the sun. In the other a hinged parabolic mirror is fitted so that it can be made to throw a narrow line of light on to the card at the side opposite to it.

An entirely different azimuth instrument was patented by Sir William Thomson, later Lord Kelvin, in 1876. This embodies an inclined tube with a 60° prism at the top and a lens lower down* (Fig. 39). The instrument can be used in either of two ways. In the first the observer keeps his eye on a horizontal level with the instrument and observes the object over the prism while the card is reflected in it. In the second method, particularly suitable for elevated objects though it can be used for low ones as well, the eye is raised to look down the tube at the card and at the same time the object is seen reflected in the prism. This instrument enables very accurate bearings to be taken but has the disadvantage of the number of surfaces which it is necessary to keep dry. The single magnifying

---

* The original instrument of 1876 had a mirror instead of the prism, which was not introduced until 1883.

prism instrument has a great advantage in this respect and is more rapid in operation. For this reason it has been preferred during the last half-century by the Royal Navy, where frequent bearings need to be observed for such purposes as station keeping, in addition to the needs of navigation. While for ordinary use at sea I much preferred it, when swinging ship for the adjustment of compasses I elected to employ the Thomson instrument using the second, eye-up, method.

Deviation of the Compass.

In the early years of the nineteenth century a new navigational hazard arose. Iron shipbuilding began to replace wood and the iron of a ship might grievously upset the accuracy of her compasses.

This was not an entirely new problem though it was one which had been unrecognised by the majority of seamen. Of course there had been iron fittings in ships for a very long time and if a compass were placed too near to these its needle would be deflected from its true direction by the magnetic influence of the iron. The trouble was however, that the effect on a compass depends not only on the distance of the magnetic material from it but also on the directions of the disturbing force from the compass. If the magnet is exactly north or south of the compass needle it should require little thought to realise that it can only increase or decrease the pull of the earth's magnetism and will not deflect the needle. If, however, the magnet is east or west of the compass the latter's needle is subjected to the conflicting pulls of the earth and of the magnet and will take up a direction between the two. If the magnet is in some intermediate direction it will still have an effect though less than that when it is at right-angles. The result of all this was that since the error of the compass was seldom noticed and when noticed would nearly always be by a different amount from that previously noted, because the ship's heading and consequently the direction of the offending iron from the compass would be different, seamen were generally led to think that the error was due to a bad compass rather than something in the ship.

An example of how an observer can be misled by this matter of the direction from the compass of a disturbing force was brought home to me on one occasion during the Second World War. We had had a great deal of trouble with compass errors owing to the fitting on the bridges of small vessels of a type of loud-hailer, whose brass trumpet concealed a particularly strong magnet. One day I was visiting a trawler in company with my senior officer who led me aside and said: "Why all this fuss about loud-hailers? I have rotated this one and though it is only a few feet from the compass the card is not disturbed." I pointed out to him that the loud-hailer at that time happened to be exactly north of the compass. When I moved it to a position the same distance from the compass but where it was now east from it, he was astounded to see that the compass was deflected up to ten degrees each way according to which side of the loud-hailer was turned towards it.

The first time that a compass error was reported, due to the proximity of iron, appears to have been in 1538 by Dom João de Castro* when he noticed that his compass needle was disturbed by the iron gun-carriages with which his ship was fitted. Thereafter the possibility of such an error appears from time to time in the literature of navigation but not nearly as often as I would have expected. I have only found it in such English books in 1599, 1627, 1669, 1685, 1696, 1721 and 1748, though the knowledge must have persisted to a certain extent, for it was referred to by Captain James Cook in 1777. Nevertheless, when in 1794 Walker's compass was being tried in the GLORY and her master, Murdo Downie, pointed out that the errors of the compass due to the presence of iron invalidated any observations for the determination of the longitude, his report was almost universally acclaimed as the first known discovery of this important fact!

The next actor in this story was Captain Matthew Flinders who in 1801 sailed in the INVESTIGATOR for a surveying voyage to Australia. In those times the compass was still extensively used by the hydrographic surveyor and Flinders soon found that his results were inconsistent. He then settled down to try to find out the why and the wherefore. His experiments showed that in his ship the error was caused by the magnetic effect of what is now usually called 'soft iron' below the level of the compass and that this could be corrected by the equal and opposite effect caused by a vertical bar of soft iron of suitable length, placed in his case abaft the compass. The amount of the error to be corrected was dependent upon the direction of the ship's head and upon the latitude, becoming zero at the magnetic equator.† The magnetism induced in Flinders' bar was

---

* João de Castro, *Roteiro de Lisboa a Goa*.
† At the Magnetic Equator the direction of the earth's magnetic field is horizontal instead of being inclined as elsewhere. The terrestrial and magnetic equators do not quite conform.

also dependent upon the ship's head and upon the latitude so that once properly adjusted it should reduce the compass error to zero under all conditions. On the return of Flinders to England in 1810 experiments were made in a number of Royal Navy ships, but no further steps were taken, possibly because of his death in 1814.

In 1820 Peter Barlow, professor at the Royal Military Academy, Woolwich, who does not seem to have heard of the work done by Flinders, became interested in the compass and its errors and produced a corrector consisting of a circular plate (Fig. 40), fitted in

Figure 40   Barlow's Plate.

the vertical plane on the side of the pillar which supported the compass. His original idea had been to fit it in a position where it doubled the error of the compass and every observation would have had to be taken twice, with and without the plate fitted, the difference in readings having to be added or subtracted from that taken without the plate. It was soon realised that this method of use was extremely clumsy and quite unnecessary and that it was possible to fit the plate in a position where it corrected rather than doubled the error. This correcting plate achieved far greater advertisement than had the Flinders Bar and was fitted in a number of ships. Unfortunately when the plate was fitted in iron ships or ships with magnetic cargoes it was found that the correction no longer remained true for all latitudes, and in southern latitudes the compass error might actually be increased. This brought the plate, and indeed all ideas of compass correction, into disrepute and though some plates were still in use at the middle of the century they were never widely fitted.*

The increased use of iron in shipbuilding led in 1836 to the Admiralty hiring an iron ship called the *Garry Owen*, and sending Commander Edward J. Johnson to carry out experiments with compasses on board her. As a result of these he proved that the ship had in fact become a huge permanent magnet and that this had probably been caused by the vibration which she sustained while she was on the building slip.† The magnetic axis of the ship depended upon the latitude and orientation of the slip.

In 1824 the French Scientist Siméon Denis Poisson had published a mathematical explanation showing the effects that the ironwork of a ship might have upon her compass and he was followed in 1851 by the barrister Archibald Smith who showed how compass errors could be analysed mathematically thereby making clearer an understanding of the factors underlying compass errors.

Meanwhile in 1838 the Admiralty had followed up the *Garry Owen* experiments by borrowing the 263-ton iron steamship *Rainbow*, from the General Steam Navigation Company and employing the Astronomer Royal, George Biddell Airy, to make experiments.

* Barlow's plate is still described in Raper's 16th edition of 1885, but it must have passed out of use by the beginning of the 1860s.
† The fact that the direction of the ship's head while on the building slip implanted a particular magnetic character upon her hull became established and universally recognised. It was not until about a century later that I was able to prove from experiments in eight destroyers that this character became considerably modified by the direction of the ship's head while in the fitting out berth.

Later in the same year at the request of her owners, Cairns & Co., he carried out further trials in their new 270-ton iron sailing ship *Ironsides*, at Liverpool where she had been built.

Airy's experiments included observations of magnetic force and deviation of the compass at a number of positions and he showed how the ship's compasses could be corrected (page 97).

In 1840 the Admiralty set up a committee to discuss the whole matter of magnetic compasses and their errors in ships of the Royal Navy. Captain E. J. Johnson did most of the work of this committee. Following its report two schools of thought emerged. The Admiralty pinned its faith on giving to each ship what was called a standard compass by which the ship was navigated and by which all courses were shaped. That standard compasses were already in use in the early years of the nineteenth century is evident from the fact that models of ships made by French prisoners of war in this country show a compass so fitted. This was contrary to the usual British practice though such a compass had been fitted by a very few captains, but it was evidently the practice in French warships. The Admiralty intended that the standard compasses should be fitted in carefully selected positions where the magnetic disturbance would be at a minimum and that each ship should be 'swung' at intervals to ascertain her compass errors, or deviations as they had come to be called, with the ship's head on each point of the compass. It was thought that if the compass positions had been carefully chosen the errors would be reasonably permanent.

A second school of thought recommended compass correction and this was enthusiastically adopted by many ship-owners to whom it seemed a cheaper way of evading compass difficulties than providing a standard compass or a carefully designed compass position where errors would be small. Unfortunately the protagonists of this school did not study their subject sufficiently and made wild claims that could not be substantiated.

It had been discovered from an intelligent appraisal of the situation that the magnetic material of a ship and her fittings came under two categories. The first, usually called hard iron, is capable of becoming magnetized by vibration in the earth's magnetic field and once magnetized its effect remains reasonably permanent, though it can be modified by fresh heavy vibrations such as gunfire or the ship being struck by lightning. It can therefore be corrected by placing a magnet, or system of magnets, of suitable strength in suitable positions near the compass. Material of the second category is usually called soft iron. Its characteristic is that when placed in a magnetic field it becomes magnetized but only remains so while it is subject to the field. When moved or removed its magnetic character will become changed in strength and direction. Consequently the effect of the soft iron in a ship upon the compass will depend upon her heading and on the horizontal and vertical components of the earth's magnetic field, these in turn depending upon her magnetic latitude. The soft iron effect of a ship can be resolved into its horizontal and vertical components and these affect the compass differently. It was the vertical component which Flinders was correcting with his bar. The horizontal component can be corrected by placing suitable masses of soft iron near the compass. We still have one more cause of error to consider, namely any magnetic source below the compass. It will be easily understood that when the ship is on an even keel a magnet below the compass needle cannot deflect it, but when the ship heels to one side or the other the magnet moves out to one side of the compass and acting more or less horizontally upon the needle can deflect it. Here again the effect can be corrected by placing a magnet vertically below the compass.

All this is reasonably straightforward for a compass adjuster who has the necessary correctors at his disposal and a compass which is reasonably well placed, but if it is placed too close to magnetic material all sorts of complicated errors can creep in which cannot be corrected.

In the *Rainbow* Airy corrected the permanent magnetism by a single magnet placed at an angle to the ship's head after calculation of the results obtained in the ship and subsequent experiments ashore. He found that the errors were over-corrected. In the *Ironsides* he used two magnets, one place athwartships and the other fore-and-aft. He adjusted their positions practically, the former until there was no deviation when the ship's head was pointing north, the latter until there was no deviation with it pointing east. In the *Rainbow* the effect of magnetism induced in soft iron was corrected by means of a scroll of soft iron plate, with which he had considerable difficulty. He decided that a box of soft iron chain would have been better. In the *Ironsides* he ignored the soft iron effect, claiming that it was small enough to be of no consequence.

In these early days of compass correction Airy stated that the effects of vertical soft iron and of heeling error though theoretically possible were negligible in practice. In this he was wrong. Compass adjusters of his school corrected the effect of vertical soft iron by fore-and-aft magnets together with the fore-and-aft portion of the permanent magnetism of the ship, from which it was indistinguishable if experiments were only conducted in one latitude. When the ship went down to the magnetic equator this effect of vertical soft iron fell to zero and the compass was left with an error caused by the correcting magnet being too strong. But worse was to come. When the ship passed into the southern hemisphere the vertical soft iron effect reappeared but with the opposite sign. The direction of the correcting magnet was of course unchanged and now its over-effect was added to the error which it was intended to correct. The result of this was that in southern latitudes it was possible for a ship to experience larger deviations of her compas than she had when in her home port before its 'correction'. Experiences of this sort threw the whole practice of compass correction into disrepute.

It was also found that heeling error did exist and not only caused the compass of a ship heeled to the wind to be in error, but if she were rolling caused the compass card to oscillate from side to side as the direction of the error changed. This latter effect became so troublesome that the Admiralty was forced to modify its 'no correction' rule to the extent that heeling error could be corrected.

In 1855 the Liverpool Compass Committee was set up by the local ship-owners at the instigation of the Privy Council for Trade to investigate the compass position in iron ships. After two preliminary reports it published its final in 1861. A strange state of affairs was revealed by this investigation. It was rare for any merchant ship officer to use an azimuth compass to discover any possible compass error, or even the variation which was instead taken from a chart. Some masters relied upon errors in the position of the ship, as revealed by their sights, to show whether or not their compasses were correct. Compass adjusters claimed that a compass they had corrected should *never* show any error and when their claim was proved to be wrong the whole system of correction became suspect. It was not realised that when a compass has large errors due to the magnetism of a ship its directive force is also affected so that on some headings the attractive force was so weak as to make the compass indications unsteady and unreliable.

The findings of the Liverpool Compass Committee were:

That the magnetic character of an iron ship depended upon the direction of her building slip and that its strength was reduced slightly during her first twelve months of service, thereafter becoming reasonably permanent. That magnetic cargoes would affect the compasses. That heeling error was a very important factor. In the iron steamship *City of Baltimore* of 2368 tons the standard compass had heeling errors which reached as much as two degrees for every degree of heel, and in some ships errors were even greater than this. That the lack of a Flinders Bar meant large changes of deviation when a ship changed her latitude appreciably. In one ship the adjuster tried to get over this difficulty by fitting adjustable magnets which the master was supposed to move out as the ship sailed southwards and in again as she returned to northern waters.

That the chain boxes recommended by Airy and commonly used would only correct about 3½° of quadrantal deviation, but more was needed and the Committee proposed the use of elongated soft iron shapes.

The work of this Committee was most valuable and made a major contribution to safety at sea. It is therefore rather surprising to find Captain S. T. S. Lecky writing in 1881 of the number of ships still at sea with standard compasses so badly placed that the initial deviations far exceeded eight points, or where iron fittings subject to frequent movement were placed so close to the compass as to cause varying errors of several degrees.

Sir William Thomson.

Sir William Thomson, afterwards Lord Kelvin, made the next great advance in the development of the compass. This gentleman had been asked in 1871 whether he would write an article on compasses. He accepted the commission and then realised that he really knew next to nothing about his subject so began to study it. As a result of these studies he patented a compass and binnacle in 1876 and an improved form in 1879 which was widely adopted. Thomson became convinced of the necessity for keeping a compass closely corrected and his binnacle was so designed as to embody all the correctors necessary and to allow of their easy adjustment. A Flinders Bar was carried in a brass case attached to the binnacle and was made up in a number of different lengths so that these could be put together to make any length required. This was a great improvement on the Flinders Bars fitted by the Liverpool Compass Committee and advocated by Lecky which were tailored for the ship and built into it at an appreciable distance from the compass (Fig. 41). Soft iron (quadrantal) correction, was made by soft iron spheres sliding on brackets on each side of the compass, and various sizes were available. Permanent magnetism could be corrected by magnets

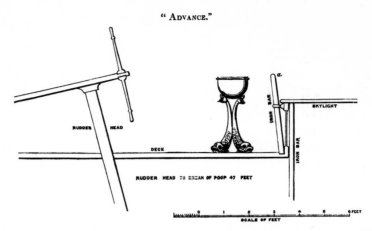

Figure 41   An arrangement of iron bars fitted in the *Advance*, c. 1860, to correct the steering compass, using the method recommended by Captain Flinders.

placed in racks which were fore-and-aft and athwartships and were adjustable for height. Finally, centrally under the compass, was a bucket in which vertical magnets could be placed to correct the heeling error, their height being adjustable by means of a graduated chain.

The introduction of the Thomson compass and binnacle revolutionised the compass situation. Henceforth it became usual to adjust compasses properly and to keep them adjusted. This had a great effect upon the accuracy of navigation.

There is, however, one last point concerning compass correction that must be discussed. If soft iron masses are used to correct quadrantal error these became magnetized from two sources—the magnetism of the earth and the magnetism of the compass needles themselves. The error which they have to correct is dependent upon the horizontal component of the earth's magnetism, which is greatest at the equator and least at the poles. If the soft iron correctors received their magnetism entirely from the earth, the correction once made would be correct all over the earth, for the magnitude of both disturbing and correcting forces would be dependent upon the same source. The masses may however receive some magnetism induced in them by the compass needles, and the amount of this will be the same at any position on the globe. Therefore, if the ship whose compass has been corrected at home moves nearer to the equator the correction will become insufficient. The consequent change in deviation can be kept to a small amount either by using large masses (the spheres on a Thomson binnacle) far out in preference to smaller ones close in, or by using weak compass needles. Thomson used very weak needles compared to those of other compasses of his time.

Spheres take up space, and are liable to be a nuisance for this reason, and in some countries it is preferred to get rid of them by substituting very small pieces of soft iron quite close to the compass which must have extremely strong needles. The navigator then has to put up with the inconvenience of having to change the size or position of his little soft iron pieces as he changes his magnetic latitude. An advantage of this system is that a compass can be corrected where errors are so large that spheres would have to be of unacceptable size. This gives the ship designer much greater latitude in his choice of a compass position but brings the disadvantage that the magnetic character of the position is much more liable to change. In my opinion it is much wiser to insist that a good compass position be provided. An example of a ship where it would have been impracticable to correct the compass with spheres came to my notice during the Second Great War. This was the French submarine *Surcouf* where the quadrantal deviations greatly exceeded 25°.

Repeating Compasses.

A ship needs more than one compass. She must have a standard compass from which bearings can be taken and by which her course is regulated, and a steering compass at each steering position. All these have to be corrected and must be in reasonable positions magnetically. It has frequently been suggested that since steering is regulated by comparison with the standard compass it does not matter how large are the errors of a steering compass, but those who make such statements forget that correction not only reduces the deviation but also equalises the directive force on all headings. If this is not done the directive force may be so weak on some headings that the compass card will become so unsteady as to be completely useless. If the magnetic compass can be made to operate repeaters at a distance, the need to provide good positions for the steering compasses is avoided.

One makeshift has been to use optical means to view the compass card at a distance. In early submarines the compass was placed outside the pressure hull and the card was viewed through a telescope. This must have given the helmsman considerable eyestrain. The next idea was to fit a lamp above the compass which, with the aid of a system of lenses, projected an image of part of the card onto a ground-glass screen before the helmsman. Electric light bulbs were fragile and could only be replaced when the submarine was on the surface and though two were often fitted so that a spare could be moved into place by a system of levers, this was not entirely satisfactory as any shock might break both. Next the projector tube was enlarged so that the whole compass and optical system could be lowered into the hull by wires for the replacement of a lamp, and finally a prism was placed above the card so that a lamp at the bottom of the tube could throw a light-ray upwards, through the prism and down again bringing the image of the card down with it. Apart from the convenience of being easily able to replace a lamp the image was much better than any other.

Shortly before the First World War a somewhat similar system was tried for projecting the image of the compass card from the lower conning tower to the upper in Dreadnought battleships. It was not very successful, chiefly owing to the difficulty of keeping the optical parts clean and dry.

Some merchant ships of recent years have adopted a standard compass which is arranged so that an image of the compass card is projected down through the roof of the wheelhouse, thus avoiding the provision of a steering compass there.

Various methods have been tried for making a magnetic compass operate repeater dials electrically. Most of these involve a scheme by which the compass bowl is driven round by a motor to keep it aligned with the card. Early types used dry-card compasses and when the card got out of line with the bowl a positive electrical contact was made energising the follow-up motor, which drove the bowl round until it was again in step with the card, at the same time driving a transmitter which operated the repeaters*. In more modern times a liquid compass is used and the signal to the bowl driving motor is given either by a light shining through an aperture in the card to activate selenium cells, or by passing a current through the compass liquid, which forms a variable resistance according to the distance between contracts on card and bowl thus affecting the balance of an electrical circuit.

* The first patent for an electrical transmitting compass was taken out by F. Jenkin in 1863.

Gyro-Compasses.

In 1852 Jean Bernard Leon Foucault used a gyroscope to demonstrate the rotation of the earth*, and soon inventors were considering how it would be possible to use one for purposes of navigation. John Kinnersley Smythies took out a patent for a gyroscopic-compass in 1856 and Trouvé followed in 1865, but neither of these ideas was ever continued.

The first experiments were made by the French Navy in 1884 with a gyroscope (not a north-seeking gyro-compass), using its constant direction in space as a datum by which to check the deviation of a magnetic compass.

In 1901 Anschütz-Kaempfe proposed to use a gyroscope in a submarine which was intended to operate below the polar ice and he spent the next few years experimenting with such an instrument. In about 1905 he realised that if the case containing the gyroscope were made pendulous this would provide a control which would precess the axis towards the meridian as soon as it started to tilt, owing to the rotation of the earth. Some form of damping would be required as otherwise the axis would tend to oscillate back and forth across the meridian instead of settling on it. Anschütz made an instrument in which the damping was achieved by the reaction of an air blast, but the first of these true gyro-compasses was found to be subject to errors if a ship rolled when steering a half-cardinal (quadrantal) course. In 1912 he introduced a new pattern in which he had three gyroscopes mounted in a frame which floated in mercury and had a circular trough in which oil flowed to introduce the necessary damping. Baffles slowed up the movement of the oil in the trough preventing its movement when the ship rolled and thereby eliminating the quadrantal error.

In 1911 the first Sperry gyro-compass had appeared with the north-seeking control provided by a weight slung below the gyro case on which it pressed eccentrically when the case was tilted. This had the same effect as the pendulousness of the first Anschütz in making the instrument north-seeking but the eccentric application provided the necessary damping factor. Unfortunately, it did not prevent the quadrantal error which when the compass was first tried in a battleship amounted to as much as 14° in heavy weather. Attempts to solve the problem were not successful until in 1919 the solid

* Foucault is always given the credit for being first in the field but on 9th March 1836 Edward Sang had proposed the experiment in a paper read to the Royal Scottish Society of Arts. *(Transactions of the Royal Scottish Society of Arts*, Vol. IV (1856), p. 418.)

weight was replaced by iron boxes on each side, from one to other of which mercury could flow through a restricted tube. In the meantime the Brown gyro-compass had appeared in 1917, another compass in which the control was provided by the flow of oil, though in this case the oil was transferred from one side to the other by air pressure instead of by gravity.

Besides these three gyro-compasses, all of which in improved forms are still generally employed, there have been several other types which it is unnecessary to discuss here.

Since the Second World War there has been a great increase in the fitting of gyro-compasses in merchant vessels. An added attraction for them is the increased need for course repeaters in radar and other instruments.

Although the great advantage claimed for a gyro-compass over magnetic is that it is unaffected by the ship's magnetism in addition to its convenience in that it can operate repeaters anywhere in the ship, this claim is not strictly true. Because of the use of steel parts in the manufacture of a gyro-compass it can be affected by magnetism if the field is sufficiently strong. Two cases of this have come to my notice. One was in the submarine PHOENIX where the main battery cables had been badly run so that they set up a strong magnetic field at the compass position and the other was in the mine-destructor ship BORDE, where a vast magnet had been built into the ship to explode magnetic mines.

NOTES.

There have been two incidents in the history of magnetic compasses which have been widely accepted by the historian on inaccurate information. These would normally have been thought to be outside the scope of this book but I have felt it desirable to discuss them in the hope that it may do something to restrict the publication of these errors.

There was at one time an idea that Alexander Neckam had described a pivoted compass needle in his work *De Utensilibus*, supposed to have been written in 1187, long before such a type of compass is believed to have been invented. The relative passage runs:

"Qui ergo munitam vult habere navem, ... habeat etiam acum jaculo suppositam, rotabitur enim et circumvolvetur acus donec cuspis acus respeciat orientem, sicque comprehendunt quo tendere debeant naute cum cinossura latet in aeris turbacione."* This may be translated: "Therefore he who wants to have a well-equipped ship . . . let him also have a needle placed under a dart; for the needle will rotate and revolve until the point of the needle looks towards the east, and thus sailors perceive in which direction they ought to go, when the Little Bear is hidden in disturbed weather."

This passage seemed very obscure, particularly relative to the mention of east, and in 1858 D'Avezac in *Anciens témoignages historiques relatifs à la boussole* suggested that there were two copyist's errors — *suppositam* for *superpositam* and *orientem* for *septentrionem*. Those following his theory would translate the passage. 'Therefore he who wants to have a well-equipped ship . . . let him also have a needle mounted on a pivot, for the needle will rotate and revolve until the point of the needle is directed towards the north, and thus sailors &c."

On this basis it has been stated by many historians that the pivoted compass needle predated Neckam. The passage has been recently re-examined and it is now generally supposed that D'Avezac's theory has no foundation. There is no reason to conclude that either of the errors which he describes have actually been made. *Jaculum* means a spear or dart and could not possibly be translated as a pivot. It might very well be applied to an arrow-headed pointer. The repetition of *acus* is very clumsy, even for dog-Latin, and it has been suggested that the error that has been perpetrated by a copyist is the second *acus* for *eius* (for it), which it would closely resemble and be an easy mistake. The passage would then probably mean: " . . . . circumvolvetur acus, donec cuspis jaculi respiciat . . . . "

If we accept this reading we should have a description of a dart mounted above a needle and at right angles to it. In other words while the needle pointed north the dart would point to the east. This is by no means as extraordinary as at first sight might be expected. I have seen a small pocket compass of a rather later date in which the card is replaced by the figure of a little bird with outstretched beak. The needle is fastened across and below the wings so that when the needle points north the beak points east. When cards were first fitted to compass needles the east point was often the most conspicuously marked.

The Brunetto Latini hoax has tricked a long list of historians during the last century and a half.

* * *

* *A Volume of Vocabularies*, edited by Thomas Wright, 1857, p.114.

In 1802 a man named William Dupré supplied the editor of the *Monthly Magazine or British Register* with a number of contributions. These he claimed were free translations from original manuscripts in his possession. He stated that Brunetto Latini had come to England from France soon after 1260 and that some of the manuscripts were letters from him to Guido Cavilcanti, a Florentine poet. Seven of these contributions were printed in the magazine in good faith.

The letters discuss such things as the standard of learning in England at the time and the climax was reached when a description was given of a visit by Latini to Roger Bacon at Oxford. The latter demonstrated gun-powder, mirrors and a burning glass. Then came the infamous passage:

> "He further showed me a black ugly stone, called a magnet, which has the surprising property of drawing iron to it; and upon which if a needle be rubbed, and afterwards fastened to a straw, so as it shall swim upon water, the needle will instantly turn towards the Pole-Star: therefore, be the night ever so dark, so as neither moon or star be visible, yet shall the mariner be able, by the help of this needle, to steer his vessel aright. [La magnete piere laide et noire. Ob ele fer volunters se joint. Lon touchet ob une aguilet. Et en festue lon fischie. Puis lon met en laigue et se tient desus. Et la point se torne contre lestoille. Quant la nuit seit tenebrous et lon ne voie estoile ni lune, poet le mariner tenir droite voie.]"
>
> "This discovery, which appears useful in so great a degree to all who travel by sea, must remain concealed until other times; because no master-mariner dares to use it lest he should fall under a supposition of his being a magician; nor would even the sailors venture themselves out to sea under his command, if he took with him an instrument which carries so great an appearance of being constructed under the influence of some infernal spirit. A time may come when these prejudices, which are of such great hindrance to researches into the secrets of nature, will probably be no more; and it will be then that mankind shall reap the benefit of the labours of such learned men as Friar Bacon, and do justice to that industry and intelligence for which he and they now meet with no other return than obloquy and reproach."

It is not clear whether it is the supposed visit to Bacon or something else which first aroused suspicion. Part of the quotation above is in fact a paraphrase of a passage in the *Bible* of Guyot de Provins. In any case Dupré was accused of having perpetrated a hoax and admitted it! Unfortunately, far too many historians have read the account of the Bacon visit and quoted from it, but though a few have noticed the similarity in the two passages it is the exception for any of them to have read the apology of the editor of the *Monthly Magazine* for having misled his readers.

This is of course a complication. Brunetto did refer to the magnetic needle in his *Li Livres dou Tresor*. This work contains two passages which have a bearing upon the history of the compass. The first of these gives the names of the winds, pointing out that sailors did not always use the same names as did landsmen and sometimes explaining their derivation. It must be made clear that these names are the names of winds and not of compass points, and there is no connection whatsoever between this part and that which mentions the magnet.

The second passage may be translated:

> "That is why sailors navigate by the stars which they call Tramontanes and the people who are in Europe and on this side navigate by the North Star and the others by the southern one. And he who wishes to know the truth should take a magnet stone and he will notice that it has two ends, one which points towards one of these stars, and the other towards the other star. And at both ends, the point of the needle lifts up towards the very star to which that end is attracted. That is how the sailor would be deceived if he were not careful, because though these two stars do not move, it happens that the other ones which are close by describe a small circle, and those which are further describe a larger one."

The only real information that we get from this is that Brunetto Latini knew that the magnet had both north-seeking and south-seeking poles and that he thought that the two poles of the compass needle were separately attracted by stars situated at both the north and south poles of the heavens.

Three
Speed and Distance

To keep the reckoning of a ship's position at sea it is necessary not only to know the course she has been making good but also the distance she has run. The earliest proposal for an instrument to register this is believed to have emanated from the Roman architect Vitruvius in about 27 B.C.* His suggestion was to fit a four-foot paddle wheel on the ship's side which would be turned by the movement of the ship through the water. At each revolution of the paddle-wheel shaft a pebble would be dropped into a hopper and if these were counted their number, multiplied by the circumference of the paddle-wheel, would show how far the vessel had moved during the time of operation. Of course speed is a function of the distance run so if the speed were reasonably constant all that was needed was to operate the apparatus over a limited known time and from this to work out the speed per hour and distance run over periods longer or shorter than an hour. It is very unlikely that the scheme proposed by Vitruvius was ever actually tried. The mechanical difficulty of making the device drop one pebble every revolution, and only one, must have been insuperable.

Even at the time of Columbus it is probable that the pilots still obtained their distance run by estimating from time to time the speed of the ship by eye. This was one of the mysteries of the trade. Long experience in vessels of the same type probably made them fairly accurate, at any rate in their own opinions. That this was formerly the case and that the practice had not entirely died out is confirmed by some condemnatory remarks made by Richard Norwood in 1637 (page 11).

It has been suggested that the first measurement of speed was made by what has come to be called the Dutchman's log, though it does not seem to have been mentioned until 1623. Two marks were set up at the ship's side and the distance between them measured. Then a chip was thrown overboard and the period that it took to pass from opposite one mark to opposite the other was timed. From

* *De Architectura*, Book x, Chap. ix.

this figure the speed of the ship could be calculated. The method must have been far from accurate because of the difficulty of measuring an arbitrary time before the introduction of watches. A sand glass will tell when the whole time for which it was made to run has elapsed, but will not measure a fraction of that time. We read of men counting their pulse beats to measure the time* or of repeating a set form of words over and over again. It was generally considered that it took thirty seconds to count up to sixty and so to do this twice would take a minute. Men even compared the time taken by the passage of the chip with the speed of their own running along the deck, taken as six miles per hour.

A similar and probably earlier alternative to the Dutchman's log was the observation of froth or anything else drifting past and it has been suggested that Iberian pilots favoured this practice. By the latter part of the seventeenth century the Dutchman's log had become extremely popular in the Netherlands, and so it received its name from other nations although it is improbable that it had originated in that country.

It is now generally accepted that the log-ship appeared before the Dutchman's log and was an English invention. It was first described by Bourne in 1574, but not as being something new. This log-ship was a piece of board in the form of the segment of a circle of about nine inches radius, the curved edge being weighted. It was attached to a long line by three branches so that it would stand at right-angles to the line. To find the ship's speed the log-ship was dropped over the stern into the water and at the same instant a minute glass was turned. As the log-ship drifted astern it was allowed to draw out the line until the sand in the glass had all run, when the line was held. As it was hauled in, the length of line that had run out was measured in fathoms by the traditional way against the stretch of the arms. Bourne tells us to multiply the result by sixty and to divide by 2500 to obtain the speed in leagues per hour. He was in fact allowing 5000 feet to the mile, which was the usual English practice, while the Spaniards and Portuguese allowed 5714 feet.

The inaccuracies of the log-ship lay in the obvious inaccuracies of the sand glass and in judging the instant to turn it and to check the line, in the difficulty of keeping the line taut without snubbing the log, and in the variation in the length of men's arms for measuring

* Edmond Gunter: *The Description and Use of the Sector, Crosse-Staffe & other Instruments*, 2nd ed., 1636, The second Book of the Crosse-Staffe, Chap. vi. The reference to the pulse does not appear in the first edition.

the fathoms. It was also possible for the eddies set up by the ship's movement to carry the log along with them, thus giving an artificially low reading.

Two improvements were introduced into the log-line. The line was marked with knots at such distance apart that the amount of line between two would be drawn out while the sand was running if the ship were proceeeding at one mile per hour. Thus the number of knots which passed the hand in one minute showed the number of miles per hour at which the ship was sailing and so the expression that the ship was 'making so many knots', came into use meaning she was making so many miles per hour. It is thus incorrect to talk of knots per hour as this is equivalent to talking of nautical miles per hour per hour, an acceleration not a speed.

The marking of the log-line probably came into being early in the seventeenth century. In March 1612 Nathaniel Marten records that he "ran fifteene leagues by the logge"* and it has been suggested that he cannot yet have been using a marked log-line or he would have referred to speed instead of distance by the log.

We first read of a marked log-line in 1632†, but it had probably been in use for some years before this. By this date also, the minute glass had given way to the half-minute glass and the distance between knots was usually forty-two feet. Richard Norwood, having measured the distance from London to York in 1635, made the length of a minute of latitude, which is equivalent to a nautical mile, to be 6120 feet. It is actually 6080 feet. A log-line should therefore be marked at fifty-one feet for a knot.

There was a great deal of conservatism over the new marking of the log-line, many navigators insisting on retaining their forty-two foot marking. Some liked to use glasses which only ran for about twenty-seven seconds and these used with the old marking gave approximately the same result as a line marked in the new fashion and used with a thirty-second glass. Actually a forty-eight marking came into fairly general use. This had two advantages. By using a line on the short side a ship's speed was always slightly over-estimated so that her reckoning tended to be ahead of her position, always an advantage when approaching land. Also if the markings were at forty-eight feet this was exactly eight fathoms. It was then easy to measure a log-line and to check for any shrinkage from time to time. If fractions were needed these would be eighths, each equivalent to

* *Purchas his Pilgrims*. Hakluyt Society Edition, Vol. III, p.310
† Champlain, *Les Voyages de la Nouvelle France Occidental*. 1632.

one fathom. In the log-book the speed columns were always headed K and F, i.e. knots and fathoms (or eighths).

If the log-line was to be marked there would have to be a zero from which to measure and in making this zero it became usual to allow what was called a 'stray line' between the log and the zero mark. The log could then be allowed to drift well astern out of the reach of any eddies before the glass was turned and the measurement began to be made.

Another refinement helped the men who had to haul in the log again after it had been streamed. Of the three strands by which the log was attached to the line two were made fast while the third was broken by a tapered plug and socket. When the sand in the glass had finished running, if the line were checked with a smart jerk the plug would come out and the log being then only attached at two points would ride in flat and be recovered with far less difficulty.

There were some writers who considered the inaccuracies of the log to be so great that as good an estimate of speed could be made without it. John Smith wrote: "Some use a log line, and a minute glass to know what way she makes, but that is so uncertain, it is not worth the labour to use it"*, and Edward Harrison agreed with him.

It was recommended that the sand-glass should be checked against the swinging of a pendulum, consisting of a bullet on a thread swinging from a nail, but writers were unable to agree as to the proper length for a half-minute pendulum!

The inaccuracy of the log-ship and of the Dutchman's log led many inventors to try to improve or replace them. As early as 1604 Robert Norton† was suggesting a wooden paddle-wheel, working in a wooden trough attached to the ship's side and recording on a dial the number of revolutions and hence the distance run. He acknowledged having got the idea from something written by Jacques Besson in 1569, but does not seem to have worked it out properly, basing his plan on one for a litter to be carried between two horses for measuring distance overland.

In 1683 Robert Hooke showed part of his way-wiser to the Royal Society.‡ He claimed that he had spoken of it to some of the Fellows about twenty years before and now exhibited a rotating vane for it. It is not clear whether he intended this to be carried on the ship's side or not, indeed it is doubtful whether he ever thought out

*   John Smith, *Seaman's Grammar*, 1627.
†   Robert Norton. *A Mathematical Appendix &c*. 1604. p.24.
‡   Thomas Birch. *The History of the Royal Society of London*. Vol. iv. p.231.

how the rotations of the vane were to be converted to indications on a dial.

Yet another of these rotators attached to the ship was actually made by Thomas Savory about 1809 but proved to be a failure.

Henry de Saumarez was convinced that the Shovel disaster (page 27) was caused by his failing to know with sufficient accuracy his distance run, owing to the imperfections of the common log. He proposed to make an accurate log, which he called the marine surveyor, and was involved in experiments with it from 1715 until at least 1729*. He made a Y of metal 2/3 inch thick with upright 27 inches long and arms 15 inches long. Attached to the end of each arm was a palm 8 × 4½ inches and these were slightly bent so that they imparted a rotary motion to the Y when it was towed through the water by a line attached to its foot. By towing the rotator with a line instead of having it mounted on the ship's hull he was striking new ground. The other end of the line was attached to the spindle of wheel-work mounted in the stern of the vessel (Fig. 42), so that the rotations of the Y were recorded on dials. De Saumarez tried three dials of which the first had three hands showing for one rotation 100, 1000 and 10,000 feet, the second showed up to 12 miles and the hands of the third registered 1 mile, 60 miles and 60 leagues.

Trials with this apparatus were made in France, England and the Netherlands, the Royal Navy being sufficiently interested to allow de Saumarez to demonstrate it during a voyage to the Netherlands and back in the WILLIAM & MARY yacht. De Saumarez also illustrated a paddle-wheel carried below a boat and having a direct vertical rod drive to a dial in-board. He does not seem to have proceeded with this variety.

Writing in 1754†, John Smeaton pointed out that the marine surveyor could never be a success because of the great weight of its rotator. This necessitated the use of a heavy line and very massive wheel-work, thus introducing enormous friction. Smeaton proposed to use, as rotator, a piece of oval plate, 10 by 2½ inches and only 1/13th inch thick, which was slightly bent to make it rotate when pulled through the water. This light rotator of course permitted the use of a much lighter line and wheel-work than had been used by de Saumarez. A spring was inserted in the line to absorb shocks.

Several trials were made with this apparatus but it was found that with more speed it increasingly under-read, due apparently to greater friction and a tendency of the oval rotator to jump out of the water.

* *Philosophical Transactions of the Royal Society.* 1725, No. 391, v; 1729, No. 408. iii.
† *Philosophical Transactions of the Royal Society*, 1754, p.532.

Figure 42   The log of Henry de Saumarez, 1725. (Adapted from *Philosophical Transactions of the Royal Society*, 1725, No. 391)

Smeaton then found that William Russell had tried a very similar apparatus some years before and this seems to have made him lose interest.

Other attempts were made to perfect mechanical logs. Among these were Joseph Gilmore's Navivium of about 1720 and Gotlieb's Perpetual Log, both of which had wheels attached to the keel which drove indicators by rods passing through the hull, and Benjamin Martin's Dromometer which differed only in the proposal to fit it on the side of the ship instead of on the keel. James Guerimand in 1776 used a paddle-wheel working horizontally on a vertical shaft. No one much liked boring holes in a ship's hull and it was foreseen that the apparatus was liable to become clogged with sea weed.

About 1747 Pierre Bouguer invented his cone and diver, which he described in his book published in 1753. This apparatus consisted of a conical float attached to a metal sinker (the diver) by a fifty-foot line, the log-line being attached to the float. The sinker consisted of two thin square iron plates, fastened together at right-angles to each other along their diagonals. The intention was that the sinker would be outside the influence of any surface motion of the sea, or of the wake of the ship, and would remain more stationary than the ordinary log-ship which it was intended to replace. Bouguer's cone and diver remained in use among some navigators for at least fifty years.

Bouguer also had an idea of a globe which would be towed astern by a line, the other end of which was attached to one end of a lever mounted inboard. The pull of the line on the lever, acting against a spring attached to the other end, inclined it. Thus the faster the ship moved through the water the stronger the pull on the line and the greater the inclination of the lever, an angle which was indicated on a scale graduated for speed. This scheme had already been proposed in about 1750 by Walter Maitland, a schoolmaster in the Royal Navy.* A similar device was proposed about the beginning of the nineteenth century by John Whitley Boswell. In an alternative arrangement the lever was mounted outboard and was much larger. The Marquis de Poleni fastened a globe to the lower end of the lever, to catch the flow of water, and the upper end moved over a scale to indicate the speed. Saverien's arrangement was similar, but a cord attached to the upper end of the lever led to a bucket into which sufficient weights had to be introduced to restore the verticality of the lever, the amount of weight needed indicating the speed. Francis Hopkinson, a judge of Pennsylvania, used a brass plate instead of the globe at the bottom end of the lever, keeping de Poleni's scale at the top but controlling the lever by means of a strong spring attached to it below the fulcrum. In 1808 Major-General Charles Grant, Viscount de Vaux, returned to Maitland's arrangement with his Hydroscope, but weighted the towed globe to submerge it and replaced the lever by a spring balance†.

The proposal of Henry de Saumarez to tow a rotator astern which would operate dials inboard by means of its towing line was never forgotten for very long. We have seen that Smeaton had heard of trials with William Russell's perpetual log by 1754 and this gentleman was still in the field twenty years later. In 1772 William Foxon patented a log‡ with a helical rotator, which was just

---

*   Walter Maitland. *An Essay towards the Improvement of Navigation.* n.d.
†   Major-General Charles Grant, *The Means of finding the Longitude at Sea*, 1808.
‡   Patent No. 1028, dated 5th December 1772.

buoyant, and a set of three dials inboard, of which one read to 12 miles and another to 288. The latter would be ample to record a whole day's run and could be reset daily at noon. The logs of Russell and Foxon were tried with the cone and diver of Bouguer by Captain Constantine Phipps during his 1773 arctic voyage in the RACEHORSE. In 1775 Captain James Cook obtained a Foxon log from Captain Rice of the East Indiaman *Dutton* and experimented with it, but neither he nor Captain Rice make any mention of it in their log-books.

All these logs with towed rotators and registering dials located inboard suffered from the same complaint. The wheelwork, at this time, could not be made free of friction which increased with the greater pull on the line at higher speeds. This resulted in a varying slip of the rotator which varied with weather conditions and the speed of the vessel. It was found that the mechanical logs were in fact far less accurate than the old log-ship which had so often been decried.

Then came a new idea. In 1792 Richard Hull Gower proposed to fit the rotator in a wooden cylinder, 18 x 8¾ inches, which also contained the registering dials. * The cylinder itself was prevented from turning and surfacing by being fastened by iron rods a foot below a 4½ ft long float. There would no longer be any question of varying slip, but there was the disadvantage that at each alteration of course or change of watch the log had to be hauled in and read. Gower does not seem to have done anything with his invention, but a rather similar idea was taken up by Edward Massey in 1802†, and pushed forward with considerable determination. Here the rotator and case containing the indicator dials were separated, being joined by four seventeen-inch lengths of cane jointed together (Fig. 43). At a later date this semi-rigid connection was replaced by a line about six feet in length. During the next sixty years several patents were taken out by the Massey family. These were usually devoted to improvements, some to prevent fouling of the rotator by sea-weed, but in 1834 there was one idea for towing the rotator from a box dropped down to the keel in a groove and operating a dial on deck. This would have necessitated structural alteration to the vessel and it is doubtful whether it was ever tried. It was the Massey towed log which for most of the century was extensively used at sea.

---

* Patent No. 1895, dated 15th July 1792.
† Patent No. 2601, dated 24th March 1802.

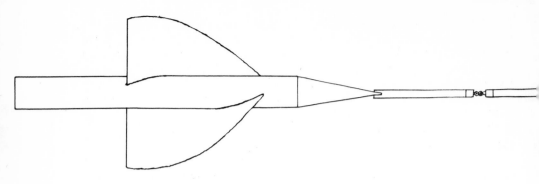

Figure 43   Massey's Log, 1802.

Another maker who made headway in this field was Thomas Walker who took out his first patent in 1846*. This was for a towed rotator and register inboard.

Thomas Walker was a nephew of the first Edward Massey and seems at one time to have made their logs for the Masseys', ultimately in 1903 acquiring their business. In 1861 the Walker harpoon log was patented† in which the rotator and dials were located in one unit. Unlike the Gower log which had had a large float above it to keep the case of the unit from turning, the harpoon log had a small heart-shaped float-plane which was quite sufficient to prevent the rotator turning the whole casing of the log (Fig. 44). In spite of more modern developments the harpoon log was still popular a century later for use in arctic waters where, unlike later types, it did not suffer from icing conditions.

By 1878 modern developments enabled Walker to go back to the old idea of having a rotator operating a register inboard through the log-line‡. This was of course far more convenient, entailing only a walk to the stern of the ship to read the dial when required, instead of the labour of hauling in the log and streaming it again. In 1884 this log acquired the name of the 'Cherub' (Fig. 45), the name having been suggested to the makers by a Tenniel cartoon in *Punch*. Ships were getting longer and even the walk to the stern of the ship to read the log was irksome to some. In 1890 Walker proposed to tow the rotator from a spar abreast the bridge and to use a special joint to

*   Patent No. 11251, dated 22nd June 1846.
†   Patent No. 3130, dated 13th December 1861.
‡   Patent No. 4369, dated 30th October 1878.

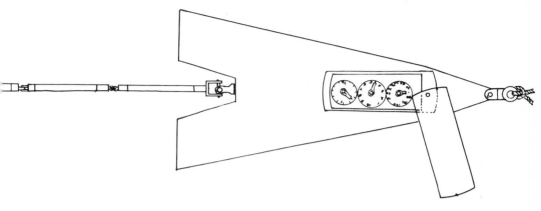

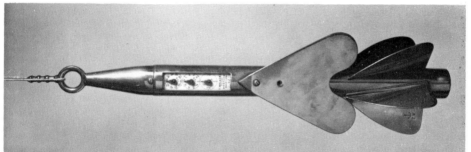

Figure 44   Walker's Harpoon Log. (Copyright: National Maritime Museum)

Figure 45   Rotator for Walker's Cherub Log. (Copyright: National Maritime Museum)

carry the motion through nearly a right-angle to the indicator on the bridge itself. This was used in many passenger liners and persisted for some time after 1902, in which year an electrical transmission from taffrail to bridge had been achieved.

Pitot Logs.

In 1730 Henri Pitot proposed the use of an L-shaped glass tube to measure current flow. It could be used either to measure the flow of rivers or the speed of ships. The toe of the L being turned into the direction from which the flow came, water would be forced up the tube to a distance which would depend on the pressure and hence on the speed of the vessel. The idea was not at that time a success. Saverien in 1753 and Captain Thomas Hamilton in about 1808 tried to introduce improvements, the latter using pewter instead of glass tubes. The idea was again resurrected in 1849 by the Rev. E. L. Berthon and trials were made in the BEE the following year.

Early in the present century the United States Navy adopted the Nicholson log on the Pitot principle but by 1917 these were being removed as being unsatisfactory. It was not until the 1950s that a Pitot log became reliable and was adopted by the Royal Navy.

Bottom Logs.

In the 1920s there was a return to the old idea of a bottom log, now in the form of a small retractable tube carrying a rotator which can be lowered a few feet below the hull to clear any eddies. This rotator drives an electrical transmitter through gearing. In 1924 the Royal Navy made successful trials with a log on this principle which had been developed by Captain B. Chernikeef of the Russian Navy in 1917. By 1928 this log was replacing the Forbes which had been used for a few years.

The Electro-Magnetic Log.

The latest development of the last twenty years is the electro-magnetic log in which a potential difference is generated in the water due to its movement relative to a magnetic field produced by an electro-magnet, the potential difference being sensed by two electrodes lowered below the hull.

Four
Instruments for Measuring Altitude

For the determination of latitude an instrument was required for measuring the altitude of the sun or a star and the first to be used was the quadrant (Fig. 46), a simple instrument which had been used for centuries by astronomers and architects. It was in the form of the quarter of a circle, made of either wood or metal, fitted with sights along one radius and having a plumb-bob suspended from the right angle. The observer held his quadrant in the vertical plane with the arc downwards, and with his eye at the arc looked up through the sights at the Pole Star. Then when his sights were properly aligned he nipped the plumb-line against the face of the quadrant between finger and thumb and read off the altitude shown there at his leisure.

The astronomer's quadrant had been graduated in degrees, but in the sea quadrant this was at first modified to be of use to the least educated seaman. At this time the need for an observation was not really to find the actual latitude but to get an idea when the ship was in the latitude of her port. For this reason the arc was only marked with the names of the principal places to which a ship might wish to sail. An observation would thus tell the navigator when he had reached the correct latitude and he could then turn and sail east or west until he found his port. In case the navigator could not even read, the names of the ports were sometimes indicated by symbols.

At this time the Pole Star circled round the pole of the heavens at a distance of three and a half degrees. It was therefore necessary always to observe when the star was in the same position and to enable this to be done the navigator was given a diagram showing the relative positions of the neighbouring stars and how they should stand at the correct time. Later he received a diagram with a volvelle which gave the correction to apply to his observed altitude, but this of course necessitated a graduation of the instrument in degrees.

We first read of the use of the sea quadrant about the year 1460.* Within about twenty years of this date degree graduations were

---

* I think that it was probably in use thirty years earlier. The rediscovery of the Azores in 1432 and the exploit of Gil Eannes in 1434, when he rounded Cape Bojador well out at sea, would have been difficult without something of the sort.

Figure 46   The Quadrant. (From Joseph Moxon's *A Tutor to Astronomie and Geographie* 1659)

coming into use and the next instrument, one in which the use of degree graduations was essential, was being adopted.

This new instrument was the mariner's astrolabe (Fig. 47). Like the quadrant, the astrolabe was originally an astronomer's instrument and its primary use was as a calculator for finding the positions of the stars and planets. Combined with the arrangements necessary for this a sight bar and a degree scale were sometimes added, so that the astronomer could observe the height of heavenly bodies. The use of this instrument is very old. At one time its invention was attributed to Hipparchus (180-125 B.C.), but more recently it has been suggested that it dates back to Eudoxus of Cnidus (409-356 B.C.).

In about 1480 the astrolabe was adapted to the needs of navigators. It was stripped of all its original reasons for existence and was left only with what was needed for the observation of altitudes. The mariner's astrolabe consisted of a heavy brass circle freely suspended from a thumb ring and weighted at the bottom so that it should hang true. At the centre of the circle was pivoted a ruler with a sight at each end and this ruler passed over a degree graduation near the edge of the ring.

Both the quadrant and the astrolabe must have been inconvenient to use. With a small vessel bucking about in even a moderate sea the standard of accuracy could not have been great. To hold a heavy astrolabe above one's head while one aligned the alidade on a star must have been practically impossible. It was a little better when using the sun, for the instrument could be held low down and the sun shining through the aperture of the upper sight threw a spot of light onto the lower. Explorers took their astrolabes ashore to observe, but the ordinary trader, trying to find his port, could not do this.

Columbus took both astrolabe and quadrant with him. It is probable that he would have used the astrolabe for sun sights and the quadrant for the Pole Star.

An offspring of the astrolabe was the Ring (Fig. 48), an instrument which had only one use — for the observation of the altitude of the sun. It consisted of a heavy metal band with the usual thumb-ring suspension. A small hole was drilled through the band on one shoulder at 45° from the top. To use the instrument it was suspended so that it hung true and turned so that the hole was

Figure 47   The Mariner's Astrolabe. (From Medina's *Arte de Navegar* 1545)

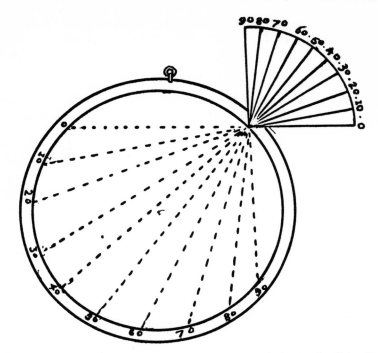

Figure 48   The Ring. (Derived from *The Seaman's Secrets* by John Davis)

towards the sun. Then the sun shining through the hole would throw
a spot of light onto the inner surface of the other side of the band,
where a graduation enabled its altitude to be read. The advantage of
this instrument over the astrolabe was that for the same diameter the
scale would be much larger. There were of course no moving parts.

Some of these instruments were made in the form of a square
instead of a ring, but this variety must have been more difficult to
balance and therefore less accurate.

I have found the ring described by various writers between 1594
and 1684 and this probably indicates its period of popularity.

When in 1497 Vasco da Gama penetrated into the Indian Ocean
and met Arab pilots he found them using the kamal. This consisted
of a length of cord attached to the centre of a rectangular plaque of
wood. Knots on the cord marked distances from the wood and were
each applicable to the latitude of a particular port. The observer held
the appropriate knot to his eye and stretched the plaque away as far
as possible, holding it so that he could see the horizon in line with its

lower edge. If then the Pole Star was in the line with the top edge he was in his correct latitude, if it was above the top edge he was too far north, if the plaque obscured the star he was too far south.

It has been suggested that the news of this instrument prompted the introduction of the cross-staff (Fig. 49), sometimes referred to as a Jacob's staff. It was first proposed for maritime use by Johann Werner in 1514, but the instrument is believed to have been invented by the Chaldeans about 400 B.C. for the use of astronomers. The cross-staff consisted of a long wooden shaft on to which could be threaded any one of four crosses of varying lengths. The observer selected and fitted the cross appropriate to the altitude that he wished to observe and held up the instrument, resting the end of the

Figure 49   The Cross-Staff. (From John Seller's *Practical Navigation* 1669)

shaft on the bone beside his eye-socket. He then slid the cross in or out until he could see, at the same time, the horizon in line with the bottom edge of the cross and the sun or star in line with the top edge. Then the position of the cross on the shaft gave the altitude. The four sides of the shaft were differently graduated — one for each cross. Apart from general awkwardness this instrument had several disadvantages. If the sun were being observed, it was dazzling and painful to look directly at it, though this inconvenience was partially surmounted by fitting a smoked glass to the upper end of the cross. This modification is described by Bourne in 1574 but had probably been adopted some years earlier. Each observer had a personal error due to the configuration of his face and the consequent variation in the actual distance between the eye and the near end of the staff. To ascertain whether there was such an error the pilot was told to put on two crosses of different lengths and to set them to the same altitude reading. If he then put the cross-staff up to his eye he should find that the ends of the two crosses appeared to coincide. If the larger cross appeared beyond the ends of the shorter, then the end of the shaft was too far from the pilot's eye and he was instructed to pare off the end of the shaft until the two crosses appeared to coincide. If the shorter cross more than masked the larger cross the eye was already too close, but we are not told how to build up the end of the shaft to deal with such a situation. The human eye is only capable of scanning a limited angle and this limited the maximum angle that could be observed with a cross-staff to about 60°, again dependent upon the observer. The form of the instrument precluded the measurement of very small angles so it was not usually graduated below 3°. For these reasons the cross-staff could not be used in low latitudes where the sun was too high and the Pole Star too low, or in high latitudes where the opposite was the case. Under such conditions the navigator had still to use his quadrant or astrolabe.

The nuisance of having four different crosses was overcome in some instruments by using a single one with holes into which two pegs could be inserted at various distances apart. The observation was then taken between two pegs instead of the ends of a cross, and the scale appropriate to the two holes used gave the angle. The first in the field with a cross-staff of this type was probably Gemma Frisius in about the year 1530. His cross-staff (Fig. 50) had a single cross of which one arm was fairly broad while the other was much thinner and carried a sliding vane. With this a number of effective lengths for the cross were available. Gemma Frisius originally suggested his modified cross-staff for measuring the angle between two stars and it was not, therefore, specifically a navigator's instrument.

In Bourne's *Regiment for the Sea*, 1574, a cross-staff is illustrated with two vanes on the cross but the author does not make any reference to them in his text.

The invention of Davis's back-staff, or Davis's quadrant as it was usually called, was first described in 1594 and was a great advance on previous instruments. His original back-staff (Fig. 51) consisted of a shaft on which slid a vertical arm A vane, called the horizon vane, was secured to the end of the shaft. The observer stood with his back

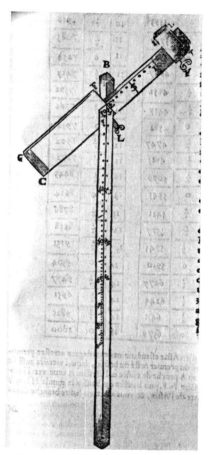

Figure 50   The Cross-Staff of Gemma Frisius.

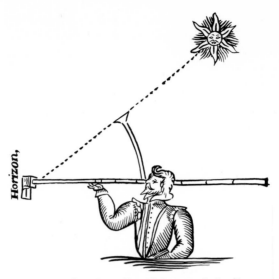

Figure 51   John Davis' first Back-Staff.

to the sun and looked along the shaft so that the horizon was viewed through a slit in the horizon vane. He then moved the vertical arm in or out until the shadow of its top edge thrown on the horizon vane, appeared to be in line with the horizon. The altitude was then read off from the position of the arm on the shaft.*

This first back-staff was not suitable for altitudes above 45° and it must have been for this reason that Davis suggested a second form (Fig. 52). This one had two arms, one above the shaft the other below it. The upper arm was fourteen inches long and straight, the lower formed the arc of a circle. There were three sets of graduations, one indicating the position of each arm on the shaft, the third showing the position of an eyepiece on the curved arm. This instrument was used in the same way as its predecessor, except that the two arms were first placed at pre-selected positions on the shaft and a fine adjustment was made by sliding the eyepiece on the lower arm. The altitude was then obtained from the sum of the three graduations but Davis does not explain this.

The first Davis back-staff, modified by fitting a sliding vane onto

* It is probable that the idea of the back observation originated with Thomas Hariot. E. G. R. Taylor, *The Doctrine of Nautical Triangles Compendious*. Journal of the Institute of Navigation, Vol. 6 (1953) p.134-5

Figure 52   John Davis' second Back-Staff.

the vertical arm and marking the staff with a set of graduations appropriate to each position of it, continued to be used until near the end of the eighteenth century, probably because of its simplicity and cheapness. It is often illustrated in the navigational notes which formed the introduction to many of the Dutch chart atlases (Fig. 53). It had however almost gone out of use, in this country at any rate, at least half a century earlier in favour of its improved form which is described by both Sturmy and Seller in 1669.

The improved Davis quadrant (Fig. 54) had two arcs with a common centre in the same plane as each other. The upper (60°) arc of smaller radius was graduated in five degree steps only and carried a shadow vane. The lower arc (30°) of much greater radius carried an eyepiece and was graduated in degrees, and by diagonals could be read off to minutes. The observer set the shadow vane on the smaller arc to an even ten degree graduation, smaller than the expected altitude, and then adjusted the position of his eyepiece on the larger arc until he got the shadow of the top of the shadow vane thrown onto the horizon vane in line with the horizon seen through the latter's slit. He then added the readings on the two arcs together to obtain his altitude.

In calculating the latitude from the meridian altitude of the sun he had to obtain the zenith distance of the sun by subtracting the altitude from 90°, and for this reason some instruments were graduated to read off zenith distance direct instead of altitude. This practice shows the decline in the popularity of the Pole Star in favour of the sun for finding the latitude. The Davis quadrant could be used the reverse way round for observing stars direct, but this can only have been an unhandy business and I have found no evidence that sailors ever resorted to this method.

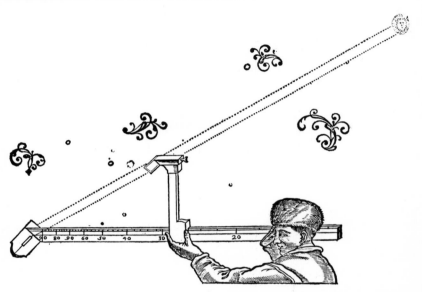

Figure 53   A form of modified Back-Staff, favoured abroad. The shadow vane could be fitted at any of three different heights.

There were two refinements to the Davis quadrant which were adopted by some users but not by all. One was to replace the shadow vane by a lens which threw a spot of light instead of a shadow upon the horizon vane, thereby greatly increasing the accuracy of observation. This seems to have been suggested by John Flamsteed, the Astronomer Royal, but it was not universally accepted.

In 1732 John Elton brought to the attention of the Royal Society an improved form of Davis quadrant with which observations could be taken without the horizon being visible (Fig. 55). The 60° arc of the Davis quadrant was replaced by a chord at whose centre was pivoted what Elton called a label. The label could be pinned to the chord at any one of three positions, 30° apart. By using these positions in conjunction with the ordinary large 30° arc, ranges of altitude of 0° to 30°, 30° to 60° or 60° to 90° could be used. The label carried a lens and also pivoted at the centre of the instrument was an index arm, carrying an eye vane and a vernier at its extremity. By means of this vernier and the graduation on the arc, which was marked every six minutes, the instrument could be read off to one minute.

Figure 54   Davis' Quadrant. (From John Seller's *Practical Navigation*, 1669)

If the horizon was visible the quadrant could be used in the same way as a Davis, the lens on the label throwing a spot of light onto the horizon plate, which Elton called the ray plate. If however the horizon was obscured the instrument was levelled by means of a spirit level on the index arm and a cross level on the ray plate.

A star sight could be taken by looking at a star just over the ray plate and levelling a third spirit level which was attached to the heel

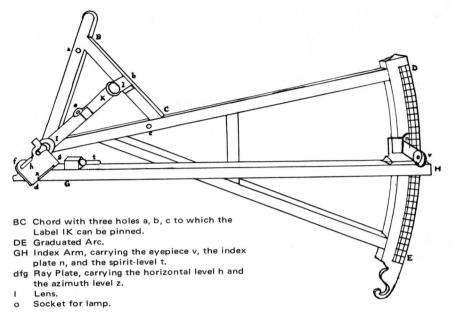

BC Chord with three holes a, b, c to which the
     Label IK can be pinned.
DE Graduated Arc.
GH Index Arm, carrying the eyepiece v, the index
     plate n, and the spirit-level t.
dfg Ray Plate, carrying the horizontal level h and
     the azimuth level z.
I   Lens.
o   Socket for lamp.

Figure 55   Elton's Quadrant.

of the label. The observer was thus looking upward at the star instead
of directing his gaze horizontally as when observing the sun.

A lamp was provided to illuminate the levels and it will be noted
that the two of these, other than the cross level, were viewed end on.
It must have been a bit tricky to be sure that the bubble had left the
near end without reaching the far end.

It is evident that some of these quadrants were used at sea, but we
hear very little of them.

The Plough (Fig. 56) was probably a transitional instrument
between the original Davis quadrant and the improved form. Seller
tells us in 1669 that it had by then almost gone out of use. The
plough was really a combination of Davis quadrant and cross-staff
with the uses of both. It had a staff graduated to twelve degrees with
a horizon vane at one end, a small radius 85° arc graduated every 10°
and fixed to the shaft, and a short arm carrying a sight vane and
sliding on the shaft. It is thus only a variation of the second
instrument described by Davis, but in addition a cross was provided
which could be slid onto the shaft at right-angles to the arc and used
with its appropriate graduations marked on another side of the shaft.

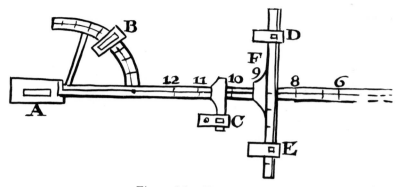

Figure 56   The Plough.

The instrument could then be used as a cross-staff but with the refinement of having vanes sliding on the cross for use as required, instead of more than one cross.

The almicanter staff was a simplification of the improved Davis quadrant having no 60° arc and carrying both the shadow and sight vanes on the 30° arc. It was thus intended for low altitudes only and would seem to have been an unnecessary instrument as it had no advantage over its parent.

Benjamin Cole's Quadrant (Fig. 57) which appeared in the middle

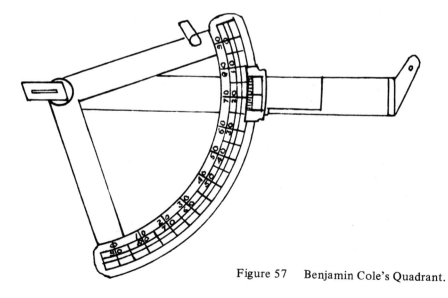

Figure 57   Benjamin Cole's Quadrant.

of the eighteenth century was another simplification of Davis's. This consisted of a two-foot staff of wood with an eyepiece at one end and an horizon vane at the other. A 90° arc of nine-inch radius was pivoted at its centre behind the horizon vane and carried the shadow vane, or a lens, on its upper radius. The arc was graduated to thirds of a degree and the altitudes could be read off to minutes by means of a vernier. The instrument was used as a back-staff in the ordinary way, the staff being pointed at the horizon and the arc moved up or down until the spot of light thrown by the lens was aligned with the horizon.

The use of the Davis Quadrant when standing with one's back to the sun so revolutionised observation that other experimental instruments using the same principle appeared, but never had much vogue. Before dealing with them it may be more convenient here to discuss some other instruments on rather different lines which competed with it. The first of these was Coignet's Nautical Hemisphere (Fig. 58) which had appeared in 1581 and seems to have

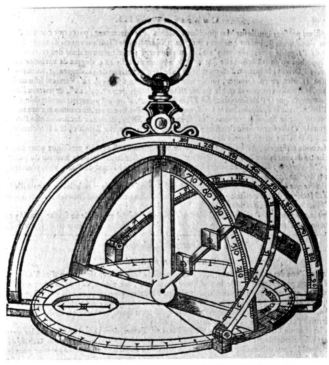

Figure 58   Coignet's Nautical Hemisphere.

lasted for half a century, though condemned by both Burrough and Fournier.

Coignet's instrument had a circular base plate, graduated in half hours and having a compass set in it. On this was erected a semicircular meridian graduated in degrees of latitude on one half of it and being fitted with a suspension ring. It is interesting to see in the illustration that this meridian was graduated for north latitude only. An Altitude Semicircle, fitted with a pivoted arm carrying sight-vanes, was mounted to turn on a vertical axis below the centre of the meridian. An Equator Semicircle was hinged on the east-west axis of the base plate and its internal radius was such that it would just clear the altitude semicircle. It carried at right-angles to it a short Declination Arc, graduated to 23° north and south.

To use this instrument it was hung by its suspension ring so that the north-south line of the base plate coincided with the direction shown by the compass needle. Then the altitude semicircle was turned and its sight arm elevated until the sun shone through the upper vane throwing a spot of light on the lower. Next the equator was raised until the declination for the day as shown on the declination arc coincided with the graduated face of the altitude semicircle. Now the edge of the equator scale indicated the latitude on the meridian scale and the position of the altitude semicircle on the base plate showed the apparent time. This instrument had many disadvantages. It depended on gravity so it could only be used in calm weather, it depended upon the compass needle pointing true north and took no account of variation, and it could not really be read off closer than to one degree.

The Universal Ring Dial (Fig. 59) was another instrument which depended upon gravity. A graduated ring was suspended from a thumb ring in such a way that it could be turned until the desired mark on it was against an index mark below the thumb ring. An inner, equinoctial, ring was pivoted on trunnions within this ring and was graduated in time, both on its upper surface and on its inner edge. A bridge with a slider travelling up and down it in a groove was mounted in the outer ring perpendicularly to the line of the trunnions of the equinoctial circle.

To observe an altitude a wire was inserted through a hole in the outer ring and this ring was turned until the zero of the graduations on the fore side was at the top index mark. The instrument was then suspended so that the outer ring was edge on to the sun, when the wire threw its shadow on the side of the ring and from this the altitude could be read off on a scale on the back surface of the ring.

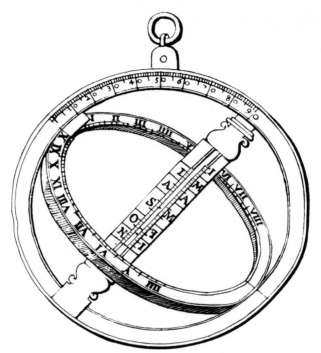

Figure 59   The Universal Ring Dial.

To find the time of day the slider was set for the date by what was in fact a sun's declination scale on the bridge. The equinoctial ring was turned on its trunnions so that it was at right-angles to the outer ring, and the latitude as shown by the scale on the fore side of the outer ring was correctly set at the index below the thumb ring. The instrument was then suspended and turned until the spot of light passing through the hole in the slide was thrown onto the centre line engraved on the inner edge of the equinoctial ring. The position of this spot of light gave the apparent time and the outer ring was then in the true north-south plane.

Edward Wright fitted this instrument to the top of a magnetic compass, calling the complete instrument his Sea-Rings, first described in 1610. By comparing the direction of the compass needle with the direction of the outer ring he obtained the variation of the compass, at the same instant as the time of day.

When the Davis Quadrant appeared someone tried to economise

by applying the principle of the back observation to the cross-staff. The largest cross was fitted to the end of the shaft and the smallest cross slid up and down from what was normally the eye-end. Then the observer stood with his back to the sun and held the cross-staff with the lower end of the large cross to his eye and used the small cross as a horizon vane, sliding it in and out until the top of the shadow of the large cross aligned itself with the horizon (Fig. 60).

The use of the cross-staff in this way was described in a number of books but the instrument does not appear to have been mentioned much after 1750. Its use persisted however in some trades, especially among Frenchmen with whom the Davis quadrant was never very popular.

An attempt was also made to apply the quadrant to the new system. A horizon vane was fixed at the right angle of the quadrant and at this point was pivoted an arm carrying a shadow vane. The observer sighted the lower radius of the quadrant on the horizon away from the sun and raised the pivoted arm until the shadow of its vane fell on the horizon vane. This form of quadrant could also be used for direct observation if the eye were applied at the right angle and the observer looked at the same time along the lower radius at

Figure 60   The Cross-Staff used as a Back-Staff.

the horizon and up along the pivoted arm at the heavenly body. This must have been very far from accurate.

An account of Hood's Cross-Staff was first published by its inventor in 1590. This cross-staff was extremely simple, consisting of two staves, a double socket and a vane. The two staves were graduated, one (the Transom) from 0° to 45°, the other (the Yard) from 45° to 90°. The two staves were fitted into the double socket so that they were at right-angles to each other, the transom vertical and the yard horizontal, with their two 45° marks together at the socket. The vane was slid onto the transom and placed at the zero mark. The observer now faced the sun and resting the 90° end of the yard on his chest pointed it in the direction of the horizon and held it as horizontal as possible, surely a most inaccurate proceeding! Then if the altitude of the sun was exactly 45° the shadow of the top of the vane would exactly reach the 90° mark, if the altitude was greater then the shadow would be further away. Now the appropriate clamp screw had to be eased so that the transom could be slid towards the observer and when the shadow reached the 90° mark the position of the socket on the yard would indicate the altitude. If on the other hand the altitude was less than 45° the shadow would initially be thrown onto the upper part of the observer's body. He would then ease the other clamp screw and slide the transom down through the socket until the shadow reached the required spot, when the position of the socket on the scale of the transom would indicate the altitude.

It would seem that after the invention of the Davis Back-staff it was realised that Hood's Cross-staff could also be used for a back observation.

The Cross-bow or Cross-bow Quadrant (Fig. 61) was invented by Edmund Gunter in about 1623 and was a development of the Davis Quadrant so designed that the actual latitude could be read off from it when taking a meridian altitude of the sun. It consisted of an arc of 120° with a shaft projecting from the centre to form a radius. Three vanes were fitted, the horizon vane fixed on the shaft at the centre of the arc and the other two sliding round the arc. The arc, of which one side was intended for the northern and the other for the southern hemisphere, was graduated from 0° near the lower end to 90° and from the 90° for 25° in each direction. On the latter graduations were superimposed the dates of the year according to the declination of the sun, onwards where the declination had the same name as the latitude and backwards when it had the opposite name.

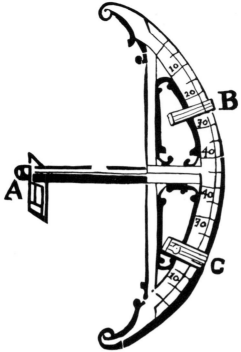

Figure 61   The Cross-Bow Quadrant. (From
John Seller's *Practical Navigation*, 1669)

The observer set the shadow vane to the date and then, turning his
back on the sun, looked through the sight vane and slid it up or
down until he saw the sun's ray shining through the slit of the
shadow vane and falling upon the horizon vane in line with the
horizon. The position of the sight vane on the arc indicated the
latitude without any calculation. Theoretically, if the names of the
bright stars were marked on the arc according to their declinations
the instrument could be used for meridian altitudes of stars, using the
horizon vane as a sight vane and looking through the instrument
in the reverse direction. It must have been difficult if not impossible
and would only have been applicable when the requisite star crossed
the meridian during twilight.

Some cross-bows were graduated from 0° at each end to 45° in the
middle of the arc, when the sum of the readings of the two vanes
gave the zenith distance.

The Removing Quadrant (Fig. 62) was another of those instruments which was intended to have more than one use. It consisted of a pair of graduated arms hinged together like a carpenter's rule, a 90° arc which was pinned to the extremity of the lower arm and a graduated rule which could be slid along the same arm. There were also three vanes, a horizon vane which plugged into a hole in the centre of the hinge and could be turned so that the apparent width of its slit was variable, a sight vane on the lower arm and a shadow vane on the upper. This instrument could be used for a back observation altitude of the sun, for a fore observation or for solving any problem in right-angled triangles, such as change of latitude and meridian distance from a course and distance run. It had the advantage that it could be folded up and taken to pieces thus taking up little space in a man's chest.

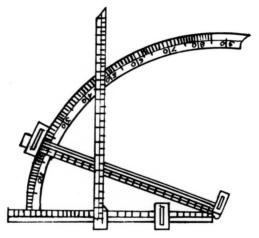

Figure 62   The Removing Quadrant. (From John Seller's *Practical Navigation*, 1669)

There were, no doubt, many other varieties of instruments which were thought up by other writers, some of whom were concerned with simplified variations which the navigator could construct for himself and to save his pocket. The Jesuit, Father Claude F. M. Dechales in his *Art de Naviger* of 1677, suggests several, some of which he admits might not be convenient to use at sea. These include a cross-staff with vanes, a simplified form of cross-bow, a modified form of Davis quadrant, a quadrant of the old type but with a weighted hanging rule instead of a plumb-line and another

variation of the quadrant which is worth describing (Fig. 64). In this
the quadrant has a long piece of wood fastened to one radius, having
a plumb bob suspended from one end and moving against a
graduated arc at the other. A sight bar was pivoted at the centre of

Figure 63   Dechales' 'T' for observing altitudes of the sun.

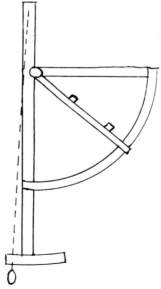

Figure 64   Dechales' Modified Quadrant.

the quadrant proper. When observing, the sight arm was roughly aligned on the object and then set to the nearest whole degree on the graduated arc. The observer then sighted on the object again and this time nipped the plumb line to its graduated arc where its position could be read off and a fine reading obtained.

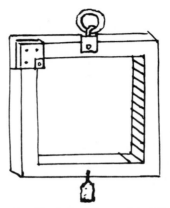

Figure 65   Dechales' Geometrical Square.

Another Dechales instrument was his Geometrical Square (Fig. 65), made of wood about three or four feet square, balanced by a two-pound weight hanging at the bottom. A pin projecting from one upper corner threw a shadow on a graduation marked inside the opposite side and along the bottom. He also proposed a simple T-form with a pinnule at the end of one arm throwing a spot of light onto a graduation on the vertical arm (Fig. 63).

In the 1730s an advance in the design of instruments for observing angles took place and was even further beyond the Davis Quadrant than the back-staff had been beyond the cross-staff.

The new instruments made use of reflection by plane mirrors and the principle that a ray of light striking such a mirror at an angle is reflected from it at the same angle. It follows that if the mirror is moved so that the angle at which the ray strikes it is altered, then the direction in which the emergent ray is reflected will be altered by an angle equal to twice that through which the mirror has been moved.

In 1730 two inventors, John Hadley in England and Thomas Godfrey in America, designed instruments which each used two mirrors and the measurement of the movement of one to measure angles. It was 1732 before either was submitted to the Royal Society and in 1734 Hadley introduced an improved pattern. There is no doubt that the two inventions were entirely independent, but some supporters of Godfrey tried to prove that his ideas had been filched by Hadley and in an endeavour to support their views claimed that Hadley had seen Godfrey's instrument while serving as a Lieutenant in the Royal Navy in the West Indies. It was easily proved that Hadley had never served in the Royal Navy or been to the West Indies.

The 1734 pattern of Hadley's Quadrant (Fig. 66), as it is usually called — though octant would be more correct — has been the basis of most instruments used at sea since that date. It consisted of an eighth part of a circle with an arm pivoted at its centre and moving over the graduations on the arc. Two mirrors were fitted, one (the index glass) placed on the arm exactly above the pivot, and the other (the horizon glass) on one radius of the octant with an eyepiece opposite it upon the other. The horizon glass was half-silvered. When the index arm was set so that the two glasses were parallel to each other the observer could see the horizon through the clear part of the horizon glass and also reflected from the index glass in the mirror of the horizon glass, so that they coincided. The arc should then have read zero. If the index arm was moved until the object to be observed was seen reflected to the eye through both mirrors so that it coincided with the horizon, then the index arm would have moved through an angle equal exactly to half the altitude of the object. The arc was graduated to minutes by means of a diagonal scale and dark glasses were provided to prevent the observer being dazzled.

It will be noted that though the arc was really only one of 45° it was graduated to 90° and could be used to observe angles up to this magnitude. By altering the angle of the horizon glass and moving the eyepiece to a position close to it on the same radius, the octant could be used for what was called the 'back observation', when the horizon opposite to the object instead of below it was used. The angle measured was then the complement of the altitude, i.e. between 90° and 180° though read off as the actual altitude. It is extremely doubtful whether the back observation was ever used in practice. Whereas the 1734 octant was held with the arc downwards, Hadley's 1730 instrument (Fig. 67) was held with the arc towards the observer and the telescope was fixed along the lower, horizontal, radius. Godfrey's instrument (Fig. 69) adopted the same arrangement, but it was not a complete octant, merely the arc and one radius.

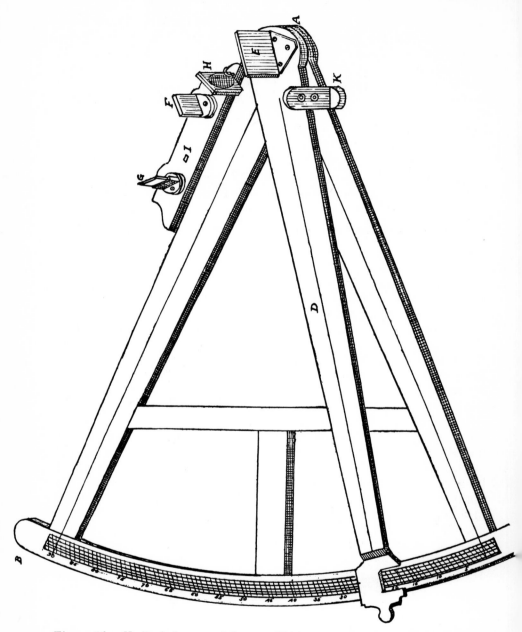

Figure 66   Hadley's Improved Octant, 1734. *ABC* the octant: *D* the index: *E* the 'great speculum' or index glass: *F* the 'small speculum' or horizontal glass for the fore observation: *G* the same for the back observation: *K* the sight vane.

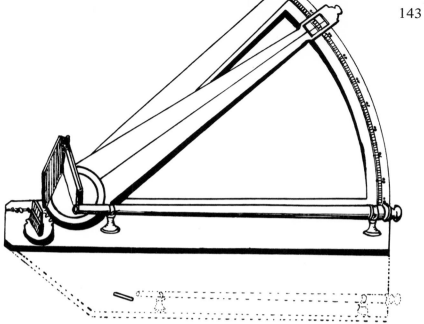

Figure 67   Hadley's Original Octant, 1730.

Figure 68   Hadley's Original Octant, alternative form, 1730.

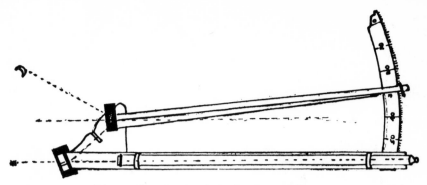

Figure 69   Godfrey's Reflecting Instrument.

These were not the first attempts to use reflection, nor the last. In 1666 Dr. Robert Hooke had suggested two instruments to the Royal Society. In one there was a fixed mirror to reflect the sun and a moving telescope to observe the horizon and the reflection in the mirror (Fig. 70). In the other there were two radial telescopes whose angle apart could be adjusted until the two objects could be seen in two mirrors set at an angle to the two eyepieces. The peculiarity of this instrument was that the observer faced the flat of it instead of the edge as in all others.

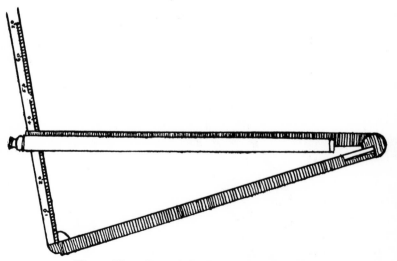

Figure 70   Hooke's Reflecting Instrument.

When Edmond Halley died in 1744 there was found among his papers a description in Sir Isaac Newton's handwriting. The arrangement of the instrument described was very similar to that of Godfrey's and of Hadley's first instrument, but had the advantage that the telescope was fixed along the upper instead of the lower radius so that it balanced better. This octant was intended to be made of solid brass with a telescope three or four feet in length so would have been far too unwieldy to use at sea (Fig. 71).

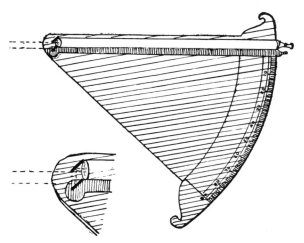

Figure 71   Newton's Reflecting Instrument.

Hadley was followed in about 1740 by Caleb Smith who did not use double reflection but, holding his octant so that the telescope was looking down at an angle of 45° along the upper radius, observed the sun in a mirror attached to the index and the horizon in a second mirror placed beyond the first (Fig. 72). If the horizon was not clear the horizon mirror could be replaced by a spirit level.

In Saverien's variation of this device the fixed and moving mirrors were both mounted at the pivot point of the index arm, instead of one being beyond it. In Bird's octant the same arrangement was adopted but the observer looked in a horizontal direction along the upper radius and the back horizon was used.

Hadley's patent expired in 1745 and it is probable that soon after this date change was made from diagonals to a vernier for fine

Mᴿ SMITHS NEW SEA-QUADRANT.

For taking Altitudes of the Sun, & Stars; without Interruption from the Ships Motion: Fr...
at Sea, and approved by Captain Christopher Middleton, Captain George Spurrel,
Captain Joseph Harrison, and several other able and experienced Navigators.

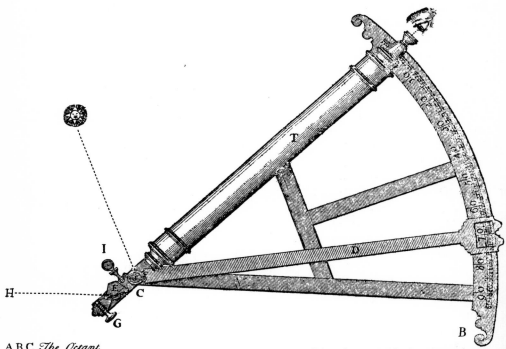

A B C, *The Octant*
A B, *The Arch graduated into Degrees & Parts of a Deg*
D, *The Label or Index.*
a b, *The chamfer'd Edge of the Index; The Divisions*
      whereof are number'd to denote Minutes.
E, *A Speculum or Prism fix'd to the Octant.*
F, *A Speculum, fix'd at the Center upon ye Index.*

I, *The red Glass to defend ye Eye from ye Sun*
G, *The Adjusting Screw.*
T, *The Telescope.*
☉, *The Sun, or Star.*
H, *A Point in the Horizon directly*
      under the Object

To be had of the Inventor at his Office for Infuring Ships &c. in Caftle Alley facing the
Weft Entrance of the Royal Exchange; or at the Crown CoffeeHoufe near Guildhall, London.
Price of the Inftrument Two Guineas & an half

Figure 72   Caleb Smith's Quadrant.

reading of the arc. The earliest mention I have found of a vernier in this connection was in a book published in 1753.

Hitherto all the instruments which I have described were intended to be used for observing altitudes of the sun or stars. In 1752 the German astronomer Johann Tobias Mayer produced his first lunar tables, which he sent to the Board of Longitude three years later, making possible the use of lunar distances in the observation for longitude. It might be necessary to measure the angle between the moon and a star when this angle was in excess of 90°, the largest angle which could be observed with Hadley's octant. Nevertheless an instrument on Hadley's principle obviously lent itself more than any other to the measuring of lunar distances. Mayer therefore proposed the use of a circle so that the index glass could move through a greater angle and also to make the horizon glass movable. With this instrument one could observe twice, with the index glass on opposite sides of the horizon glass, and then read off the double angle, thus halving any instrument errors. John Bird made the first instrument to be tried in England. As the circle had a diameter of sixteen inches it was so heavy that it had to be supported in a fitting attached to a belt. The circle was divided into 360° instead of 720° so that the reading given was half the double angle, saving the observer the labour of dividing the figure read off by two!

This circle was given for trial to Captain John Campbell who had been experimenting with lunar distances observed with Hadley's octant. He saw that if the octant were increased to a sextant, so that angles up to 120° could be measured, and the instrument were made of a radius equal to the diameter of the Mayer/Bird circle, then the weight would be little more than one third of that of the circle — much more convenient — while the greater radius would double the accuracy of the ordinary quadrant so that the double observation would no longer be necessary. So was born our modern sextant, made of metal instead of wood to avoid distortion and stripped of the fittings for the back observation. Improved methods of graduation have permitted its reduction in size to a radius less than that of the usual Hadley octant.

Until quite late in the nineteenth century it was usual for a navigator to keep two instruments. His sextant, always handled with the greatest care, was strictly reserved for the taking of lunar distances. His octant was used daily for his meridian altitudes. Gradually the sextant came to be used for all purposes and this usage was no doubt accelerated by the growing use of the Sumner Method (page 172). The reduction of radius to some six or eight inches to which we have already referred had also a great deal to do with it.

In its later days the octant lost its back observation fittings and copied the sextant by acquiring a tangent screw to enable the index to be moved more smoothly to obtain conjunction. The tangent screws had only a limited travel so that if care were not taken to centre it before the observation was begun one was liable to come up to the end before the sight was completed. Many modern sextants now have endless-tangent-screws to obviate this and in some the knob which operates the screw is large and graduated so that the angle can be read off closely without the necessity of using a lens for reading the fine graduations of a vernier.

Although the manufacture of octants had ceased in this country by 1900 I was told by a well-known instrument maker that he had had one sent in for repair as late as 1943. Old habits die hard!

Although it was never popular in this country the circle was often preferred to the sextant by the seamen of other lands and used in lightened and modified forms.

The sextant shares one disability with the Davis back-staff. The horizon must be visible. This prevents the accurate taking of star sights during the period from about an hour after sunset to an hour before dawn, unless there is bright moonlight. Several attempts have been made to overcome this difficulty and to produce a sextant that does not use the horizon.

If an observation is taken with the aid of an artificial horizon the angle observed between a heavenly body and its reflection in the artificial horizon will be double the actual altitude. The difficulty is to make an artificial horizon which will remain truly horizontal in a ship at sea.

Ashore, a mirror can be levelled by the aid of a spirit level, or a bowl of mercury can be used, but these are seldom of value for purposes of navigation.

It is only very occasionally that a ship is steady enough for any liquid to remain level, but there have been cases when its use has been valuable. In September 1746 the CHESTER had been in fog for many days in the vicinity of Cape Sable and ultimately struck soundings. When the sun appeared but the horizon remained very indeterminate the Commander-in-Chief, Sir Peter Warren, asked the schoolmaster, Walter Maitland, to see if he could get a sight for latitude. Maitland tried a bowl of water as an artificial horizon and was pleasurably surprised to find that he got very good results which were confirmed later by a sighting of the land.

Lecky, in 1881, considered that no artificial horizon could ever be satisfactorily used at sea and suggested that if ever a sight was needed when the horizon was obscured it would be better to lower a boat and to observe while sitting in the bottom of it. One's horizon would then be so near that it should be reasonably visible in conditions when the sun could be observed.

When I was a midshipman in 1915 we were made to take artificial horizon sights on the upper deck of the ship while in harbour in calm weather. In an 18,000-ton battleship a levelled mirror gave quite satisfactory results, provided that the officer-of-the-watch did not hoist a boat in the middle of the sight. Mercury was never of any use for the surface had always a tremor caused by the slight vibration of auxiliary machinery.

Serson's Horizontal Speculum.

In 1743 Serson produced an instrument which he called his Horizontal Speculum (Fig. 73). This was a species of top carrying a mirror and forming an artificial horizon to enable altitudes to be observed at sea with Hadley's octant when the horizon was obscured.

The mirror was just over three inches in diameter, set in the upper edge of a brass hoop, and had a hardened steel axis projecting a little way above and below it. The lower end of the axis was formed into a cone with its apex rounded off and rested in a bearing. This pivoting point needed to be at the centre of gravity. The upper end of the axis was formed into a square and when the speculum was required a shaft was fitted onto this and the top was then spun by means of a cord. The shaft was subsequently removed and the top should have levelled the mirror in a short time.

The Horizontal Speculum was tried at the Nore on 13th September 1743 on board one of His Majesty's Yachts, Captains John Russell and Christopher Middleton attending. This trial seems to have been very successful and it was decided that a more extended trial under seagoing conditions was required. Serson was accordingly embarked in the VICTORY, but returning up Channel in October 1744 she was wrecked upon the Casquets and lost with all hands. It would seem, however, that the instrument did not quite die with its inventor. Graham made one but does not seem to have done anything with it, another was made by Smeaton and a third by Shelton which was sold in France. It was described by Saverien in 1758 in his *Dictionnaire de Marine*. This has recently given rise to an amusing error. An English author, who had only read the description

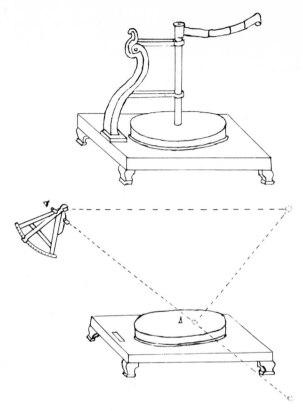

Figure 73   Serson's Horizontal Speculum. The upper sketch shows the shaft in place for rotating the speculum by means of a tape or cord. The lower sketch shows the observation of a double altitude of the sun by measuring the angle between the sun and its reflection in the speculum.

given by Saverien and whose knowledge of French was insufficient, saw that that writer had used the French word *Toupie* for a top and not knowing its meaning annnounced that Serson had called his instrument a Toupie!

Artificial Horizons.

When using an artificial horizon the angle observed is actually double the altitude, a fact that increases the accuracy of a sight observed by its means.

During the middle part of the nineteenth century many attempts were made to produce artificial horizons that could be used at sea, at any rate in smooth weather. These usually had some form of mirror for an horizon secured to the top of a pendulum which was itself carried by the sextant. None of them had any real success. During the Second Great War the Germans needed to be able to obtain altitudes of stars at night, when alone their submarines could safely surface to fix their positions. They perfected a sextant which embodied a gyroscope spun up by air pressure. The instrument was very heavy and the observer was advised either to take the weight by some suspension around the neck or to rest his elbows upon the rail with some sort of cushion under them.

Bubble sextants, where a spirit level provided the artificial horizons, have also been used at sea, but were not accurate within ten minutes. These instruments were originally designed for use in the air where the difficulty is not so much the inability to see a horizon as to allow for its dip.

Refraction.

We must now turn our attention to the four errors which must be allowed for if accurate altitudes are to be used in calculations. These are refraction, semi-diameter, parallax and dip.

The line of sight from an observer to a heavenly body is not straight but curved, being bent by refraction as it passes through the atmosphere. The amount of this bending is dependent upon the amount of atmosphere that the line of sight passes through and hence it increases considerably as the body sinks in the heavens. At horizontal the refraction amounts to thirty-five minutes of arc and makes it possible for us to see bodies which are actually below the horizon. To obtain a true altitude the amount of the refraction must be subtracted from the altitude observed.

The first man to note the existence of refraction is believed to have been the Arab astronomer Al Hazen (died 1038 A.D.). Tycho Brache, who had read the comments of Bernard Walther on the matter, observed its existence in 1575 and during the years 1585—1589 made some measurements. He compiled a table which was not published until 1598, but it is probable that it was distributed in manuscript and appeared in this country at an earlier date.

Thomas Hariot referred to refraction in 1595 but considered that it could be ignored. Edward Wright in 1599 gave warning of errors from this cause but gave no indication of its magnitude until in the second (1610) edition of his book he gave a table derived from that of Tycho Brache.

William Baffin, that indefatigable experimentalist, tried on 15th August 1613 to measure the refraction. At midnight that day the sun remained below the pole with one fifth of its diameter showing above the horizon. Having already discovered his latitude to be 78° 47' N. and knowing the declination, he calculated how far the sun's centre should actually be below the horizon and hence made the refraction to be twenty-six minutes. It should have been about thirty-four minutes, but it was a very good attempt.

At the end of the century Flamsteed made observations of the refraction and produced a table. His figure for the refraction on the horizon was thirty-three minutes and was therefore less accurate than that of Wright who had given thirty-four, the modern determination being 35' 23''. At 10° altitude Flamsteed made it four and a half minutes against the modern 5' 18''.

Wright committed one serious error in believing that the refraction for a star would be less than that for the sun. He gave thirty minutes for a star on the horizon.

Dip, or the Correction for the Height of Eye above Sea Level.

When measuring the altitude of a heavenly body with instruments which measure the angle between it and the sea horizon, we are trying to measure the angle between it and the horizontal. If the eye of the observer were only just above sea level, or if the earth were flat and not spherical, the result would be near enough for practical purposes, but the observer is usually standing fairly high up in the ship and is looking down upon the horizon. This error must be subtracted from the observed altitude.

The first tables giving the amount of correction needed for various heights of eye above sea level were produced by Thomas Hariot in 1595 and printed by Edward Wright in his *Certaine Errors in Navigation* in 1599. Both contain some small errors of which the greatest, by Wright, is 2' 38'', due probably in part to a misprint. They were based on experiments made at Plymouth in 1589.

Semi-Diameter.

When observing the altitude of the sun or moon one wishes to observe the altitude of its centre. This is obtained when using the astrolabe or any other instrument where the sun is throwing a spot of light, but otherwise it is usually more convenient, besides being more accurate, to observe the lower limb, or edge, of the sun or moon and to add half the diameter to the observed altitude. As usual, the first man who seems to have mentioned semi-diameter was Thomas Hariot who, in 1584, compiled a manual of navigation which is now lost, following it with some advice on navigation in instructions for Raleigh's voyage in 1595. This advice is believed to have closely followed the missing manual. In it he objects to the coloured glass commonly used on the upper edge of the cross of the cross-staff to enable the altitude of the sun's centre to be observed without the eye being dazzled. The imperfect glass obtainable at that time might well cause errors from refraction in it. Instead he recommended that the observation should be made with the cross just obscuring the sun so that the altitude of its upper limb is measured. His semi-diameter (sixteen minutes) had then to be subtracted from the observed altitude.

Parallax.

In any tables of the positions of heavenly bodies it is necessary to assume that the observer is at the centre of the earth. In consequence there must be some error in observing from the earth's surface and this error will be greatest when the body is low and zero when it is in the zenith. Attention was first drawn to this error by Edward Wright in 1599. Owing to the great distance of stars from the earth, parallax is negligible in their case. Wright said that parallax for the sun was 2′ 58″ at zero altitude but that for the altitudes normally used in observations it could be ignored. Actually the figure is always under ten seconds. It was not until moon sights came into use that parallax had to be considered.

General Note on these Errors.

The treatment of these errors by writers on navigation was somewhat extraordinary. Sturmy (1669) refers to correction for semi-diameter only. Seller (1669) says that parallax can be ignored but quotes

Tycho Brache as saying that refraction causes an error of thirty minutes on the horizon but disappears at 20° altitude. We have seen that it is actually about thirty-five and a half minutes on the horizon.

Several of the English writers of the first half of the eighteenth century ignored all these errors, but the French authors whom I have consulted give tables for refraction and height of eye.

No wonder the errors were often imperfectly understood by navigators, some of whom were content to apply an arbitrary correction. For example Captain T. H. Sumner tells us that among his acquaintances it was usual to add twelve minutes to all altitudes of the sun as a combined correction for all occasions.*

---

* *A New Method of finding a Ship's Position at Sea*, by Captain Thomas H. Sumner, 1843.

Five
Longitude and Position Line Navigation

Latitude and longitude are used to describe a position on the surface of the earth. The fixing of latitude has never presented any real problem, for it is measured north or south from the equator and, since the position of heavenly bodies relative to that line is known, the latitude of an observer can always be obtained by measuring their altitude, provided that the body required is visible and that he has available an instrument of sufficient accuracy.

Longitude, measured in an east-west direction, is a very different matter, for as by the rotation of the earth the sun and stars seem to travel around it, there is no datum from which their positions in this direction can be measured. If the position of one of them relative to the east or west point of the horizon is measured one can obtain the time of day at the place of observation, but nothing more.

This then was the age old problem for sailors — to be able to determine how far east or west they were from an arbitrary meridian.

The Prime Meridian.

Even the prime meridian from which to measure was a problem. The first recorded proposal was that of Alexandria by Eratosthenes. Then to avoid the nuisance of having both east and west longitude Ptolemy suggested a meridian at the western extreme of the world, which he took as being two degrees west of the Fortunate (Canary) Islands, but of course he did not know how far they were out in the Atlantic.

During the sixteenth century the prime meridian was variously taken as the meridian of Ferro — the most westerly of the Canaries — and the line of demarcation laid down by the Pope between the Spanish and Portuguese spheres of influence which ran 270 leagues westward of Cape Verde. Mercator, in 1569, used the Cape Verde Islands because he thought that this would be the line of no variation, while Plancius, in 1612, used the Azores for the same reason.

By the eighteenth century prime meridians were proliferating. A French chart of 1750 showed no less than six scales of longitude, those measured from the meridians of Paris, London, the Lizard, Madeira, Teneriffe and Ferro, and charts with four scales were not uncommon, though many charts had none at all. In England, in a list of geographical positions given by Sturmy in his *Mariner's Magazine*, 1669, the longitudes are measured from the Lizard, while in a similar list in Seller's *Practical Navigation* of the same date they are measured from Teneriffe. In English eighteenth century charts the prime meridians used were usually London (St Pauls), the Lizard, or Ferro. The first to use Greenwich seems to have been one by Fearon & Eyes in 1738, but Sayer & Bennett were still using London in 1777. However, in that year the *Atlantic Neptune* came out using Greenwich and from that time Greenwich rapidly displaced London on English charts. The first publication of the *Nautical Almanac* ten years earlier and the spreading use of lunars giving longitude from Greenwich no doubt influenced the use of that meridian on charts.

It had been the custom for sailors to take their departure from the last land seen at the beginning of a voyage, and so English sailors usually started their reckoning from the Lizard. They usually took a fresh departure from each port of call and might do the same on passing any particularly noticeable land, but practice was by no means uniform. For example, in the log-books of the PHOENIX returning from India in 1687, the master measured his longitude throughout the latter part of the voyage from the island of Ascension, but after they had sighted Corvo Lieutenant Legge could not make up his mind whether to record his longitude from Ascension or Corvo, so he used one on some days and one on others! In 1773 the East Indiaman *Royal Charlotte* on her way to China even took a fresh departure from a sounding on the Macclesfield Bank, though that shoal is seventy-five miles in width. From the 1790s the use of longitude sights meant that the recording of longitudes became more standardised.

As nations became less secretive about their hydrographical information and allowed their charts to be sold abroad the multiplicity of prime meridians became an increasing nuisance to seamen. Many countries were now using the prime meridians through their capitals and were loth to give them up. There were several conferences which recommended the general adoption of some completely neutral meridian, such as those of Jerusalem or the Great Pyramid. At a geodetic conference in Rome in 1883 it was decided that delegates should recommend the use of Greenwich to their governments, but these were uninterested. In the following year the United States convened a conference at Washington, expressedly to come to a decision, and their representatives proposed Greenwich. On their own charts they were already using Greenwich and British Admiralty charts were the ones most frequently used by other nations. At first there was a move to demand a meridian which was completely neutral and passing over sea only. How its advocates thought that such a meridian could be independently defined is not revealed. In the end the Greenwich meridian was adopted by a vote of twenty-one nations to one, France and Brazil abstaining.

Measuring the Longitude.

The instant of apparent noon occurs as the sun, appearing to travel around the earth, becomes due south of the observer (north in the southern hemisphere). Travelling westwards the sun will bring noon to each meridian in turn until after twenty-four hours have elapsed the sun will have traversed the full 360° of longitude and returned to its original meridian. It will have covered 15° in each hour. If we could know the exact time at the prime meridian when we ascertained that it was noon or any other time at our own, the difference of time would give us our difference of longitude from the prime meridian.

So much had been obvious for a long time. The difficulty was to be able to determine the time at the prime meridian. The means which would leap immediately to mind would be a good clock. This was, in fact, first suggested by Gemma Frisius in 1530, but no one knew how to make a clock which had anything like sufficient accuracy. To obtain an observational accuracy of only one degree it would have been necessary to know the error of the clock within four minutes, and in the sixteenth century no clock would be guaranteed to show the time with a greater accuracy than four minutes after one day since it was checked, let alone after the periods over which one would have need of it at sea.

Another way to know the time is by the position of the moon in the heavens, for the moon's motion around the earth causes its place relative to the stars to change with considerable celerity. If the motions of the moon could be forecast with accuracy there are several ways in which it should be possible to time its movement and by comparing the time of observation with the times forecast for the prime meridian the difference of longitude could be obtained. Times at which the exact positions of the moon in the heavens can be determined are:

> Beginning and end of solar and lunar eclipses.
> Occultations of stars or planets by the moon.
> Measurement of the distance between the moon and a selected star, known as a lunar distance.

The use of eclipses to determine the longitude of places was proposed by Hipparchus as long ago as 150 B.C. At that time eclipses had, of course, no value for navigation for though astronomers had reached the stage when they could forecast that an eclipse would occur they could not forecast at what time. An explorer could observe an eclipse and obtain its local time, and then, on his return home, provided that an astronomer had also been lucky with clear weather, the two observations could be compared and the difference of longitude determined. One case where this procedure was carried out took place on 29th October 1631 when Captain Thomas James observed an eclipse of the moon in Hudson's Bay. A modern determination has shown that he was about a degree in error.

Another occasion on which eclipses are known to have been used was during the (1669-1671) voyage to the South Seas in the SWEEPSTAKES by Sir John Narborough. Narborough relates* that on 26th March 1670 an eclipse of the moon observed at sea gave him the longitude of Cape Blanco as 69° 16′ W. of London. Its correct longitude is 65° 45′ W. of Greenwich.† The account of this observation is obscure as he implies that the moon had already set and that it was partially obscured by clouds. Another observation was made on 18th September of the same year at Port Desire. This gave the longitude of that place as 73° W. of London, the correct longitude being 65° 54′ W. of Greenwich. The complete calculation is given in a manuscript account‡. This was probably written by the master, for the writer was obviously of some standing in the ship and refers to the captain and both lieutenants. He also claims to have obtained the longitude of St. Julians on 14th August and 9th September by the 'continuacon' (conjunction) of the moon and Mars, making it 67° W. of the Lizard, which as he puts the Lizard 7° W. of London instead of its correct 5° 12′ W. of Greenwich makes it

*   *Account of several late Voyages and Discoveries*, 1711, p.40-41.
†   'London' usually meant St. Pauls Cathedral which is 0° 5′ W. of Greenwich.
‡   Ministry of Defence Library (Naval) M.S.4

74° W. of London against the true value of 67° 36' W. of Greenwich. These large errors show how little use eclipses could really be to the navigator at this time, even on the few occasions when they could be observed.

Edmond Halley was of the opinion that the occultation of stars by the moon offered the best chance of success. He himself tried the method during his two voyages in 1698-1700 in pursuit of the variation. Making use of the tables for the moon published in 1661 by Thomas Street in *Astronomia Carolina* to forecast its position, the only instruments needed were a strong telescope to observe the instant of ocultation and a quadrant to observe the altitude of a star so that local time could be calculated. Unfortunately he found that the tables were insufficiently accurate for his purpose.

It had long been recognised that a more accurate knowledge of the heavens, and in particular of the motions of the moon, could not fail to be of the greatest aid to navigation. Accordingly in 1675 the Royal Observatory at Greenwich was founded with the object of the 'rectifying of the tables of the motions of the heavens, and the places of the fixed stars, in order to find out the so much desired longitude at sea, for perfecting the art of navigation.' Writing in 1731 Edmond Halley complained that had Flamsteed, the first Astronomer Royal, kept continuous records of the moon it would by then have been possible to forecast her movements.

The observation of the exact instant of occultation of a star by the moon was not easy at sea, requiring a powerful telescope, and the greater the magnification of a telescope the larger it becomes and the more difficult it is to control in a seaway. For this reason it was better to measure the distance of the moon from some fixed star. The method was first suggested by Johann Werner in 1514, who proposed the use of the cross-staff to measure the actual lunar distance. Two things made the method quite useless at that time; the cross-staff would not measure the distance with sufficient accuracy and no one could correctly foretell the movements of the moon.

In the eighteenth century all this changed. In 1730, Hadley's octant was the first instrument which would measure angles with sufficient accuracy (page 141). It is true that the largest angle that could be measured with this instrument was 90° and it would sometimes be desirable to measure angles as large as 120°, but this disability was removed by the introduction of the reflecting circle on the same principle in 1755 and the expansion of the octant to a sextant in 1759.

In 1755 Professor Tobias Mayer of Göttingen sent a copy of his lunar tables to the Admiralty and when they had been tested at the Royal Observatory it was found that by their aid the position of the moon could be forecast within one minute of arc. With the aid of these it would be possible to discover the longitude of a ship within thirty minutes. This does not seem a great standard of accuracy but with errors of several degrees being quite common it represented a very definite step in the right direction.

In 1761 Dr Nevil Maskelyne made a voyage to St Helena, during which he tried out the method and found it good. After his return, he published in 1763 *The British Mariner's Guide* explaining how the longitude could be discovered by the use of lunars. He claimed that whereas errors of longitude of up to 15° were not uncommon on long voyages it should now always be possible to know it within one degree and usually within half that amount.

The first British *Nautical Almanac* was published in 1766 for the year 1767 and contained, besides astronomical information covering the positions of the sun, moon and stars, the times of the eclipses of Jupiter's Satellites and the distances of the moon from seven bright stars at regular intervals of time. The French *Connaissance de Temps*, an equivalent publication, had been first published in 1679.

The navigator was now adequately provided with everything necessary for him to undertake the observation of lunars. But it was not quite as easy as all that. It was said later that the observation and subsequent computation were both difficult and that it was most unusual to find a man who was competent at both. At first it was considered necessary for the observer to have three assistants. At the instant that he himself observed the lunar distance, one assistant took the altitude of the moon and another that of the star. The third noted the time. This procedure was usually repeated five times, after which the means of the five readings were taken to form the basis of the calculation. It might be thought: why the altitudes and the time, when all that is wanted is to compare the lunar distance with a similar one at Greenwich? The reason is that the distance observed is not the true one and must be corrected.

The true position of a heavenly body is always lower than that in which it appears to be, owing to refraction which causes a bending of the line of sight as it passes through the earth's atmosphere. The position of the moon is calculated as if it were viewed from the centre of the earth so because it is actually observed from the earth's surface there is an error known as parallax (see page 153). Since the parallax is always greater than the refraction the true position of the moon is always higher than it appears. Thus the position of the moon and star must both be corrected for the altitude, and the lunar distance observed must also be corrected for the true positions. This is known as 'clearing the distance'. During the years a large number of different solutions to the problem were suggested.

It was possible for one man to take all the observations with the aid of a single assistant to take times and to write down the figures. In this case he would observe the two altitudes, then the distance and then repeat the two altitudes in the reverse order.

All the angles taken had to be corrected for any index error of the sextant or sextants, besides the semi-diameter of the moon and the dip of the sea horizon as appropriate.

From the altitude of the body most nearly in the east or west the apparent time could be calculated for the same time of observation. If this were not convenient a good watch was needed for the comparison of the time between that when the lunar was taken and that when a time sight could be observed. In calculating the longitude from the difference of time between that at Greenwich and that on the meridian of observation it was essential to use the same kind of time for both. Apparent time is the time as measured by the sun and which is obtained from an observation. The length of a day, i.e. the time taken by a rotation of the earth between two meridian passages of the sun, varies throughout the year. This is inconvenient for purposes of calculation or of ordinary day to day timekeeping. Mean Time is therefore used by which the length of the day is always the same. The difference between Mean and Apparent Time is known as the Equation of Time. Its existence was ignored by writers on navigation until the advent of lunars. One could have obtained it earlier from the *Connaissance de Temps*.

As with other methods of navigation it is difficult to ascertain the extent to which lunars were actually used at sea. The experience of four battleships in 1802 has been discussed earlier (page 34), besides that of some East Indiamen (page 33). Their use gradually declined as the chronometer came into its own and from 1906 the tables required for lunars were omitted from the *Nautical Almanac*.

Other methods of using the moon for the determination of longitude were suggested but none was really applicable for use at sea. One was the Moon's Culmination, i.e. the highest altitude which she reaches when crossing the meridian. If the instant of culmination could be determined and its time obtained by the observation of some other body, this time could be compared with the forecasted time of the moon's passage of some other meridian, adjusted for the motion of the moon in the time interval, and then the difference of longitude would be obtained. The difficulty was of course to determine the instant of the moon's culmination, for the rate of change of altitude at this time was too small for the instant to be apparent. In 1612 William Baffin tried to use the moon's culmination on two occasions during his arctic expedition. He decided on the instant of the moon's culmination by observing its bearing with a magnetic compass, having previously determined the variation from a number of observations. His estimate of the longitude of Cockin's Sound is now known to have been about 7½° in error! On these occasions he used John Searle's *Ephemeris* giving the time of the moon's transit of the meridian at London from 1609 to 1617, and that of David Origanus giving the figures for Wittenberg from 1595 to 1650. It is obvious that the method has no value for navigation, because of the impossibility of determining the instant of the moon's culmination when at sea.

On one occasion Baffin also tried the lunar distance method, observing the difference of azimuth between the sun and moon and their altitudes, from which he calculated their distance apart. He probably did this because the lunar distance from the sun was about 104° and no instrument which he possessed could have measured such a large angle. In the end he did not work out this sight, preferring his culmination observations.

Moon's Right Ascension.

This method was described in the *Nautical Almanac* for 1769.

A telescope had to be set up in the meridian, and the time elapsed between the transits of one side of the moon and of a star noted. The star selected had to have approximately the same declination as the moon and its right ascension had to be known. Thus the right ascension of the moon at this time could be calculated. As her right ascension was given in the *Nautical Almanac* for every twelve hours the Greenwich time of the observed right ascension at the time of her transit could be calculated. By comparing this with local time the longitude could be obtained. It was pointed out that as the observation was for difference of time between the two transits an error of up to half a degree in setting up the direction of the telescope would be immaterial. The method was, of course, useless at sea but seemed to hold out possibilities for surveyors.

Meteors and Shooting Stars.

When Edmond Halley in 1719 reported on the sighting of a great meteor he suggested their possible use for measuring difference of longitude over relatively short distances. The idea was taken up in 1727 by George Lynn, who proposed the determination of the longitude of several places in this country by their aid. His idea was that observers should, during a prearranged period each night, watch the heavens and record the exact time and locality of every shooting star seen. By subsequent comparisons of these records differences of local times and hence of longitudes could be determined. This method also was useless at sea.

Jupiter's Satellites.

The four largest satellites of Jupiter were discovered by Galileo Galilei in 1610 and shortly afterwards he suggested that it might be possible to forecast the times of their eclipses and if this could be done they could be used as clocks for the discovery of the longitude. The first tables giving the times of their eclipses were published in *Ephemeridies Bononienses Mediceorum* in 1668.

Eclipses of the first satellite occur about four times a week but then Jupiter might be below the horizon or there might be clouds which would reduce the occasions on which the method could be used. In addition during about three months in the year Jupiter is too close to the sun. Nevertheless, there seemed to be some hope that the method would be useful.

Edmond Halley gave some consideration to the matter but rejected it because of the difficulty of handling a telescope of sufficiently large size to give the necessary magnification in a ship at sea. In 1762 Christopher Irwin designed a marine chair in which the observer could sit and be freed from the motion of the vessel. It was tried in the PRINCESS LOUISA in 1764 but was a failure, as were other similar attempts. Nevertheless, the forecast times of the eclipses of Jupiter's satellites were always published annually in the *Nautical Almanac* since its inception.

Captain Christopher Middleton of the FURNACE used the

satellites to determine the longitude of Fort Churchill in 1742, with an error of forty-five minutes. Nevil Maskelyne at St. Helena in 1761 and Captain James Cook a few years later seem to have had better success. These observations were all made ashore. I have been unable to find any case of the method being used at sea though William Emerson, writing in 1764, expressed surprise that it was not in constant use. He, however, had no practical experience of the sea.

Declination of the Sun.

This method of finding the longitude is mentioned by some writers merely to be able to show its impracticability. If the latitude of an observer is accurately known a meridian altitude of the sun can be used to calculate his declination. Then since the declination at the time of meridian passage at the prime meridian is known, and the change of declination in twenty-four hours, the difference would enable the difference of longitude to be obtained by proportion. The absurdity of the method is shown by the fact that the daily change of declination is at most twenty-four minutes at the equinoxes and nothing at the solstices. Thus at best a difference of declination of one minute would only give an accuracy of fifteen degrees of longitude. Seldom was any navigator's reckoning as far out as that!

Variation of the Compass.

It is probable that it was during the second of the voyages of Columbus that seamen first appreciated that the variation of the compass was not the same, or in the same direction, on both sides of the Atlantic. In fact, it was at that time easterly on the European and westerly on the American side with zero near to the position of the Azores. Although Pedro de Medina in his *Arte de Navegar*, 1545, denied that the compass pointed anything but true, anywhere, it is probable that the Spanish navigators used the variation of the compass as a very rough guide to their progress when on a voyage across the Atlantic. William Bourne, in 1574, recommended navigators who might visit ports abroad to make a note of the variation there, so that if they returned the fact that the variation was approaching the figure found before, would give them an indication that they were nearing their destination.

Two things hampered proposals to make use of variation as a guide to the longitude. First there was the uncertainty as to whether or not the values of the variation were uniformly disposed on the surface of the globe, enabling it to be forecast for any spot where it had not yet been observed, or whether their distribution was purely arbitrary, depending perhaps as William Gilbert expected upon the proximity of land masses. A second problem was whether or not it was true that a compass would indicate a direction for north which would depend upon the locality in which it had been 'touched'. William Bourne implored sailors who might be visiting America or the East Indies to settle this point for him. It was not really until 1667 that John Seller settled this problem once and for all by communicating to the Royal Society that he had made the requisite experiments which showed that neither geographical position nor the idiosyncrasy of a particular lodestone had any effect upon the pointing of the needle.*

John Davis, on his voyage to the East Indies in 1604, found that the variation of the compass was sometimes a more reliable guide than his reckoning to warn him of his approach to the Cape of Good Hope. A chronicler of the voyage wrote:

> "The first of Aprill [1605], toward night, wee descried Land from the maine top, which bare off us South South-East, when according to our reckoning and accounts, wee were not neere by fortie leagues, but yet the variation of the Compasse did tell us we were on Land thirtie leagues before we saw the Land."

A new complication appeared. In 1580 William Borough had found the variation at Limehouse, in London, to be 11° 15' East. In 1622 Edmund Gunter, observing at the same place, found it to be 6° 13' East. At first it was thought that Borough had been careless, but someone checking Gunter's figure found the variation smaller still. This led Henry Gellibrand to look into the matter and in 1634 he found it to be but 4°. It thus became clear that the variation at London was steadily decreasing and Henry Bond, writing in 1648, forecast that it would be zero in 1657. It was.

There were other navigators besides Davis who used the variation to warn them when they were approaching the Cape of Good Hope. Edward Harrison tells us that in 1688 the variation at the Cape was 10° West, while at St. Helena it was 1° 4'. Here we have a difference of variation of 8° 56' during a change of longitude of 21° 54', i.e. of about 1° for every 3 1/3 degrees of longitude. It does not sound of

---

* *Philosophical Transactions of the Royal Society*, No. 26, p.478.

very great help but since St. Helena was about 18° North of the Cape and the isogonic lines ran in a N.N.W.-S.S.E. direction the change of longitude per degree of variation decreased when the latitude of the Cape was reached and it was actually needed.

It is evident from the log-books of ships of the Royal Navy and of the East India Company that in the middle of the eighteenth century it was usual to take care to observe the variation daily when the latitude of the Cape was reached and land was still some way off. An examination of the log-books of the ships of Rear-Admiral Boscawen's squadron on its way to India in 1748 shows that a change of variation of 1° corresponded to about 1¾° of longitude. By this time the variation at the Cape had increased to about 18° West.

Ships making for the Straits of Sunda usually steered on an easterly course from the Cape of Good Hope until the island of St. Paul was sighted. Those who missed the island used the variation as a check on their easting before altering course to the north-eastwards.*

In 1698 Edmond Halley, later to be Astronomer Royal, was given a commission as a captain in the Royal Navy and the command of the PARAMOUR, pink, for a voyage to investigate the variation. He made two voyages, returning from the second in 1700, and then published two charts showing the isogonic lines, or lines of equal variation. The first, published in 1701, covered the Atlantic only, but the second, published in the following year, was extended to include the Indian Ocean. As an example of the difficulty accompanying such an endeavour, due to the lack of means to determine the longitude, I will quote from some remarks concerning the longitude of the Cape of Good Hope made by Halley in 1719†. In 1685 some missionaries recorded 20° E., their method of determining it not being stated. In 1694 Alexander Brown made it 16½° using a lunar distance. On 5th March 1718 the East Indiaman *Emperor* observed an eclipse of the moon when 180 leagues east of the Cape and from this Halley subsequently calculated the longitude as 15°. It is actually about 18½°. The missionaries had been nearest to the truth after all!

Halley's charts became out of date and were followed in 1744 and 1756 by charts compiled by James Dodson and William Mountaine. Bouguer provided a useful little chart in *Nouveau Traité de*

* Captain Frederick Vincent of the East Indiaman *Osterley* about 1760 always used the variation as a check on his longitude. (India Office Library. L/MAR/B.400A)
† *Philosophical Transactions of the Royal Society*, XX, No.361, p.992.

Navigation, 1753, showing isogonic lines for both 1700 and 1744. Later variation charts were intended for correcting compass courses and bearings and not for aid in obtaining the longitude.

The last endeavour to use the variation to obtain the longitude was made by Ralph Walker, an officer in the merchant service who became a planter in Jamaica and later planned the London Docks.

While he was living in Jamaica, Walker designed an instrument for very accurate observation of the sun's magnetic bearing (page 87). It was, in fact, a compass onto which a universal sun dial was mounted, very much on the same lines as Edward Wright's sea-rings, but the compass was a gimballed compass suitable for use at sea instead of being suspended from a ring. Walker hoped to interest the Admiralty in his plans and in 1793 managed to obtain a passage to England in the PROVIDENCE, in which ship Captain William Bligh was returning from his second, and this time successful, bread-fruit voyage. Unfortunately Walker made two miscalculations. he imagined that the distribution of the lines of equal variation would be quite regularly disposed throughout the world and that it would be possible to find its value for any position on the earth's surface by means of a diagram which he provided. In the book which he published in 1794* he gave a long list of variations observed. Had he plotted these on a chart, or even consulted one of the variation charts which had been published, he would have realised that few would have fitted his diagram. His second miscalculation was when he failed to realize that the magnetic material in a ship would cause compass errors and that if these were not accurately known his compass observations would not give the variation.

Magnetic Dip.

Henry Bond in *The Longitude Found* (1676) proposed that the magnetic dip should be of help in finding the longitude and this method has been suggested by others but is not a practical proposition. The use of the dip had earlier been suggested as a means of determing latitude.

---

* *A Treatise on Magnetism with a Description and Explanation of a Meridional and Azimuth Compass.*

The Chronometer.

The suggestion that a clock could be made of sufficient accuracy to carry to sea the time at the prime meridian and that this could be compared with the observed local time to give the longitude has been ascribed to Gemma Frisius in 1530, but at that time no such clock could be devised.

The first clock specially designed for the purpose and actually tried at sea was constructed by Christian Huyghens in Holland. Some of these clocks were tried in 1663 and 1664, in the latter year by Major (afterwards Admiral Sir Robert) Holmes. During his voyage to Guinea a question arose of whether they could get to the Cape Verde Islands before running short of water, or whether they would be wiser to make for Barbados. Holmes trusted to his clocks which gave a longitude differing to that of the masters' reckoning by about three hundred miles, and this trust proved well-placed. Nevertheless these clocks never succeeded in establishing themselves as being sufficiently reliable to be continued.

Other inventors, notably Gottfried Wilhelm von Leibnitz in 1675, John Hutchinson in 1712, Jeremy Thacker in 1714, and William Hobbs in 1715, apparently never got further than airing their ideas. Of more importance was Henry Sully, an Englishman resident in Paris, who made a number of timekeepers and carried out several unsuccessful trials at sea in the years which preceded his death in 1728.

The first successful inventor was John Harrison, who was brought up to follow his father's trade as a carpenter, but took to making clocks and then turned his attention to a timekeeper for use at sea. His first was ready for sea trial in 1735 and in the following spring was sent to Lisbon in the CENTURION, returning in the ORFORD. On this return voyage of four weeks the timekeeper demonstrated its utility, for by its aid they identified her first landfall as the Lizard whereas the master's reckoning made it the Start, one degree twenty-six minutes further east!

Harrison tried to improve this timekeeper and in 1739 had his second edition ready for sea. It is not clear why it never had a sea trial. Probably the outbreak of war with Spain in the same year as its completion had something to do with it, though it is possible that Harrison found his intended improvements less successful than he had hoped.

Harrison tried further betterments but he experienced a great deal of trouble with his H.3, as it is usually called, and it was 1757 before it was ready. He then proposed to make a miniature version and this, known as H.4, was completed in 1759.* This smaller timekeeper, or watch, was so successful that Harrison decided to rely on it alone in subsequent trials.

The timekeeper was to be tried on a voyage to Jamaica and it was not until November 1761 that the DEPTFORD was ready to sail with it. On the outward passage the watch proved that the ship had overrun the reckoning by about a degree and a half during the nine day voyage to Madeira. At Jamaica the longitude by the watch differed only from the known longitude by one and a quarter minutes. The watch came home in the MERLIN and on its return to Portsmouth after an absence of five months had an error of 1 minute 53½ seconds, equivalent to 28½ minutes of longitude, still within the Board of Longitude requirement of half a degree.

The Board would not believe that such an accuracy could be anything but a fluke and a second trial was demanded. For this the watch was embarked in the TARTAR in March 1764 and she proceeeded to Barbados, where the longitude was specially observed anew using the method of the occultation of Jupiter's satellites. On this occasion Barbados was chosen instead of Jamaica because Nevil Maskelyne†, who with Charles Green was to make the observations, considered Jamaica to be unsuitable in view of his state of health. Harrison was bitterly incensed at Maskelyne being chosen for this duty because he had openly boasted that he expected to be awarded the Board of Longitude prize of £20,000 for his lunar distance method which he considered to be far superior to the timekeeper method. However the longitude of Barbados by the watch was found to be only 9.6 minutes in error. On its return to Portsmouth the watch was found to have gained fifty-four seconds in the 156 days, after allowing an expected mean rate of one second per day, gaining. However, before sailing Harrison forecast that the rate would be affected by change of temperature and when these predetermined corrections were applied the total error over the five months was only fifteen seconds! This was a great triumph but it was not until

---

* H.1 occupies about a three foot cube and weighs 72 lb.
  H.2 is rather taller than H.1 and weighs 103 lb.; 165 with case and gimbals.
  H.3 is 2ft. by 16 in. by 10 in. and weighs 66 lb.; 101 with case and gimbals.
  H.4 looks like a large watch 5¼ in. diameter and weighs 2 lb. 14 oz.
† Maskelyne became Astronomer Royal after his return.

1772 that Harrison received the final instalment of his £20,000 prize. Harrison died in 1776, aged 83.

One of the requirements of the Board of Longitude had been that Harrison should instruct Larcom Kendall in how to make a copy of H.4 and this duty was duly performed.

Kendall's copy of H.4 was delivered in 1769 and was used by Captain James Cook during his second and third voyages (1772-1775 and 1776-1779) and by George Vancouver during his survey of the west coast of North America (1791-1795). Kendall then told the Board that the design must be simplified if watches were to be made at anything like £200 apiece. He was told to try what improvements he could and produced two more watches at £200 and £100 respectively. Neither of these performed as well as his K.1.

K.2 had a strange history. In 1787 it was lent to Captain William Bligh for his bread-fruit voyage in the BOUNTY. When he was set adrift in the Pacific by mutineers he was refused permission to take the watch with him on the grounds that by its aid he might be able to find his way home. In 1808 the mutineers were found at Pitcairn Island by an American whaler captain who acquired K.2 from them but soon after had it stolen from him in South America. It turned up again in 1840 when it was bought by Captain Thomas Herbert, R.N., for fifty guineas. He brought it home in 1843 and the Admiralty then lent it to the Royal United Service Institution. A few years ago there was a proposal to sell it but it was discovered that it was not the property of the Institution to sell and the Admiralty transferred the loan to the National Maritime Museum where it is now exhibited with the first four Harrisons and K.1.

The success of Harrison's timekeeper encouraged others, in particular John Arnold and Thomas Earnshaw, of whom the former sent three of his watches on Cook's second voyage (1772-1775) but their performance did not compare with that of K.1. Thereafter the use of chronometers, as they came to be called, increased considerably and by the beginning of the nineteenth century they were to be found in many ships, being normally provided by the ships' officers. It was not until 1825 that they were generally issued to ships of the Royal Navy.

England was not the only country interested in the chronometer. In France sea trials were held in 1766, 1768 and 1771 at which the instruments of Pierre le Roy and Ferdinand Berthoud were the most successful. The latter continued to improve his chronometers and was soon turning them out in large numbers.

To find the longitude by the aid of a chronometer necessitates the calculation of the apparent time of an observation, corrected for the equation of time, and its comparison with the time shown by the chronometer, allowance having been made for its rate. The apparent time can be derived from the solution of what has come to be called the PZX triangle, where P is the pole of the heavens, Z the zenith of the observer and X the sun. Then the angle at P is the apparent time.* By the ordinary cosine formula:

Cosine P (time)

$$= \frac{\cos XZ \,(90 - \text{altitude}) \pm \cos PZ \,(90 - \text{latitude}) \,.\, \cos PX \,(90 - \text{declination})}{\sin PZ \,(90 - \text{latitude}) \times \sin PX \,(90 - \text{declination})}$$

The sign is negative where the latitude and declination have the same name and positive if they are of different name. The presence of this positive or negative sign makes the formula unhandy as it cannot be directly solved by using logarithms. Several practitioners introduced other formulae, some of which required the use of special tables.

By 1880 the use of chronometers had become so widespread that lunars were rarely used.

A complication of the longitude by chronometer sight was that the latitude came into the calculation. If the latitude used were incorrect, the further the body observed might be from east or west the greater became the consequent error in longitude. This fact was often overlooked by navigators. One such case was brought out by the court-martial on the loss of the CHALLENGER on the coast of Chile in 1835. This ship had fixed her position by good sights on 17th May as 41° 41' S., 80° 43½' W. and had sailed in a N.E. by N. direction for two days in hazy weather. At 9.00 a.m. on the 19th through a gap in the clouds a reasonable sight was obtained and using the dead reckoning latitude a longitude by chronometer was obtained. No noon sight was possible and shortly before 10.00 p.m. the ship ran ashore and became a total wreck. It then transpired that an adverse current had made the ship thirty-four miles south of her reckoning and the result of using a latitude thirty-four miles too far north had given a longitude a whole degree too far to the west of her actual position.

---

* It would be more accurate to say P is the time interval from noon. Stars can be used with some additional complication.

The Sumner Position Line.

On 17th December 1837 Captain T. H. Sumner, of Boston, U.S.A., on passage from Charleston to Greenock was approaching the south coast of Ireland. He had had no sights for some time and, with a south-westerly wind, the south coast of Ireland was an unpleasant lee shore not forty miles away. At 10.00 a.m. the sun appeared through a break in the clouds, and Sumner hastily took a sight and used his dead reckoning latitude to work out a longitude. The calculation placed him nine miles farther east than he had expected. Worried about his imperfectly known latitude and knowing how this might affect his longitude he reworked his sight using another latitude ten miles further north and obtained a position twenty-seven miles E.N.E. of the first. A third attempt using another latitude ten miles still further north put him yet another twenty-seven miles to the E.N.E. He plotted these three positions on the chart and musing over them realised that they all three lay on a straight line running E.N.E. with the second close inshore of the Smalls Light* and the third on the Welsh coast (Fig. 74). In a flash he realised that even if he did not know his latitude and longitude he did know that his ship must be on that line and that if he steered on along this E.N.E. course he was bound to sight the Smalls Lighthouse almost right ahead.

Six years later Captain Sumner published a pamphlet describing the method he had evolved from this experience. After taking a sight he worked out two longitudes using two different latitudes, of exact degrees for convenience of computation, and plotting the two resulting positions upon his chart joined them by a line which he called a position line. The ship had to be on this position line and if it were transferred bodily by allowing the course and distance run between the time of this sight and noon, the point where it cut the latitude derived from the meridian altitude would give a position line at noon with far greater accuracy than that obtained by merely carrying on a longitude derived from a sight for which an erroneous latitude could have been used.

If a noon sight were not obtainable it was still possible to get a running fix by making a second observation and obtaining a second Sumner position line, the ship's position being the point of intersection between this second Sumner line and the first transferred for the run between. In either case of course, the

---

* Sumner, in his pamphlet published later, shows it to seaward, but he charts the Smalls Light some miles north-eastward of its true position.

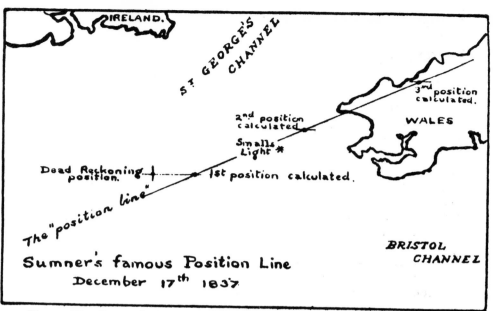

Figure 74   Sumner's Position Line. In the diagram published in Sumner's pamphlet his second position is shown to seaward of the Smalls Light, but he charts the light some miles northeastward of its true position.

accuracy of the final fix was dependent upon the accuracy of the run between but any inaccuracy here was negligible compared with that caused by using a longitude derived from a very inaccurate latitude.

Staff Commander W. R. Martin in his *Treatise on Navigation and Nautical Astronomy* (1888), records that the Sumner method had been practised by officers of the Royal Navy under the name of Cross Bearings of the Sun for some time before he had his experience off the Smalls. I have been unable to find any published account which can have guided them.

In his most valuable book, *Wrinkles in Practical Navigation* (1881), Captain S. T. S. Lecky pointed out how the calculation could be shortened. The Sumner line is at right-angles to the direction of the sun. Tables were now available giving the true bearing of the sun for any time, latitude and declination. All that was necessary was to work out one longitude from the sight and to look up the sun's azimuth. Then the line at right-angles to the direction of the sun drawn through the position worked out from the sight would be identical with the Sumner position line.

The Sumner method could be used for a star instead of the sun and if two stars were observed simultaneously, two Sumner lines could be obtained whose intersection would give an instant fix.

The Double-Chronometer Method.

Yet another method of obtaining a position was practiced in the nineteenth century, known as the double-chronometer. It is said to have been suggested by Lalande. Two altitudes of the sun were taken on the same side of the meridian with a time interval between and the apparent time obtained from each. Then if the latitudes used had been correct the chronometer interval between the two sights would be the same as the difference between the apparent times, provided the first had been corrected for the change of longitude between them. If there was a discrepancy, a formula would give the error in latitude and a second sight worked out with the true latitude would give the true longitude. Tables shortened the calculation, but it seems unwieldy and could only be practiced with advantage in the leisurely days of sail.

The Marcq St. Hilaire Method.

In 1875 the French Captain Marcq de Saint Hilaire published another way of obtaining a position line from a single sight. His method was to calculate the distance of the sun from the zenith of his dead reckoning position at the instant when he took his sight. His corrected altitude, subtracted from 90°, gave him an observed zenith distance at the same instant. Now the zenith distance is also the distance on the earth's surface between the place of observation and the spot immediately below the sun at that instant. It follows that if the observed zenith distance is greater or less than the calculated, the observer must be farther from or closer to the sun than the dead reckoning position by the difference between the two. This quantity is called the intercept. Under normal circumstances the ship will be so far from the sub-solar spot that the position of the circle of equal zenith distances, in which we are interested, will be a straight line at right-angles to the line joining ship to sun.

When using the St. Hilaire method the navigator works out his calculated and observed zenith distances and obtains the bearing of the sun from a book of azimuth tables. From his dead reckoning position on the chart he then measures off the length of his intercept

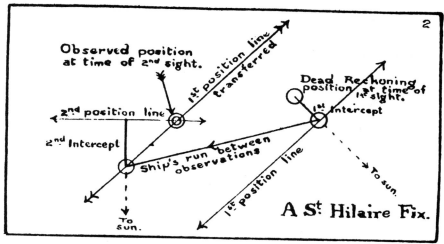

Figure 75   A Marcq St. Hilaire fix.

towards or away from the sun according to whether his observed distance is smaller or larger than the other. Through the end of the intercept he draws a line at right-angles, and this is the same position line which would be produced by the Sumner method of calculation (Fig. 75).

Of course, one position line will not give a fix and a second must be obtained later. An advantage of the St. Hilaire over the Sumner is that the same method of working can very conveniently be used for a sight near the meridian so the inexperienced can always use the same method of working without having to think of any other.

The St. Hilaire method was introduced to the Royal Navy in a book wherein it is called *New Navigation** and consequently became known by that name. The calculation required the use of haversines and these appeared from 1845 in James Inman's *Nautical Tables* which, having been originally compiled by the Professor of Mathematics at the Royal Navy College, Portsmouth, 1808-1839, had always been extensively used by naval officers. On the other hand the introduction of the method into the Merchant Navy was probably delayed by the absence of haversines until about 1908 from Norie's tables, for these tables were much more popular in nautical schools and were therefore extensively used by their former pupils.

---

* *A Shorter and Accurate Method of obtaining the Longitude at Sea . . . . . to which is added a Brief Explanation of the New Navigation*, by Charles Brent, A. F. Walter & George Williams, 1886.

Six
Charts and Sailing Directions

The earliest sailing directions known are contained in the *Periplus* of Scylax, believed to have been compiled in about the fourth century B.C. but to have been derived from earlier material dating from at least a couple of centuries earlier. These directions give information about ports in the Mediterranean and the distances from one to the next, but give no bearings or courses. In a few cases soundings appear. It was probably usual for a master who was going on a voyage to collect information from those of his friends who had previously made the journey and to make his own notes which he might correct on his return home. From time to time such a man as Scylax or those who followed him might collect together such notes as he could find into a comprehensive periplus.

What would seem to be the earliest report of a map is given us by Herodotus who says that about 500 B.C. Aristagoras, the tyrant of Miletus, had a 'bronze tablet, whereupon the whole circuit of the earth was engraved, with all its seas and rivers.' Herodotus, who wrote in about 430 B.C., also tells us that Darius (died 486 B.C.) sent two triremes and a cargo boat from Phoenicia to explore the sea-coasts of Greece taking notes of all they saw. Surely this is the earliest example of an attempt to carry out a survey, incomplete though it was? Herodotus condemns the maps of his time: 'For my part, I cannot but laugh when I see numbers of persons drawing maps of the world without having any reason to guide them; making as they do, the ocean-stream to run all round the earth, and the earth itself to be an exact circle, as if described by a pair of compasses, with Europe and Asia just of the same size.'*

There were others after Scylax who compiled sailing directions; of some we know nothing but their names. Then in the second century A.D. came Marinus of Tyre, all of whose work has disappeared. He seems to have compiled sailing directions and drawn charts which were extensively copied and used. Perhaps his were the first true navigational charts for we hear that one was still in use as late as the

---

* *The History of Herodotus*, English version by George Rawlinson, 1859. Book IV, Chap. 36.

tenth century A.D. It has been said that Marinus should have the credit for first making use of the idea of locating places on the earth's surface by latitude and longitude, first suggested by Eratosthenes.

The type of wheel map deplored by Herodotus persisted even into the fifteenth century; it was used by Andrea Bianco for his world map of 1436. Already, however, a more valuable type of map, or early chart, was making its appearance. This was the so-called portolan map of the Mediterranean. Though these charts are often referred to as portolans, or portolani *tout court*, this is an incorrect term, for *portolano* is the Italian name for sailing directions and the charts which we are discussing were drawn to illustrate and to accompany these works. There is one great peculiarity about these charts of the Mediterranean: they show considerable evidence that they are all descended and copied from a single source. The earliest known example dates from near the end of the thirteenth century and they lasted for about three hundred years. A clue to their age curiously enough is contained in the last wheel maps. Those of Petrus Vesconti, 1320, and Andrea Bianco, 1436, have as their centre pieces a more or less accurately shaped representation of the Mediterranean, obviously derived from the same source as the portolan maps, while on the other hand the Hereford map of the thirteenth century has a Mediterranean which is scarcely recognisable (Fig. 76).

The portolan maps were drawn on sheepskins, usually a whole skin with the neck showing at one end, and kept rolled (Fig. 77). They were intended for hard use and must have got it, being thrown away when worn out. Many of those that have survived show much sign of wear and fading. The distinctive feature of these charts is that they were covered with a network of lines, known as loxodromes or loxodromic lines. These radiate from perhaps half a dozen or more points scattered about the chart from each of which the thirty-two wind directions radiate. There is much argument about these lines. One school of thought considers that the lines were first drawn and then used for the accurate plotting of the coast line, suggesting that this proves that they were derived from a survey made by compass after that instrument had reached a sophisticated form. Protagonists of this line of reasoning have been slightly strengthened by the discovery of sheets on which the loxodromes have been already drawn but no coastline has yet been inserted. The other school claims that the survey is much more likely to have been compiled from astronomically obtained latitudes and from distances run from

Figure 76   Outline from the Hereford Map, circa 1285, a typical wheel map.
(Copyright: British Museum)

place to place and that the loxodromes were added later. I suggest
that there were in fact two methods used. The original map was
probably drawn as suggested by the second school of thought, but
when it came to a question of duplicating maps, which had to be
done by hand in quantity, it would have been easier to draw the
loxodromes first and to add the coast later, and this would usually,

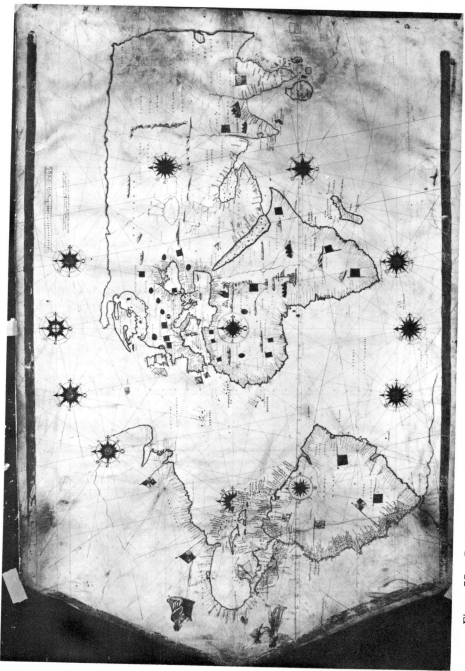

Figure 77 Portolan Chart of the World, by Verrazano, c. 1529. (Copyright: National Maritime Museum)

though not always, have been done. It is similar to the method of squaring down, which is often practiced.

There is another great peculiarity of these charts. When Eratosthenes propounded his ideas which were to become the system of latitudes and longitudes used later, he placed his central parallel running through the Straits of Gibraltar, the Straits of Messina, the southern extremity of the Peloponnisos, and the island of Rhodes. Except for the Straits of Messina, which are about two degrees further to the north, this is in fact the line of the thirty-sixth parallel of latitude. If we examine any of the early portolan charts we would expect to find an east-west loxodrome following approximately the line of this parallel, but we will find that the chart seems to have been tilted. This has suggested to some writers that the portolan charts must be based on an original which was derived from a magnetic compass at a time when there was about ten degrees easterly variation in the Mediterranean, and that the magnetic compass was assumed to be pointing true north. I do not consider that this is by any means proved. A close examination of these charts shows that not only does the tilt differ for different parts of the same chart, which might well be expected as the variation would not be the same throughout, but it appears to differ for the same area on different charts! For example, on a chart of 1456 an east-west loxodrome runs from the Straits of Gibraltar through the northern part of Tunisia, and this is the line of the thirty-sixth parallel, but thereafter the line runs to just north of Egypt as though based on a compass with 10° easterly variation. The E. by N. loxodrome runs from Gibraltar to Messina, which is correct, but then dips to the southern edge of Asia Minor, which is really due east of Messina. These lines give the idea that the western Mediterranean was surveyed with a true compass, the eastern with one having about a point of easterly variation. If now we examine another chart of 1486 we shall find the opposite, for here it is the western Mediterranean which seems to have been surveyed with a compass having easterly variation while it is the eastern Mediterranean which is true. There is no doubt that far more research in this field is needed before any definite statement can be made. Besides, we have no evidence yet that the variation of the compass was known until long after these charts had come into general use. It is very puzzling.

In the earlier charts the centres of radiation of the loxodromic lines were merely points. Starting with the charts of the Catalan atlas of 1375 one of these meeting points was embellished by a drawing of a wind-rose. By the early years of the sixteenth century it had become customary to decorate each starting point in this way, some with large and most ornate wind-roses, some with representations of compass-roses.

The loxodromes had their own system of colours, those for the cardinal and half-cardinal points were usually black, those for the intermediate points were green and those for by-points were red.

The loxodromes were very useful for determining a course on which to sail. All that was necessary was for the pilot to find on his chart the ports of his departure and destination and then to find, probably with the aid of dividers (or compasses as they were called at that time), a loxodrome near by which appeared to be parallel to the line joining the ports, and there was the course to steer.

The first use of a chart which has been definitely noted is in the account of the Crusade of St. Louis in 1270 when the pilots showed one to the King.

There is in existence a manuscript of 1296 entitled *Lo Compasso de Navegare**. This interesting title shows a use of *compasso* in the sense of a circuit and indicates the possibility that some writers have been misled by taking the word compass, when it appears in ship's inventories and similar documents, as necessarily meaning the mariner's magnetic compass though it may mean a book of sailing directions, as in the title of the work just referred to. For example in *Arbor Scientiae* by Raimondo Lullo, written about the same time as the *Compasso* occurs the passage:

> *"El ad hoc instrumentum habent Chartam, Compassum, Acum et Stellam Maris."*

Here some have thought that *Compassum* and *Acum* must refer to the same object but it seems more likely that the *Compassum* was a volume of sailing directions, complementory to the *Chartam*. The *Compasso de Navegare* differs in one remarkable particular from the *Periplus* of Scylax. In addition to the distance from place to place one is given the course as well.

Printed sailing directions appeared in Venice in 1490. This print of an earlier work was not confined to the Mediterranean and there is no doubt that manuscript sailing directions had been appearing in northern Europe for some time. The first printed volume devoted

---

* *Il Compasso da Navigare*, by Bacchisio R. Motzo, Cagliari, 1947.

exclusively to northern waters was published in France about 1502, being followed by an expanded work in 1520. The latter book was translated into English and published by Richard Copland in 1528. The French book was called a *Routier* which the English converted to *Rutter*, a word which was commonly used to describe a volume of sailing directions during the next sixty years, after which it gave place to *Waggoner*.

The charts being produced in the sixteenth century were all plane charts. They took no account of the fact that the earth is a sphere, but tried to show areas of the earth as a flat surface. If two ships were to start from two places on the equator one hundred miles apart and to steer due north they would gradually get closer together until they met at the north pole. When they reached the latitude of Gibraltar they would be eighty-one miles apart, when they reached that of the English Channel they would be only sixty-four miles apart. If however their positions were plotted on a plane chart they would still be shown as one hundred miles apart, for on these charts the meridians were shown parallel to each other instead of converging as the pole was approached. While navigation was confined to the Mediterranean this did not matter very much. The extremes of latitude in that sea are 31° and 45° so the change of distance apart for the two ships we have supposed above would only be from eighty-six to seventy-one miles. During the early Spanish and Portuguese voyages the use of the plane chart still did not cause any very great inconvenience for they were, in general, operating within the limits of 35° north and south. In northern latitudes, such as our own, matters were very different. There was also another complication. This was the difference in the variation of the compass on the two sides of the Atlantic. In the sixteenth century the variation on this side of the Atlantic was easterly, but on the coast of Newfoundland it was 22° west. If a ship steered from England due west by compass, without making any allowance for the variation, she would reach a point on the American coast in a more southerly latitude than that of her point of departure and the coast would appear to trend by compass in a more north-easterly direction than it actually did. The plane charts of the Atlantic were definitely plotted by compass and so on the further side the latitude scale was incorrect and the coast trended away too much towards this side. If the navigator should be sufficiently expert to observe the latitude accurately he would not be able to reconcile it with the latitude of his position shown on the chart. To overcome this, the charts were given another scale off the coast of America which was drawn true north and south and carried a scale of true latitude. This scale is now usually referred to as the oblique meridian by modern historians (Fig. 78).

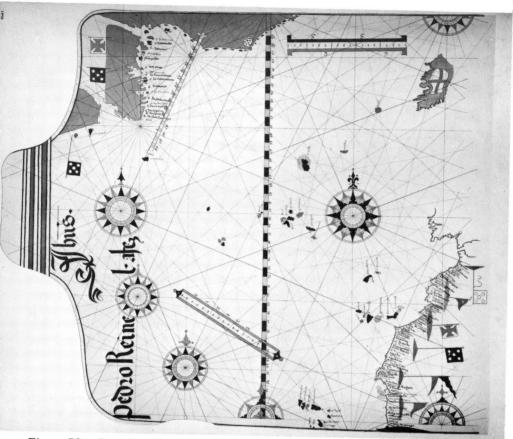

Figure 78   Portolan Chart showing the Oblique Meridian. (Copyright: British Museum)

Even if the variation were taken into account, and the plane chart were drawn with true latitudes and bearings, the errors that I have referred to persisted. The first writer to draw attention to its imperfection was probably Pedro Nunez in 1537. The first attempt to overcome it was made by Mercator in his world map of 1569. In this he kept his meridians parallel to each other, thereby keeping the length of a minute of longitude constant throughout the chart, and stretched his latitudes so that in any latitude the proportion between a minute of latitude and one of longitude would still be correct. It is not known on what principle he worked but his chart did show errors in high latitudes.

In 1599 Edward Wright published his *Certaine Errors of Navigation* in which he demonstrated that for the properly constructed Mercator chart the length of a minute of latitude should equal the length of a minute of longitude multiplied by the secant of the latitude. Wright had communicated with Jodocus Hondius, who brought out Mercator's charts after the latter's death in 1594, and he was already producing charts on the new principle before the publication of Wright's book. For this reason the projection is usually known as Mercator's.

It was a long while before this projection came into general use and even in the beginning of the eighteenth century about half of the contents of chart atlases were still plane charts.

As we have seen, the making of charts started in the Mediterranean but by the end of the fifteenth century manuscript charts of northern seas were also being made in the Netherlands. The earliest, however, which has survived is the *Caerte van de Oostercher Zee* of Jan van Hoirne, 1526.

The first printed maps were woodcuts, but these were world maps like that of Martin Waldseemüller published in 1507, or land maps, and not sea charts, until 1543 when Cornelis Anthonisz produced his *Caerte van Oostlandt**. His chart covered the Baltic and North Seas with Denmark at its centre and was made up in nine leaves after the fashion of the wall maps of the time. It introduced the innovation of showing profiles of the coast, as was already done in sailing directions. They were of the greatest value to seamen when approaching an unknown shore.

In Italy about 1540 copper engraving began to replace woodcuts and the use of this process soon spread to the Netherlands.

In the low countries the first printed *Leeskaart*, or sailing directions, was the work of Jan Severszoon Cruepel van der Schellinc in 1532. The first cartographer to produce a combined chart atlas and sailing directions was Lucas Janszoon Waghenaer, who published the first part of his *Spieghel der Zeevaerdt* in 1584 and the second in the following year. His charts were confined to the coasts of Europe,

---

* *Cornelis Anthonis*, by Johannes Keuning. *Imago Mundi*, VII (1950).

but their value was immediately recognised in England where Anthony Ashley was ordered to produce an English edition and this appeared in 1588 under the title of *The Mariner's Mirrour*.

The text of Ashley's work was translated from Waghenaer's Latin edition of 1586 and the charts were mostly taken from Dutch originals although Richard Caundish had made a good manuscript chart of the Thames Estuary in 1533 as had Robert Norman in 1580, while in 1584 Richard Polter had made a chart of the coast from the Thames to the Humber. Other English manuscript charts were available, but these were mostly engineers' surveys of harbours made for particular purposes and not for navigation.

The Mariner's Mirrour was extremely popular, the atlas form being very convenient to use and store besides being much more durable than the old sheepskins. Waghenaer's name was anglicized as Waggoner and this became the generic name for chart atlases in England.

No steps were taken to bring *The Mariner's Mirrour* up to date and the initiative for supplying charts to the English reverted to the Netherlanders. Most of their principal cartographers issued English editions of their works, often under fanciful names*.

One of the first comprehensive volumes of engraved charts of the world appeared in 1646 under the name of the *Arcano del Mare*, by Robert Dudley. Manuscript charts were, however, still being used at this time. One distinctive series was produced in England between about 1650 and 1670 by cartographers who included Nicholas Cumberford, John Burston and John Thornton. The particular peculiarity of these charts was that they were drawn on paper which was pasted onto two boards, these being hinged like a chess-board for convenient stowage (Fig. 79).

As we have seen, the Netherlanders still had a monopoly, or almost a monopoly, of the English chart trade and in an attempt to secure a share of it John Seller published his *English Pilot* in 1671 and followed it up with other volumes to cover the rest of the world†. These ran into many editions and were still in common use

---

* For example:
Fierie Sea-Columne, by Jacob Colom, 2nd ed. 1637
Lighting Colomne, or Sea Mirrour, by Jan van Loon, 1654.
Burning Fen, by Arent Roggeveen, 1675
† *The English Pilot – The Oriental Navigation*, 1675
The English Pilot – The North America and West Indies Navigation, 1689
The original *English Pilot* was at first divided into two parts – *The Northern Navigation* and the *Southern Navigation*. The second of these two parts was later split up, the *English Pilot – Mediterranean Sea* appearing in 1677.

Figure 79   Part of Chart by John Burston, 1664. (Copyright: National Maritime Museum)

at the end of the next century. The accuracy of the charts still left much to be desired and in some cases second-hand chart plates are said to have been purchased in Holland. The charts did not even cover the whole of the British Isles and when in 1689 it was necessary to send ships of the Royal Navy to Scotland at the time of Argyle's rebellion pilots who knew the coast had to be obtained for there were no charts of that area. It is evident that these ships were using Seller's *English Pilot* where the charts extended to the north of Ireland, for one of their officers in his log-book uses the name Knockforgus for Carrickfergus, a form which appears in Seller's chart.

In 1683 Greenville Collins was ordered to carry out a survey of the British coasts and appointed to command the yacht MERLIN. Samuel Pepys had drawn attention to the fact that the Isles of Scilly were generally placed about ten miles too far to the northward, so causing an unnecessary hazard for ships approaching the English Channel. This may have had something to do with the appointment of Collins, whose task was completed in 1688. One would have expected the results of this government-sponsored survey to have been published by government agency but this was not done and the work was left to a private printer who issued *Great Britain's Coasting Pilot* in 1693. Like Seller's *English Pilot* this survey did not include the north and west coasts of Scotland but covered the coast from Shetland to the Mull of Galloway, clockwise.

Collins put St. Agnes Light in the Scillies in 50° 2′ N. and the Lizard in 49° 59′ N. Seller had put them in 50° 7′ and 50° 10′ respectively and modern determinations are 49° 53′ and 49° 58′. Collins' result was an improvement, but it was not nearly good enough.

From time to time the Admiralty made attempts to survey foreign parts and occasionally officers made their own surveys and sent them in. Captain Benjamin Candler was ordered to make surveys in the West Indies in 1717-1718 and 1721-1722, and although his ship had other duties, such as the suppression of piracy, he did achieve quite a lot of work, including the determination of the longitude of Virgin Gorda by an eclipse of the moon on 16th March 1717.* His charts were not published. During the years 1728-1734 the ALBOROUGH, captained by John Gascoigne, was based at Charleston and employed exclusively, usually with the help of a small vessel, on the survey of

---

* His determination was about a degree too far to the eastward. His manuscript charts of 1717-1718 are in the Ministry of Defence (Navy) Library.

the coasts and harbours of South Carolina, Georgia, the Bahamas and part of Cuba. In spite of all these years of hard work nothing was done about the publication of Gascoigne's charts either, until some were engraved by a private firm about forty years afterwards. There was nevertheless, a serious need for more accurate charts of this area and Gascoigne had revealed many grave errors in those in use. For an example, Cay Sal Bank at the southern end of the Florida Strait was incorrectly charted too far to the eastward and Gascoigne showed the error. Yet no correction to existing charts was made and in 1748 the FOWEY, trusting to them, took her departure from Cay Sal and steered northwards for the centre of the Strait, only to go ashore on the Florida side. An examination of modern charts shows that she had in fact steered exactly for the spot where she had stranded!

For the next serious attempt to survey the coasts of the British Isles the Admiralty employed Murdoch Mackenzie I (born 1712) who spent the years from 1741 to 1749 in a survey of the Orkneys and the island of Lewis. The results were published by Emmanuel Bowen in the following year under the title: *Orcades, or a Geographic and Hydrographic Survey of the Orkney and Lewis Islands*. For this the north coast of Scotland was taken from a survey by the Rev. Alexander Bryce, published in 1744.

Mackenzie was then sent to tackle the west coasts of Scotland and England with the islands and the coasts of Ireland. Starting at Cape Wrath in 1751, by 1770, when ill health forced him to retire, he had got as far south as Pembrokeshire, having completed Ireland on his way.

Mackenzie was succeeded by his nephew, Murdoch Mackenzie II (born 1743), whom he had trained. The latter continued his uncle's work surveying the Bristol Channel and the north coasts of Devon and Cornwall, with a detour to Plymouth, during the years 1771-1773. He was then diverted to carry out a survey of channels off the Kent coast in 1774-1777. This survey marks a distinct step in the history of hydrographic surveying. Whereas before it had been usual to fix the soundings by compass bearings they were now fixed by sextant angles and, it is believed, with some form of station pointer. This instrument enables a fix to be quickly and accurately effected by means of two angles measured between a single fixed object and two others, one on each side of it. Henceforth the number of soundings taken greatly increased, to such an extent that when the chart was engraved a selection had to be made. This multiplicity of soundings enabled the limits of a shoal to be shown with far greater accuracy and reduced the likelihood of overlooking some isolated danger.

During the years 1777-1788 Mackenzie made extensive surveys of the south coast of England and was followed until 1803 by Graeme Spence (born 1757), another relative trained in the family tradition. Murdoch Mackenzie II had been given a commission as Lieutenant in 1779, no doubt to facilitate his position in ships of the Royal Navy while carrying out his surveys. At one time he commanded the PETEREL.

Throughout the century, isolated surveys were carried out by various individuals but even if these were naval officers their work, like that of the Mackenzies, had still to be published by private publishers, if they were to be published at all.

In 1758 a chance encounter was to have a profound effect on British chartmaking. After the fall of Louisbourg, James Cook, then master of the PEMBROKE, met Samuel Holland and Des Barres, two military engineers and surveyors, with the result that the three collaborated in making a chart of the St. Lawrence which enabled the fleet to get up to Quebec in the following year. For this chart Cook took the soundings and he was subsequently sent, when the war was over, to survey the coasts of Newfoundland. Des Barres was also employed upon the American coast and ultimately in 1777 published all the charts of North America on which he could lay his hands under the name of *The Atlantic Neptune.*

Cook was recalled before his Newfoundland survey was completed so that he might take command on the first of those three voyages to the Pacific which ensured his everlasting fame and set a new standard of surveying for voyages of discovery. He was followed by George Vancouver who surveyed the west coast of North America in 1791-1795, by William Broughton who was off the east coast of Asia in 1795-1797 and by Matthew Flinders who circumnavigated Australia in 1801-1803.

All these officers had still to have their charts engraved and published by private enterprise, but a new era was dawning.

The French Navy had set up their Depôt de Cartes et Plans in 1720 and Captain Gascoigne had proposed to the Admiralty back in 1737 that they should appoint a 'Surveyor-General of the Sea' whose duty it should be to collect, collate and publish charts and other hydrographic information. It appears that some years later the Board did get as far as considering the idea but it was not until 1795 that a Hydrographer of the Navy was actually appointed.

The man chosen for this post was Alexander Dalrymple, then fifty-eight years of age. In those days age was not considered an obstacle to employment and one of his successors, Francis Beaufort, was destined to hold the post of Hydrographer for twenty-six years until he reached the age of eighty-one. Dalrymple had spent his early years in the East Indies in the service of the Hon. East India Company and had made good use of his time himself surveying whenever opportunity occurred and collecting information from others when he could not see for himself. In 1779 the Company appointed him their Hydrographer and in a short time he had made available to them an excellent collection of charts.

Dalrymple's selection as Hydrographer of the Navy was an obvious choice, in spite of the fact that he could not get on with naval officers and nursed a continuous grudge that it was James Cook and not he who had been given command of the ENDEAVOUR in 1768, but he did not give complete satisfaction. It was thought that he was far too slow in providing the Navy with charts, so much needed in war-time, and that few had reached the fleet. It has been said that he was a perfectionist and objected to any chart going out which was in his view incomplete or might contain inaccuracies, but it is more likely that it was his ridiculously small staff which limited his output. At last he realised that something more must be done quickly and that it was necessary to purchase charts from independent publishers if the Navy was to obtain anything approaching world coverage. He admitted that he knew little of the coasts of Europe and America and sought the appointment of a committee to advise him on purchases. The Committee was appointed in 1808 and rather exceeded its terms of reference. It recommended the production of chart sets for each station, the formation of chart depots at the dockyards, and the appointment of a younger man as Hydrographer with the requisite drive to put all this through.

Dalrymple, now seventy-three, was replaced by Captain Thomas Hurd who had had much surveying experience and had also seen something of his predecessor's organisation. Within six months he was able to report that he had the issue of chart-boxes arranged and had already sent out 134, besides making arrangements for their return and refurbishing for further issue when no longer required. He was convinced that much must be done to provide more and better surveys. In 1810 he selected George Thomas to carry out a survey of the east coast of England and for the next thirty-six years this master, originally pressed into the Navy, was to be similarly employed. Other officers were sent out as opportunity offered.

The coming of peace in 1815 was Hurd's opportunity. He laid a report before the Admiralty showing the vast areas of the globe that still required adequate examination. The Admiralty was not particularly averse to employing as surveyors, some of the many officers which the peace establishment had made redundant. They would provide a suitable reserve in the event of another war. It was not so ready to spend money in providing them with adequate ships and established the rule, which was to be maintained for some 140 years, that any vessel of no value for anything else would do for a surveying ship. Another and much better tradition was established by Hurd and the officers he selected, that of a strange devotion to their survey from which neither the difficulties of inadequate and unsuitable vessels nor those of climate and weather were to deter them. They sometimes sacrificed their lives, often their health, their families and their small savings in that service. They spent long periods abroad, commissions of six years were not considered unusual. An example of such long service that may be quoted is the career of John Lort Stokes. He joined the BEAGLE as a midshipman in October 1825 and served in her until 1830 and again from 1831 to 1836 surveying the Straits of Magellan and the coasts of South America. In January 1837 he was promoted to Lieutenant and immediately reappointed to the BEAGLE for the survey of Australia. Six years later he brought her home, now in command after his former captain had been invalided three years before. He himself had been desperately wounded in the lung by the spear of an aborigine. The coat that he wore on this occasion was carefully mended by his wife and preserved in the family, being now in the National Maritime Museum. Having thus served for eighteen years in one vessel, almost continuously abroad, he now spent four years at home before sailing again in the ACHERON to survey New Zealand, being this time away from 1847-1853. To the great benefit of the seamen of the world this kind of dedication has been passed down to the surveying officers of the present day, better served as they are now with improved ships and equipment. Even when I was employed in the MERLIN on the Singapore survey in the early 1920s her officers thought nothing of working a ninety-two hour week and our crew but little less.

Throughout all the years in peace and war the surveying service has never missed an opportunity to show its worth and to improve its charts. When in 1854 Sir Charles Napier commanded the fleet in the Baltic during the Russian War he greeted the captain of the LIGHTNING with the remark: "I do not know what you have come out for, or what is the use of a surveying ship, unless to make a fire vessel of." It was not long before Napier had changed his tune, finding the LIGHTNING's surveys of immense value to the fleet in those previously badly-charted waters.

One of Hurd's great achievements was his persuasion of the Board of Admiralty to allow the Admiralty charts to be sold commercially. This he achieved in 1823 after years of argument. His original plan had been to make his surveying service self-supporting, but the production of accurate charts at a very reasonable price was to prove of inestimable value to the commerce of this country and indeed of the whole world. At first no attempt was made to keep charts that had been issued up to date and the only way of insuring that one had the latest information was to buy a new chart. In 1832 the introduction of the *Nautical Magazine*, for which the then Hydrographer was largely responsible, provided a means of promulgating the latest information, enabling the holders of charts to correct them themselves. Two years later the Hydrographic Department began the issue of its *Notices to Mariners* with the same object.

The Blue Back Chart.

In the second half of the eighteenth century Robert Sayer had become an important publisher of charts. He was in business from 1745-1795, being partnered from 1770-1787 by John Bennett, and was succeeded by Robert Laurie and James Whittle, a firm which ultimately became Imray, Laurie, Norie & Wilson. The excellent charts which this firm produced during the nineteenth century were usually mounted with a blue backing so that they naturally became known as blue back charts. It is possible that the dislike of all things naval which seems to have been widespread during the century had something to do with their success. Nevertheless, Lecky, writing in 1881, recommended the Admiralty chart for its cheapness, its convenient size and scale (the blue back charts were often of unwieldy size), and the probability that however hard a commercial concern tried to ensure that its charts were up to date, it was unlikely ever to be able to compete with a government department on which it had to rely greatly for its information. It would appear that the First World War dealt a heavy blow to the production of these charts though some special charts of use to fishermen are still sold.

Sailing Directions.

The production of sailing directions has proceeded from the earliest times, usually preceding that of charts, for where no charts existed records of the experiences of other men could not fail to be useful. In fact, where not even sailing directions were available, log-books and accounts of previous voyages might go some way to fill the lack. As an example of such, Anson during his voyage of 1740-1744 carried with him the account of Frezier's voyage of 1712-1714 which had been rendered into English in 1717.

The Spaniards were very secretive with their information concerning the Pacific coasts of the New World and when Bartholomew Sharp during his voyage of 1681 was lucky enough to capture a book of Spanish sailing directions it was looked upon as a great prize, translated into English, and copied by William Hack. Three examples of this work are known to me* and exhibit considerable differences. Each contains about 260 pages of sketches, they can hardly be called charts, showing the shape and profile of the coasts (Fig. 80). These are accompanied by notes giving courses, bearings and distances. There are no scales of latitudes, longitudes, or distance, but one latitude is sometimes given. The first two copies include a chart of Juan Fernandez (Fig. 81), made by Basil Ringrose when he was there with Sharp, but the third, which is actually the oldest, does not. The Ringrose chart is of higher quality than any of the others and in the second copy is the only one to give a wind-rose and a scale. The first copy shows a large number of wind-roses, the second none, except for that on the Ringrose chart, while the third copy has six. This last example, alone of the three, also features a translation by Phillip Dassigny of sailing directions, running to ninety-three manuscript pages.

Much of the information concerning the dangers of the Indian Ocean was built up by the experiences gained by the Portuguese on their voyages to India. It was included in their *Roteiros* which like those of the Spaniards were jealously guarded. Occasionally, however, these leaked out and were translated into other tongues, such as the *Roteiro da carreira da India* of about 1622, by Aleixo da Mota, which appeared in *Relations de divers Voyages curieux*, published in Paris in 1663.

* 1. National Maritime Museum, Gosse, Collection, MS.P/33; 2. British Museum, Sloane MS.44; 3. British Museum, King's Collection, K.Mar. VIII.15

Figure 80   Chart from Hack's Waggoner for the South Seas. (Copyright: National Maritime Museum)

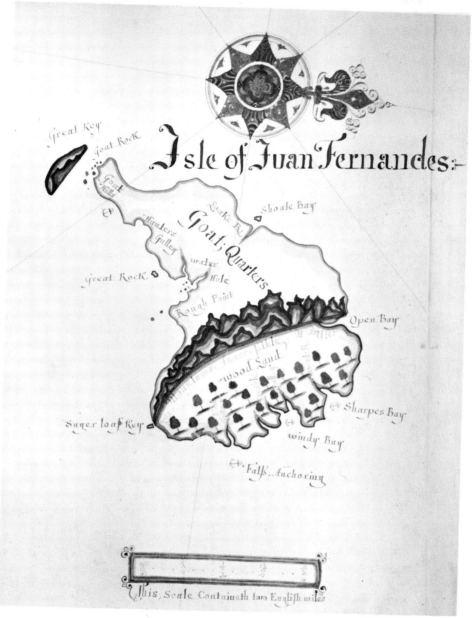

Figure 81   Ringrose's Chart of Juan Fernandez, from Hack's Waggoner. (Copyright: National Maritime Museum)

There were three traditional routes from the Cape of Good Hope to India (Fig. 82). One was the inner passage, used by Vasco da Gama, where ships sailed inside Madagascar and some way up the coast of Africa before stretching across to Goa. The middle passage became known to the French as Boscawen's Passage after he had used it with success in 1748, when after reconnoitring Mauritius he took a squadron of more than twenty ships to India without

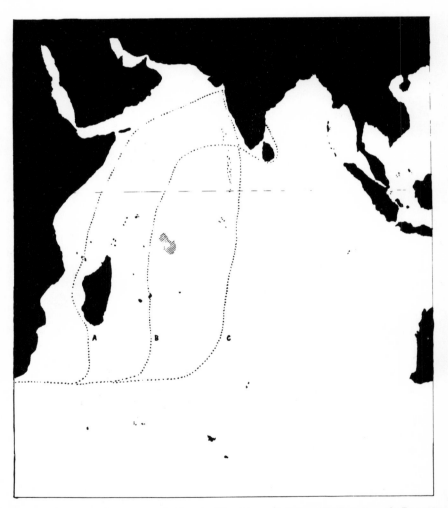

Figure 82   The Routes to India. A, The Inner Passage: B, Boscawen's Passage: C, the Outer Passage. The shaded area represents Saya da Malha Shoals.

encountering any danger. This route took ships eastward of Madagascar and of the great Saya da Malha Shoals and would, one might think, have seemed highly dangerous because of the uncertainty of the exact locality of hazards. As an example of this, the island which appeared under a variety of names, such as Roquepires and Roquepiz to mention two of them, was given twice over on some charts, the two positions sometimes differing by as much as four degrees of latitude and six degrees of longitude. It was visited by Lancaster in 1601 and was renowned for its odoriferous plants and flowers which spread their fragrance off shore. It was expunged from the Admiralty charts in the 1870s as non-existent and was probably Agalega.

In spite of its possible dangers the middle passage was very commonly used by ships returning home from India. In 1736 the *Scarborough*, East Indiaman, sighted Diego Rais (Rodriguez) right ahead when expecting to reach its latitude some 120 leagues to the eastward. It seems incredible.

A ship using the outer passage sailed eastwards from the Cape of Good Hope until in 70° or 75° East, and then turned northwards to pass east of the Maldives. This last route was not mentioned by da Mota.

During the second half of the eighteenth century the East Indiamen relied to a great extent upon William Herbert's *New Directory for the East Indies*, which was largely based upon the French *Neptune Oriental* of Lieutenant D'Apres de Mannivillette, besides other sources. A rather amusing example of how information passed back and forth is in the first (1745) edition of the *Neptune Oriental* where its compiler states that he had undertaken the work because he did not think it right that his countrymen should have to rely upon English and Dutch charts.

To consider Herbert's third edition (1767), the resultant charts were rather mixed, some having a longitude scale emanating from Paris, some originating from London, and many having no longitude scale at all. The charts, which are in a separate volume from the text and therefore far more convenient to use than when bound together, are quite well chosen. There are comprehensive charts of large areas — the Atlantic, the Indian Ocean, the South China Sea — some larger scale charts of important areas and some on even larger scale of anchorages and their approaches and of narrow straits. Lines of soundings are given along the principal sea routes, and at focal points.

One of the difficulties of navigators in those distant seas at that

time is emphasised by a note on the difference of longitude between
Pulo Condore and Manila. Herbert says that this is 13° and points
out that the *English Pilot* makes it only 11½°. It is actually about
14°.

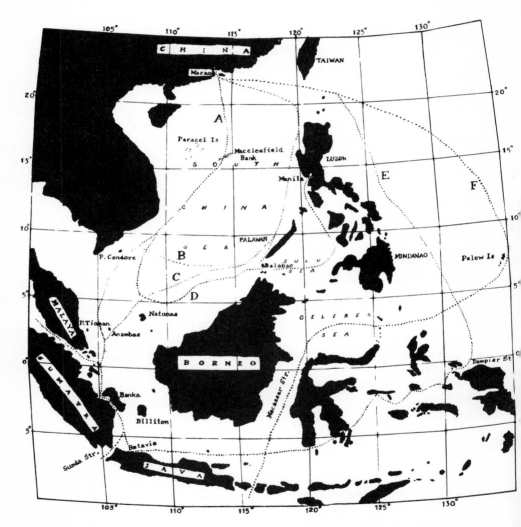

Figure 83   The Routes to China. *A*. the usual route: *B*. the *Royal Bishop*,
Mars, and *York* in 1786: *C*. the *Walpole* in 1783-4: *D*. the *Osterley, Glatton,
Abergavenny*, and *Lord Thurlow* in 1793: *E*. the *Pitt* in 1758: *F*. the Armiston
in 1797.

The normal passage to China (Fig. 83) took a ship by the same route as the outer passage to India, eastwards from the Cape of Good Hope, but she generally aimed at sighting St Paul Island (38° 43′ S., 77° 31′ E.) before turning to the north-eastwards for the Straits of Sunda. If she missed the island she waited until the variation was found to be 7° W. After passing through the Straits of Sunda, she turned northward, through Banca Strait between the islands of Banca and Sumatra, past the end of the Malay Peninsula, and outside Pulo Tioman, across the Gulf of Siam to the coast of Indo-China. Here ships passed outside but in sight of Pulo Condore and Pulo Sapata and after this two ways were available. A ship might hug the coast for a while and after passing inside the Paracels strike across to Hainan Island and thence to China near Macao. Herbert's *Directory* however said that winds were unreliable inside the Paracels and recommended to go outside and to endeavour to strike soundings on the Macclesfield Bank, so named after the ship who discovered it in 1701. Finding the Macclesfield Bank gave the ship a point of departure from which to make Macao. It is interesting to note that in modern' times the navigator is advised to keep to the westward of the bank as there may well be less depths than the five fathoms so far discovered.

The great problem of a ship on passage to China was that she had to get through the South China Sea before the north-east monsoon set in about the end of October and adverse winds became too strong. Ships which for any reason were late in arriving might have to wait for months at Malacca or Batavia.

Just as the Portuguese had tried to keep secret any navigational information about the Indian Ocean, so the Dutch kept to themselves all that they knew of the East Indies. This was reflected by the *Directory* which has nothing to say about any of the straits through the islands, save the Banca Strait and a chart showing an alternative route sounded by the *Osterley* in 1758-9. This passed close to the island of Billiton.

In 1758 an attempt was made to find another way to China which could be used late in the season, and the *Pitt* was sent by the East India Company to see what could be done. Reaching Batavia in December she made her careful way through the islands, finally emerging into the Pacific Ocean through Pitt and Dampier Straits. She then sailed without difficulty well to the eastwards of the Philippines so that she could weather them comfortably during the north-east monsoon and so passed to China which she reached in April. In this investigation and his subsequent report Captain Wilson was no doubt aided by charts and information obtained unofficially from Dutch sources in Batavia.

The *Pitt's* route became an established one for the Company's ships who were sailing late*. It had an additional advantage that ships could avoid Sunda Strait, which in time of war was liable to be watched by French ships. The Straits of Bali or Lombok could conveniently be used by anyone making passage through these eastern channels.

A glance at the chart might suggest that a more obvious route than that of the *Pitt* would have been that through Macassar Strait and the Celebes Sea, but Horsburgh stated† that the winds are adverse that way in January and February and though Macassar Strait is suitable in December thereafter Pitt and Dampier Straits are to be preferred. Macassar Strait seems to have been first used by East Indiamen in December 1783 to January 1784 when the *Earl of Sandwich* and *Ganges* passed that way, and it was recommended by Dalrymple in 1788. The *Arniston* made a quick passage, passing through Lombok Strait on 30th October 1797 and continuing through Macassar Strait and the Celebes Sea reached Macao on 4th December.

In 1759-1762 Alexander Dalrymple in the schooner *Cuddalore* carried out considerable surveys off the north coast of Borneo and in neighbouring seas. His charts were not published until 1771 but information which he had collected must have been available to East India Company ships. In 1762 and 1763 in the *Cuddalore* and *London* he proved the possibility of a route to Balabac Strait passing close to the north of the Anambas and Natunas and his instructions were responsible for the voyage of the *Royal Captain* in 1762. Passing Pulo Tioman on 2nd September she only went as far north as 7° and then, while still more than a degree south of Pulo Condore, turned almost due east to the northern tip of Borneo. The master had Dalrymple's manuscript chart of this area and seems to have expected to meet him, or at any rate to have found a pilot to aid him. In default of one he was afraid to try to enter any harbour in Borneo. He therefore blundered on, beyond the confines of Dampier's chart, across the Sulu Sea. A fortnight's sailing during which he did not even record the latitude, brought him to the eastern boundaries of the sea, and then, managing to get a pilot and a

---

*   One ship which went this way was the *Ganges* in December 1762.
†   James Horsburgh, *Directions for Sailing to and from the East Indies, China New Holland, Cape of Good Hope and the interadjacent Ports*, 1816.

Spanish chart, the *Royal Captain* got out between Mindanao and Leyte to the Pacific and thence to China.

In December 1761 Dalrymple in his schooner made a running survey of the coast of Palawan which, while showing that the Palawan Passage north-west of that island was a possibility, indicated that some serious dangers existed. In the *Sailing Directions for the East India or Oriental Pilot for the Navigation between England and the Cape of Good Hope*, published by R. Sayer & J. Bennett in 1781, the route north of the Natunas and then by the Palawan Passage was recommended for the late season. The first East Indiaman to try this is believed to have been the *Walpole* which did not reach the China Sea until the beginning of December in 1783. After being delayed by lack of wind for about a fortnight in the vicinity of the Anambas, she passed north of the Great Natunas and then sailed east-north-eastwards until opposite the Balabac Strait and then by the Palawan Passage, west of the Philippines and so to Macao. Three years later a variation of this route was tried by the *Royal Bishop, Mars* and *York*. A month earlier than the *Walpole* these ships took the old way but when they were off the coast of Cambodia the monsoon set in earlier than usual and held them back. On the 19th October they turned east-south-eastwards and steered right across the China Sea, sighting more than one danger on the way, until they saw Balabac and turned into the Palawan Passage with a long-boat sounding ahead. They reached China on 30th November.

In 1793 the *Glatton, Osterley, Abergavenny* and *Lord Thurlow* were caught by adverse weather even earlier than the *Royal Bishop* and her consorts had been. It is true that they got a degree further north but it was only 12th October when they had to turn back. Then not relishing the dangers which the other ships had seen they turned southwards again to near the Anambas and followed the *Walpole's* track. On sighting the island of Balabac they made another departure from precedent and instead of turning into the Palawan Passage continued eastwards through the Balabac Strait and crossed the Sulu Sea until in sight of Mindanao and Negros they turned north-north-westwards and coasting along came to Manila.

These explorations were of great value and the Company made the resulting information available to their ships. There was however generally some delay before it got into print or appeared on charts and reached the general shipping fraternity.

As we have seen, the practice of including sailing directions in chart atlases, following the example of Wagenhaer and Seller, was generally continued until the middle of the eighteenth century. The two were then becoming separated. In the better known areas the sailing directions described coasts but in the less known areas they tended to become a collection of descriptions of routes. With better chart coverage with the extension of Admiralty surveys these descriptions of routes waned in importance and the production of the Admiralty series of *Pilots* brought in the systematic description of coasts and adjacent waters. The first of the Admiralty series was the Channel Pilots, published in 1856, and the set was gradually extended to cover the whole globe. Other nations have now produced very similar collections.

Seven
Sounding

The lead and line was probably the oldest of all navigational instruments. That we hear little about it is not surprising, for it is so simple that no one would think it necessary to describe it. The earliest mention that I have been able to find is in the History of Herodotus, written in the fifth century B.C. In his Book II, Chapter 5 there appears a passage which has been translated as: "In the first place, on approaching it [Egypt] by sea, when you are still a day's sail from the land, if you let down a sounding line you will bring up mud, and find yourself in eleven fathoms' water."*

In mediaeval records the only occasions where leads occur are when mentioned in lists of ships' stores. For example in 1345 we read that the *Plenty* of Hull was supplied with two sounding lines with the leads.

The lead was made with a recess in the bottom which could be armed (or filled) with tallow. This would pick up a sample from the sea bed and from the look, and sometimes even the smell, of this, taken with the depth, the experienced pilot might often estimate his position. We have seen Herodotus referring to the bottom off the Egyptian coast. At a much later date, in areas where the soundings and the nature of the bottom were of value to pilots, these were recorded in books of sailing directions and when Trinity House began to examine Masters for the Royal Navy it was common to ask the candidate to recite the depths and bottom to be encountered when approaching the English Channel from the westward and running along the coast.

For a long time the line was unmarked. The leadsman either estimated the amount of the line he had had to let out to allow the lead to reach the bottom or he measured it, hand over hand, fathom by fathom, as he hauled it in. After all, with a ship moving but slowly there was plenty of time. However, after a while someone did think to mark the line and markings, once introduced, became fairly well standardised.

---

* *The History of Herodotus*, English version by George Rawlinson, 1859.

I suggest that the date of this introduction was most likely to have been about 1600. On the title page of Wagenhaer's *Spieghel der Zeevaerdt*, 1584, two leadsmen appear (Fig. 84), but their leadlines are unmarked. The drawing has every indication of being attributable to an artist who knew his subject and one would therefore have expected him to put in some markings, had they existed. Later title pages of similar works also lack the markings, but these drawings have indications of having been derived from Wagenhaer and are not necessarily drawn by knowledgeable artists.

The first list of markings is given by Sir Henry Mainwaring, who wrote his *Seaman's Dictionary* in about 1620 but continued to polish it until it was published in 1644. He gives:

2 fathoms	black leather
3 fathoms	black leather*
5 fathoms	white
7 fathoms	red
10 fathoms	leather
15 fathoms	white or leather

This handline, with its 7 lb. lead, was only twenty or thirty fathoms in length. For deep water there was a deep-sea line, marked at twenty fathoms with two knots, thirty fathoms with three knots, and so on. With this a 14 lb. lead was used. The leads were found to be insufficiently heavy. A 14 lb. lead is sometimes used on a hand line and one of about 30 lb. for the deep-sea line was already being used by the middle of the eighteenth century. As much as 60 or 70 lb. leads were sometimes recommended for very deep water.

There have been various modifications to the markings. Methods have never been completely standardised but the following will give some indication of practice:

By 1860 the two and three fathom markings of leather had become differentiated by being split into two and three tails respectively, although some writers advocated their being marked by one or two tails only.

The leather mark at ten fathoms had a hole in it by the same period, although Alfred H. Alston's *Seamanship* of 1860 uses the leather with the hole for two fathoms.

---

* Captain John Smith in his *Sea-man's Grammar*, 1627, says that this piece of leather was split. He also says that seven fathoms was marked by 'a piece of red in a piece of leather', but as he does not mention ten fathoms I am of opinion that his printer has left out a few words from the middle of this quotation.

Figure 84   Title page of Wagenhaer's *Spieghel der Zeevaerdt*, 1586, showing leadsmen with unmarked lead-lines.

205

A thirteen fathom mark was added by 1763 and here there was another divergence, either blue or leather being used. The British seem finally to have adopted blue while the Americans stuck to leather, ultimately giving it three tails like three fathoms.

By 1763, marking at seventeen fathoms (red) and by 1810 at twenty fathoms (two knots) were also used. By this latter date also it had become usual to mark the deep-sea line with a single knot at 25, 35, 45, fathoms, &c. In some ships it was common to use white calico, red bunting and blue cloth for the marks so that they could be detected by feel at night.

When sounding with the hand lead, it is necessary for the leadsman to stand clear of the ship's side. In a sailing ship he stood on one of the chain-wales on the weather side. These were stout timbers, bolted to the side of the ship, to which the shrouds for the mast were secured. A rope passed round his waist and made fast at each end to the shrouds, left him with his hands free. In steam ships a small platform is built over the ship's side for this purpose and has inherited the name of 'leadsman's chains'. The leadsman takes a turn with the line around his hand and after swinging the lead back and forth heaves it around his head until it has sufficient momentum when released to fly well ahead. Provided that the ship is not going too fast for the depth of water, the lead will reach the bottom before the chains have come above it and the leadsman can gather up the slack line and note the mark on the surface of the water, or that nearest to it. He then calls out the depth. If a mark is on the surface the call will be for example, 'by the mark five'. If the sounding should be judged at an unmarked fathom the call will be, for example, 'by the deep eight'. If the sounding is not an exact fathom the call will be in the form 'a quarter less seven' or 'and a half five'.

When the deep-sea lead was in use a number of men were stationed along the ship's side, each holding a coil of the line, and the lead was taken right forward. It was thrown overboard and as each man felt the strain coming on to his coil he let it go and to warn the next man called out 'watch there watch'. Finally when the lead reached the bottom the line was checked from running out and the mark on the water noted and reported by a quarter-master. It was usual to heave the ship to when using the deep-sea lead.

From about the end of the nineteenth century various mechanical methods of using the deep-sea lead were used in surveying ships of the Royal Navy so that a continuous line of soundings could be run without stopping the ship or using undue labour. In one method the lead was hauled to a boom rigged forward, by means of a wire and winch. The end of the marked line was also attached to the lead and, passing over a block at the top of a second boom rigged over the quarter, was attached at the other end to a float towing astern. The lead was hauled forward by the winch and then the turns of the wire were thrown off the drum so that the lead was free to sink quickly to the bottom. The float kept the lead-line taught so that, when the lead had reached the bottom and come aft under the leadsman, the line was vertical and the depth could be read off easily. The leadsman then signalled to the winch operator to haul away and the cycle of operations was repeated. It was, of course, necessary to adjust the speed of the ship so that the lead had time to reach the bottom before coming under the leadsman.

The surveying rig just described was not suited to ordinary navigation and was not available before the introduction of effective power winches.

For some time inventors had examined the problem of how to measure a true up-and-down sounding without stopping the ship for each cast. Jonas Moore tried sounding with wooden balls. The intention was that one of these balls should be thrown overboard attached to a weight and would therefore sink at a constant speed. On reaching the bottom the weight would be automatically released and the ball would return to the surface. The time taken for its double journey would be proportional to the depth. The attempt was a failure, partly because the releasing gear for the weights was unreliable and partly because it was difficult to be sure of the instant when the ball broke surface.*

A more successful, but much later, device was Burt's Buoy and Nipper which was in use through most of the nineteenth century†. With this apparatus the sounding line was led through a block secured below a buoy, which was thrown overboard with the lead. When the lead reached the bottom the strain on the line was reduced and this caused the line to be nipped and held at the buoy. Buoy and lead were then hauled in and the depth read off by the markings on the line at the nipper. Of course as the buoy remained over the lead an up-and-down sounding was obtained.

In 1802 Edward Massey patented his sounding apparatus‡. This

---

*   Thomas Birch, *The History of the Royal Society of London*, 1756, Vol.III, p.399
†   Henry Raper, *The Practice of Navigation*, 1840, Art. 399, and later editions.
‡   Patent No.2601, dated 24th March 1802.

consisted of a frame containing a rotator, rather similar to that of his log, and a lead. As the lead sank the movement of the rotator through the water caused it to turn and this movement was transmitted by rods to dials attached to the lead (Fig. 85). In improvements to the original design the rotator became a propellor mounted in the same unit as its dials, and this unit was attached about three feet above an ordinary lead by a length of line. The pressure of the water upon a flap arrangement released the propellor when the apparatus began to sink but locked it, and its dials, when the lead was lifted off the bottom. This was, of course, a necessity or when the lead was being hauled in the propellor would have turned in the reverse direction and would have wound the dials back to zero again and beyond.

A trial of Massey's sounding gear was made in the TRINCULO, Captain James R. Booth, in September 1832, but it was then a failure because the lack of a stop on the rotator allowed it to overrun by 40%.*

The Massey sounding apparatus when perfected was very successful and extensively used, though after 1846 it had competition from Walker's which operated on a very similar plan.

With all these deep-sea sounding gears great exertion was needed in hauling in the long thick line after each cast, and this was exacerbated by the additional line necessarily used when the ship was not hove to and some such device as Burt's, Massey's or Walker's was employed.

To lighten the task, proposals were made for the use of wire instead of a hemp sounding line. In 1834 a trial was made in H.M. Steam Vessel MEDEA, Commander H. T. Austin, of a sounding machine which recorded the length of copper wire run out. This had been designed by an American named Reid. When the lead reached the bottom one of its two halves dropped off thus lightening the load to be hauled in†. The idea of a copper wire was again put forward in 1837 by a Captain Taylor, but it was not until 1848 that further trials of a wire were made. This was in the THUNDER, Captain Edward Barnett. Four years earlier Lieutenant William Mooney had brought on board a drum on which was wound 3000 fathoms of iron wire. It was not tried until 1848 and the wire then broke when 2000 fathoms had run out. It was not tried again.‡

* *Nautical Magazine*, Vol. I (1832), page 498
† *Nautical Magazine*, Vol. III (1834), page 444.
‡ *Nautical Magazine*, 18 (1849), pp. 121-124.

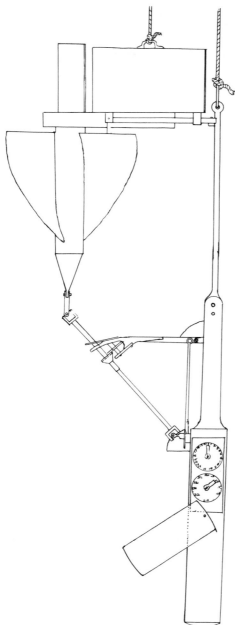

Figure 85   Massey's Sounding Apparatus, 1802.

In June 1872 Sir William Thomson experimented with a sounding machine of his own design, on the drum of which was wound three miles of piano wire. Using a 30-lb. lead he successfully obtained a sounding of 2700 fathoms. When he came to heave in, however, he found that there was far more strain on the wire than he had anticipated and this collapsed the drum of the machine. In his report of this trial Thomson mentioned the possibility of disconnecting part of the lead when it hit the bottom, leaving less weight to be hauled in, as had been proposed by Reid forty years earlier. This idea seems to have been adopted in America.

Thomson's experiment promised success and he went on to perfect his sounding machine. It was patented in 1876[*] and was soon universally adopted. Its final modified form appeared in 1905 [†] .

While Thomson's machine registered the amount of wire out and with this and the known speed of the ship an approximate depth could be obtained from a table, to obtain an accurate depth while steaming a thin glass tube was attached to the 28-lb. lead. The tube was sealed at one end and in its final form the inside was coated with chromate of silver. As the tube sank to the bottom with the lead, the air in it was compressed allowing the salt water to enter. The distance to which the salt water penetrated was dependent upon the depth of the water and was marked by the chromate of silver becoming discoloured by the salt. When the lead had been recovered all that was necessary was to measure the length of the tube which had not been discoloured against a special scale.

The use of compression of air to show the depth was not new. In 1678 a somewhat similar proposal had been made to the Royal Society[‡]. This was to use a glass tube with its lower end sealed. It was thought that, under pressure at depth water would force its way in, compressing the air, and when the lead was raised and the pressure reduced the expanding air would come out past the water without expelling any. In Burney's 1815 edition of Falconer's *Marine Dictionary* the self acting sounder is described. This also was a glass tube with one end sealed, but the free end housed a non-return valve. This allowed sufficient water to enter to compress the air according to depth, but when a start was made in hauling up the lead the non-return valve trapped the water whose amount would subsequently be measured. A variation to this device was invented by

[*]   Patent No. 3452 dated 1st December 1876.
[†]   Patent No. 20813 dated 14th October 1905.
[‡]   Thomas Birch, *The History of the Royal Society of London*, 1756, Vol. III, p. 395.

John Ericsson in 1835*. In this a restriction in the tube took the place of the non-return valve.

Thomson's original intention had been to paint the inside of his tube with aniline blue which would wash off as the water entered and reached it. He later adopted the chemical tube which had in fact been patented by T. F. Walker in 1879 †.

The Thomson sounding machine was widely adopted and, until the perfection of echo sounding, remained the most convenient apparatus for the purpose, especially after the addition of an electric motor made the drudgery of deep water sounding a thing of the past.

Echo Sounding.

In 1911, Alexander Behm, a German, showed that it might be possible to measure depth of water by timing the echo of an underwater explosion. Other countries began experiments. The United States Navy took up the idea in 1917 and by 1922 echo sounders were a practical proposition and were being fitted. In 1924,

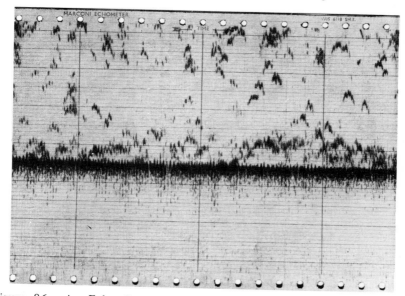

Figure 86   An Echo Sounder Trace, showing echoes from fish above the bottom echo. (Copyright: Marconi International Marine)

* *Nautical Magazine*, 5 (1836), p.390.
† Patent No. 3487, dated 30th Aug. 1879.

the Behm system was being tried in the United Kingdom. In this system a cartridge was fired on one side of the ship and the echo was recorded by a hydrophone on the other. An instrument measured the time between the two sounds and consequently the depth of water. In the same year the Royal Navy was experimenting with other equipment which had been developed on its behalf by Henry Hughes. In this system the sound was produced by a gong. In both these systems single soundings only were measured and there was a possibility of a human error. However, by 1931 the Admiralty equipment had been greatly improved by the addition of a continuous automatic record which provided a traced curve showing the depth of water at all times. If the bottom is very soft over rock it is possible to get a double trace and a similar result can be obtained when passing over a shoal of fish (Fig. 86).

Even with the original set the Admiralty was sufficiently encouraged to push on with its introduction into the Navy and starting with the M.V. *Asturias* in 1925 a large number of merchant vessels followed suit. Once the depth recorder became a success the echo sounder became almost a must. It has been found of particular value in surveying ships.

Eight
Tides

The Mediterranean sailor was not much bothered by tides. The maximum rise and fall in the sea was only about three feet at Gibraltar and Venice while in other places it is much less. In north European waters it was a very different matter. With a possible rise and fall, such as ten feet at the Isle of Wight, twenty feet at Dover and over thirty feet at Liverpool, and tidal streams which might reach three knots off the coast and much more in narrow channels, the navigator was presented with two problems. There might not be sufficient depth of water to allow his ship to pass over shoals to reach his port, or the tidal stream might be so strong that he could not get in against it or even make progress along the coast. For example, in light winds a vessel coming up the English Channel might need to anchor while the ebb tide was running towards the west. For these reasons one needed to know the time of high water.

In spite of the small tidal rise and fall in the Mediterranean the existence of the tides was known to the Greeks from quite early times. The first mention of them which has been traced is by Herodotus (484-428 B.C.) who refers to those in the Red Sea, where a range of about twelve feet occurs. The connection between the moon and tides was noted by Pytheas of Massilia (Marseilles) about a century later. He is said to have been the first man to make tidal observations and to have recognised the link between the phases of the moon and the height of the tide. Aristotle had also heard it said that there was some connection.*

When Julius Caesar landed in Britain in 55 B.C., he hauled his ships above the high-water mark and thought that they would be safe. Unfortunately he apparently did this at neap tides, and when springs came round some floated away and were lost and others were damaged.†

Strabo (c.54 B.C.-24 A.D.) describes the tides of Denmark, Britain, Portugal, Spain, Italy and the Persian Gulf. He tells us that

---

* The information in this and the next two paragraphs is mainly derived from the historical introduction, by Harold D. Warburg, in the *Admiralty Tide Tables*, 1916.
† Caesar's *Commentaries on the Gallic War* Bk. IV, Chap. xxix.

the nature of the ebb and flow of the tides had been fully treated by Poseidonius (c.135 − 50 B.C.) and his pupil Athenodorus Cananites (c.74 B.C.-7 A.D.). The works of both of these are now unfortunately lost. He points out that the direction of the current in the Straits of Messina seems to be connected with the tides and discusses their effect upon shipping using the estuaries between Cape St. Vincent and the Straits of Gibraltar.*

Pliny in his *Natural History* gives a detailed account of the tides and comments that those at the equinoxes rise higher than those at the solstices. He refers to the effect of confined waters upon the tides and claims that in the Eubœa Channel there can be as many as seven in the twenty-four hours.† This would appear to be an exaggeration but in these very confined waters curious effects do occur, especially in high winds, and though the spring range is only about two and a half feet, tidal currents of up to eight knots occur.

The first tide tables forecasting the times of high water are believed to have been compiled by the Monks of St. Albans in the thirteenth century. They give the time of high water at London Bridge for each day of the lunation. These must have been very useful to the watermen who thronged the river. To use these tables it was of course necessary to know the age of the moon and the time of day, but the first of these would always have been known to anyone whose constant business was on the water and the time could be guessed with sufficient accuracy for the purpose.

The production of these tide tables for London Bridge must have continued, for Flamsteed noted in 1683 that 'hitherto our tide tables have only shown the time of one high water',‡ presumably that occurring during daylight.

When tidal information began to be available to seamen it was customary to state the bearing of the moon when it was 'full sea', instead of giving the time of high water, for the various ports frequented. Though this bearing is generally taken as that of the moon on the days of new and full it did, in fact, give a rough indication of when it would be high water throughout the lunation, sufficient for ordinary purposes. As the time of high water would get

---

* Strabo, *Geography*, Book I, Chap. iii, ∮ 11 & 12; Book III, Chap. ii. ∮. 4.
† Pliny, *Natural History*, Book II, Chap. xcvii.
‡ *Philosophical Transactions of the Royal Society* , Vol. XIII. p. 10. Of this Halley wrote: "Mr Flamstead's Tide Table is wholly owing to one Phillips Observations long sinse, who living upon London Bridge had thereby particular Opertunitys of making the same." British Museum Ad.MS. 30221, page 184.

later each day, so the time at which the moon would reach the appropriate bearing would come later also.

An early form of tide-table was a diagram, consisting of a map of the British Isles with adjacent coasts of Europe and a drawing of a compass card, the various points of which were joined by lines to those parts of the coast where it would be full sea when the moon was on that particular bearing. Tidal diagrams of this sort are known to have been produced by the Breton Guillaume Brouscon in the 1540s, but the device may well be older. From Chaucer we hear that the Shipman could:

But of his craft to rekene wel his tydes

His stremes and his daungers him besydes*

so it is evident that the tides were reasonably well understood by 1390.

This method of linking times of high water with the bearings of the moon was still used as late as the beginning of the seventeenth century. In 1574 Bourne is giving us lists of ports under each point of the compass at which it would be high water when the moon, new or full, was on that bearing. In 1594 Davis still uses an illustration of a compass card with the places appropriate to a full sea marked against each point. Polter, in 1605, tells us that sailors often made mistakes because they thought that the bearing of the moon for full sea was a compass bearing instead of a true one so did not allow for the variation.

Gradually the sailor broke away from the habit of linking high water with the bearing of the moon and began to connect it with time. At first we find the two concepts running concurrently. Seller in 1669 and Newhouse in 1701 give a section for each point of the compass under which appears the time of high water for each day of the lunation, besides a list of places to which each bearing is applicable. They also introduce an innovation — details of the areas where the main tidal stream sets in the given direction.

By the first quarter of the eighteenth century manuals of navigation were only giving times of high water on the days of full and new moon, usually called the H. W. F. & C (High Water Full & Change) of the port. At a rather later date this came to be called the Establishment of the Port. From these times that of high water at any other period of the lunation could be found by adding

* *Canterbury Tales*, Prologue, lines 401, 402.

forty-eight minutes for each day of the moon's age. Many seamen ran into some small error by allowing forty-five minutes only.

Some books introduced a most complicated calculation. To obtain the time of high water it was necessary first to obtain the time of the Moon's Southing, i.e. the time when the moon was on the meridian of the place. First there had to be obtained the Golden Number, a figure relating to the 19-year cycle before the moon returns to the same position in the heavens. This was the remainder after adding one to the year and dividing the sum by nineteen. Next the Epact was the remainder after multiplying the Golden Number by eleven and dividing the product by thirty. The Epact is actually the age of the moon at the beginning of the year. The Moon's Age was the remainder after adding the Epact to the day of the month and the Figure for the Month and dividing the sum by thirty. The Figure for the Month was zero for January, one for March, two for February or April, three for May, four for June, five for July, six for August, eight for September or October and ten for November or December. Lastly, the time of the Moon's Southing was four-fifths of her age with twelve minutes added for each hour. This rather complicated calculation was avoided by many books which gave tables of the times of the moon's southing.

According to William Hutchinson in *A Treatise on Practical Seamanship*, 1777, the normal way of forecasting the time of high water at Liverpool was found to be very inaccurate, so after keeping records for many years Richard and George Holden published predictions for that port from 1773.

Liverpool was by no means the only port where tides were found to be irregular. The river Thames also has irregular tides as had been noted by the monks of St. Albans long ago. It is therefore not surprising, especially in view of the busyness of the port, that when the Admiralty considered the issue of predictions their first should be for London Bridge. From 1834 to 1916 the *Nautical Almanac* contained the times and heights of high water at London Bridge for every day of the year. In addition it contained a list of places throughout the world with their establishments.

Already the *Admiralty Tide Tables* were appearing. In 1833, a small pamphlet was issued giving the times of high water at London Bridge and at three other places in the United Kingdom. In 1835, the tables were expanded to give both times and heights of high water at nine ports in Britain and at Brest. In addition a list was provided of tidal differences for thirty-three other ports enabling the navigator to obtain the times and heights of high water at these by applying the correct difference to the predictions for the appropriate standard port. Through the years the number of ports with predictions and with tidal differences was steadily increased, the secondary ports being extended to northern Europe in 1841, to the Bay of Biscay in 1850 and to Gibraltar in 1853.

In 1858, a section giving ports throughout the world at which the High Water Full and Change had been ascertained was added to the *Admiralty Tide Tables*. For the first two years the range of the tide at springs and neaps was given for some of the ports, but from 1860 the rise above datum was substituted.

In 1897, the times and heights of low water as well as those for high water were given for the more important ports and this feature was gradually extended.

In 1910, predictions for five German ports were added and in the following year other foreign and some colonial ports appeared. There were still very few, fourteen for the rest of the world compared with twenty-six for the British Isles.

Starting in 1835 a few notes were given on the direction of tidal streams in the vicinity of ports. This feature grew until it became quite extensive. In 1909 this information was transferred to a new publication entitled *Tides and Tidal Streams* and after that year this section disappeared from the *Tide Tables*.

By 1920, low water was being predicted for all standard ports, of which there were now twenty-eight in the British Isles and thirty-four abroad. In this year there was a further innovation. The tables of tidal differences became amalgamated with those of the establishments of ports in a separate volume which had been started for the latter in 1910.

Harmonic Method of Computation.

The tide is considered as being made up of a large series of harmonic constituents. While these are all taken into account in the predictions for a standard port, for ordinary purposes predictions for a secondary port can be advantageously obtained from the more important ones only.

Since 1927 the principal harmonic constitutents for various ports have been provided in the *Admiralty Tide Tables* together with necessary tables to enable the height of the tide at any particular time to be calculated. The times of high and low water are not given directly by this method and the navigator has to compute the height of the tide for several exact hours and then to plot the results to find out what he requires.

By 1971, the *Admiralty Tide Tables* have been so expanded that they now require three volumes to cover the world. In the first, which is for European waters, there are now thirty-four standard ports in the British Isles and twenty-four for the rest of Europe, besides well over a thousand secondary ports. The other two volumes are even larger. Truly, the progress over the last sixty years has been remarkable.

To find the height of the tide at any time intermediate between high and low water a simple table was originally provided assuming a regular rise and fall. This was followed after some years by a diagram on the same assumption. Few places however conform to simple rules. The first move to improve knowledge in this respect was made in 1911 when tables giving the tides inside the Isle of Wight appeared, followed in 1917 by one showing the stand of the tide at Rosyth. Improvements in this respect culminated in 1964 with the inclusion, for each standard port in the British Isles, of a diagram illustrating the rise and fall.

It must not be thought that the British *Admiralty Tide Tables* are the only ones in existence, for other nations produce their own publications. An early example was the *Annuaire des Marées des Côtes de France,* first compiled in 1839 by A. M. R. Chazallon, not, however, the first venture in that country. There are also unofficial publications such as *Brown's Nautical Almanac,* which prints tide tables for a number of ports, some not included in the Admiralty publications.

The Survey of India issued *Tide Tables for the Ports of Bombay and Kurrachee* from at least as early as 1873. Tidal ovservations had been made since the beginning of the century. In 1880 Edward Roberts, who was to remain an assistant in the Nautical Almanac Office until 1907, took over the calculations of the predictions for this publication and continued to be associated with it until 1906, by which date it had been extended to include forty ports. Roberts also worked out the predictions for Halifax (Nova Scotia), Singapore and Hong Kong.

Another regular publication, issued since 1903, is *New Zealand Nautical Almanac & Tide Tables,* and the list of such could be considerably extended.

As ships become larger tides have more and more effect upon their movements. An early example was in the spring of 1916 when it was decided to send the battleship TEMERAIRE to Belfast for a brief refit. This had to be timed between two spring tides, for even if she were lightened by being run short of coal she could only get in at high water on a few days each side of the highest tides. One of the principal jobs to be tackled was the fitting of a new bridge, for the original one had proved inadequate for wartime conditions in northern seas. The new bridge had been prefabricated in one of the southern yards at which it had originally been intended that the ship should refit, and it was now planned to send the component parts to Scapa Flow by a collier and that the TEMERAIRE should then take it with her to Belfast. The collier was delayed on her voyage north by a series of heavy gales and kept the battleship waiting so that she did not reach Belfast until the last possible high water for her entry during that part of the lunation. It of course followed that her late arrival curtailed the length of her stay, limited as it was by the necessity of getting her out during the next spring tides. The time was too short for the bridge to be fitted and the ship's officers had to shiver when at sea for the rest of the war!

Fifty years ago few ships exceeded a draught of thirty feet. Increase was at first steady and it was only during very recent years that the figure has risen sharply. In the near future draughts will reach ninety and even one hundred feet, introducing new problems.

There are parts of the world where such factors as strong winds may affect the height of the tide. The *Admiralty Tide Tables* from 1921-1937 provided special tables for estimating the height of the tide under such conditions at Wilhemshaven and from 1924-1937 in the Rio de la Plata. Most people will be familiar, if only through their newspapers, with occasions where a combination of strong winds and high spring tides has caused disastrous flooding on the North Sea coasts. In 1953, high water in the Netherlands was ten feet above prediction. It is not generally recognised, because less apparent, that exceptionally low tides are just as common. In 1967, a low water seven feet below prediction, occurred at Southend. Although on a normal day predictions about the British Isles may be considered accurate within four inches and ten minutes, in an average year there will be several occasions on which the best predictions may err by as much as two or three feet.

As to the question of chart accuracy, this must of course depend upon the standard of the survey and this will probably be affected by its age and the importance of the area. The chart of a much frequented port will usually be kept extremely accurate by frequent resurveys, though depths may even be reduced by careless dumping. Even in a very careful survey something may be missed. I had an experience of an unexpectedly shallow sounding in the early 1920s. A merchant ship in charge of a pilot passed through Keppel Harbour, Singapore, at dead low water springs and should have had five feet under her bottom, but just touched. The pilot was accused of taking the ship too close to a reef, which he of course denied. One of His Majesty's Surveying Vessels, being in the neighbourhood, was asked to investigate and I went away in a steam cutter to sound the area. The first time that I crossed it one of my leadsmen called a single sounding which was five feet less than those immediately before or after it, or than the depth shown on the chart. Challenged, he was certain that he was right. I spent the day crossing and recrossing the area and was unable to repeat the shallow sounding, but nevertheless I was convinced that I could trust the leadsman and there must be something there. In the end a diver went down to look and he found two slender columns of rock standing on the bottom, one being three feet and the other five feet high and neither more than a foot in diameter. It was upon the summit of the higher of these that the leadsman had lodged his lead.

When the navigator had only to consider a draught of thirty feet things were seldom difficult. Except at dead low water, spring tides, the five-fathom line always represented a safety limit for him. Most navigators reckoned to allow at least six feet under their ships' bottoms, considering that that margin gave amply protection against inaccuracy in their tidal predictions or in their charts. Waters where the height of the tide was of importance were usually close inshore and pilotage, with the local knowledge involved, would be compulsory.

With ships which now require the fifteen fathom line or thereabouts as their safety margin, matters are very different. The fifteen fathom line is much further out at sea than the five and with increasing distance from the shore the charting of waters which are just safe becomes more difficult. Tidal predictions which are based on observations made near to the shore become less accurate at a distance from the coast. At the bottom of these deeper waters water movement can often cause sand waves which may reduce the depth of the water by as much as three feet. Yet at this time there is a demand from ship owners for an increased accuracy of prediction which would enable their ships to operate with a reduced safety allowance under their bottoms. The demand is understandable. If not met, some channels may be unusable for very large ships. Whereas the lightening of a 10,000-ton ship, sufficiently to reduce her draught by a foot might be no great matter, to reduce the draught of a ship of 200,000 tons by a similar amount might mean the reduction of cargo by something like 4000 tons.

Nine
Modern Developments in Navigation

By Captain Leonard Holder

A general review of the last 30 years.

The changes which took place in navigation up to 1939 were comparatively slow. Any ingenious device which was proposed was allowed a long period for development, and even then the introduction was slow, because the cautious, conservative mariner tended to rely on his well tried methods. For example, the gyro-compass was fitted in some merchant ships from about 1919, but the magnetic compass was still favoured by many mariners twenty years later.

The urgent needs of the Second World War and the rapid advances in technology which arose from and followed them, accelerated changes in navigation, to such an extent that the mariner has found it hard to keep abreast of developments.

The years 1934 and 1935 saw the independent invention of radar in Britain and the U.S.A. It was referred to as "RDF" (Radio Direction Finding) in Britain; the word RADAR (Radio Detection and Ranging) was coined in America. Radar went to sea in 1937 in U.S.S. *Leary*, and in 1939 in H.M. Ships RODNEY and SHEFFIELD. These radars were fitted mainly to give warning of the approach of enemy craft and could not be termed "navigational radar".

The needs of bombers for an accurate position fixing system led to the rapid development in Britain, in 1940, of the hyperbolic system called Gee (Fig. 87). A similar system, Loran, was proposed in the U.S.A.. By 1942 Loran chains were established in the North Atlantic, Gee was in full operation around Britain and over North West Europe and, on the other side of the conflict, the German "Sonne" rotating long range radio beacon had been established. These navigational aids were used by aircraft and ships as soon as the equipment became available, and as with radar, there was often a conflicting demand on supplies. In 1943 and 1944 marine navigation made great advances. The invasion of Europe called for accurate navigation in conditions of great difficulty, with cross tides, the possibility of rough seas, and

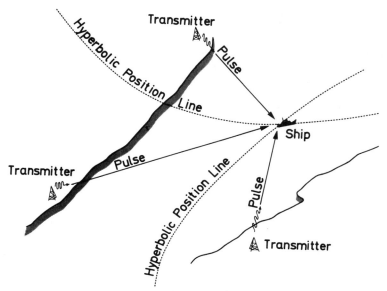

Figure 87   A Hyperbolic Navigation System.

no guarantee of good visibility, even though D-Day was in June. Electronic aids played a vital part in this operation. New 9 cm. wavelength radar, which gave improved definition over the older 1½ metre sets, was used, and the presentation was also improved by plan position indicators which gave an all-round "picture" rather than the older A-scan displays which only looked in one direction at a time (Figs. 88 and 89). The Decca navigator system (referred to as "QM"), which was a new phase-comparison hyperbolic navigational aid, was available for the first time.

The end of hostilities left the navigators of the world with a selection of new navigational aids, none of which had been designed for peacetime use. Great initiative was shown by Britain in arranging the 1946 "International Meeting on Radio Aids to Marine Navigation" (I.M.R.A.M.N.). The conclusions arrived at by delegates to this meeting provided the basis for specifications of radar and radio navigational aids, and most of their work remains valid today.

The first of the Consol radio beacons were set up in 1946. These beacons radiate a pattern of coded signals and were developed from the German Sonne beacon. Many merchant ships had surplus Admiralty type 268 radar sets, and the specifications for a navigation

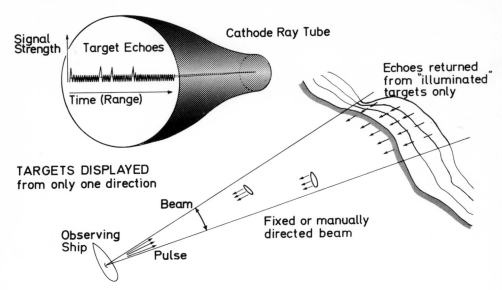

Figure 88   A-Scan Display.

and collision avoidance radar suitable for merchant ships was drawn up. Prototype sets were produced and installed aboard H.M. Ship FLEETWOOD for demonstration purposes and manufacturers soon followed with commercial equipment which embodied all, or most of, the suggested features.

The first Decca Navigator equipment produced for commercial marine use was the Mark IV, introduced in 1947 (Fig. 90). It was designed to operate on the Decca English chain — the only one existing at that time. Coverage of the world by the Decca system is still far from complete, but there were thirty-eight chains in 1971, in Europe, North America, South Africa, Australia, Japan, India and the Persian Gulf.

The port of Liverpool created a precedent in 1948 by establishing a port radar service to give advice to vessels, particularly to those navigating in poor visibility without shipboard radar. In the same year the Decca Navigator Company improved their system by the introduction of lane identification which enabled the mariner to set up, or reset, the receiving equipment without reference to an accurate fix by some other method.

There followed a period of gradual development and greater use of electronic navigational aids, and in the case of radar, several cases of misuse, or rather misinterpretation. Relative motion radar, with a display on which "own ship" stays fixed at the centre, and all other targets show their *relative motion,* was in general use (Fig. 91). This type of display needs an associated plotting board and a plot to show the heading of any other ship. Hence, the introduction in 1957 of true motion radar which gave this information very quickly was heralded as an end to plotting problems.

The year 1957 also marked the setting up of an operational Loran C chain in the Eastern U.S.A. This system was developed to combine the long range performance of Loran (the original Loran is termed Loran A), with the accuracy of phase comparison techniques. Whilst it achieves this aim, the receivers are very expensive, and though the range exceeds 1000 nautical miles, it would require very many stations for world-wide coverage.

The harnessing of nuclear power led to the development of new types of naval craft in the U.S.A., USSR and in Britain, including the nuclear submarine. These missile-launching vessels could remain submerged for long periods, in fact the crew's endurance became

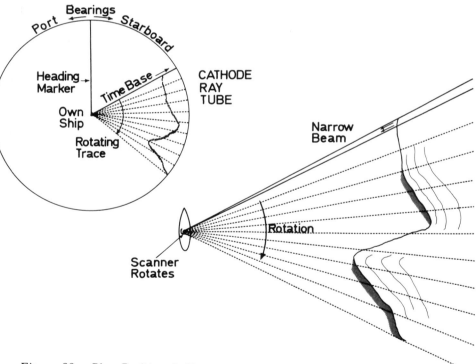

Figure 89   Plan Position Indicator Display. Continuous rotation of scanner produces all-round picture.

Figure 90   Decca Navigator Mk IV Display, 1947. (Courtesy of the Decca Navigator Co.)

more important than the fuel consumption. This versatility would be seriously curtailed if the submarine had to be brought to periscope (or aerial) depths to fix its position by astronomical or radio methods. This problem was solved by the use of inertial navigation. This system is very simple in concept: if the vessel's position is known at the start of a passage, and if the acceleration in two directions can be measured. then speeds and distances can be calculated and a final position ascertained. This is really an improved dead reckoning device using accelerometers. Beneath this simple statement there lies an almost incredible engineering feat. The accelerations due to speed and course changes on the vessel are very small compared with those associated with pitching, rolling, yawing etc. and compared with gravitational attraction, so that it is quite remarkable that these large items are eliminated and the remaining positional data is not only useable but highly accurate

The voyages of U.S.S. *Nautilus* and U.S.S. *Skate* under the polar icecap in 1958, using the American inertial navigation system marked one of the major milestones of post-war marine navigation.

Russia launched Sputnik I on 4th October 1957, and astonished the world. The signals which the satellite emitted were monitored in the U.S.A. by Dr. W. H. Guier and Dr. G. C. Weiffenbach of John Hopkins University, and within a year such signals were not only used to accurately track satellites, but Dr. F. T. McClure of that University had proposed an inversion of the problem, that is to navigate on earth by using the signals from an accurately tracked satellite. The first test satellite in the Transit series was launched in September 1959. Unfortunately it was unsuccessful, but the Transit navigation system now known as the Navy Navigation Satellite System (Fig. 92) has been in use for accurately positioning naval vessels since 1964, and was released for commercial use in 1967. This is a remarkable example of applied space technology and will probably be the first of many. Satellites which survey the earth from great heights are ideally placed to act as relay stations for messages, as weather stations, and navigational beacons. This potential is being explored, but the mariner must share the new technology with others — military and air force users, television networks, telephone subscribers etc. In 1967, the successful launch of A.T.S. 3 took place. This applied technology satellite is one of many in synchronous (stationary) orbit over the equator and has been used for navigation and communications tests with ships.

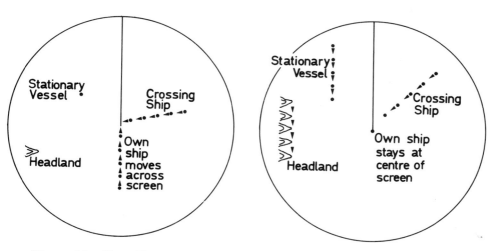

Figure 91   True Motion Radar, and Relative Motion Radar. *Left:* own ship tracks across the screen. All vessels show true course and speed. The same situation *Right:* displayed on Relative Motion Radar. Targets show motion relative to own ship.

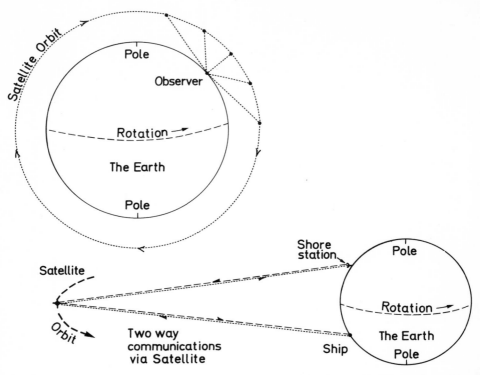

Figure 92   *Above* Navigation Satellite System. (Transit). Height about 600
nautical miles. Orbit takes about 90 minutes. Satellite in view up to about
fifteen minutes. Observer measures rate of approach by doppler technique.
Orbital data calculated on earth and re-transmitted by satellite.
Below A Geostationary Satellite in Equatorial Orbit. Orbital Period about
twenty-four hours (height 19,000 nautical miles). Rotates at the same rate as the
earth, and in the same direction. Position calculated by shore station using time
delay measurements on signals passed via two satellites. One satellite gives only
one position line.

Another navigation system is Omega (Fig. 93). It is a long range
phase-comparison system working in the very low frequency (VLF)
band. The radio waves in this band tend to follow the curvature of
the earth and world-wide coverage can be achieved with about eight
stations. By 1966 the Omega system was in limited use by the U.S.
Navy but in 1967 this great navy placed orders for more than one
hundred receivers for naval vessels.

Four stations are situated in Norway, Trinidad, New York and
Hawaii. It is hoped to complete world-wide coverage by building new

permanent stations in the following places: North Dakota, Norway, Hawaii, La Reunion, Argentina, Tasmania, Trinidad and Japan.

One of the main reasons for the development of the Omega system has been the need to up-date inertial systems in nuclear submarines with an external fix. The advantage of Omega is that the VLF signals can be received at considerable depths (about 20 metres below the surface), thus reducing the chances of detection.

In commercial spheres, 1967 saw the effects of a navigational disaster when the tanker *Torrey Canyon* spilled out her crude oil cargo in the western approaches to the English Channel, after stranding on the Seven Stones rocks off Lands End (Fig. 94). This has everywhere highlighted the dangers of environmental pollution and has created a public awareness of the problems of navigation and collision.

In 1968, various manufacturers of commercial radar introduced a new generation of displays with sophisticated plotting devices so that the data can be extracted more rapidly and accurately when the ship

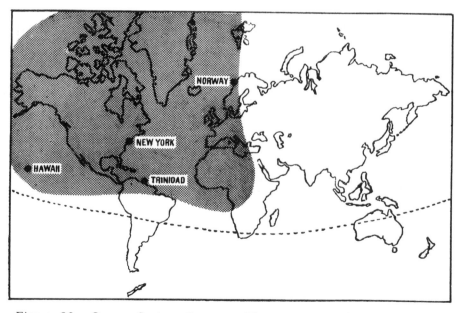

Figure 93   Omega System Coverage. The shaded area indicates present coverage using four transmitters. When the next two transmitters are installed this will extend to the whole area north of the dotted line.

Figure 94   The wreck of the *Torrey Canyon* broken in two and awash. (Crown Copyright Reproduced by permission of the Controller H.M. Stationery Office)

is in heavy traffic areas, such as the Dover Strait or Tokyo Bay. These include video-tape and computer-based systems. This concentration on collision avoidance is the result of experience, following many collisions (Fig. 95). It seems to indicate that true motion radar did not solve all the problems in radar presentation.

In 1968, the *Queen Elizabeth 2* was fitted with the very successful Navy Navigation Satellite System (Military version). This year was also marked by the availability of the commercial Omega receivers, one of which was also evaluated in the QE2.

The year 1969 saw another milestone in navigation when the tanker *Manhattan*, equipped with an integrated satellite/doppler sonar navigation system, sailed through the North West passage. This venture was to test the feasibility of exporting Alaskan oil to Atlantic refineries using this route (Fig. 96).

The introduction of a less accurate, cheaper version of the satellite navigation system for marine users began in 1971. Although less accurate than the military version, the accuracy is quite sufficient for ocean and landfall stages of the voyage. The sets on the liner *Prometheus* and tanker *Esso Scotia* may be forerunners of many more. The satellite system is the only worldwide all-weather system available now, but the needs of some ships will probably be better met by Omega, which is slightly cheaper, when it becomes available.

The introduction of electronic navigational aids has changed navigation in the last thirty years. However, there is still a great deal of art in the science of navigation and new projects, such as methods of farming the sea for food, will bring new challenges for the navigator.

Radio Direction Finding.

The great advances in wireless telegraphy made during the First World War led to attempts being made to use wireless station bearings as a means of fixing the position of a ship. This would have the great advantage of extending methods of coastal navigation to some distance out at sea.

Figure 95 *The Andrea Doria* goes down in Atlantic. The Italian liner of 29,083 tons lists heavily in the Atlantic off the coast of Massachusetts before sinking on the 26 July 1956. She had been in collision with the 12,644 ton Swedish liner *Stockholm*.

Figure 96 *The Manhattan* in ice conditions in the North West Passage.
(Copyright: Esso Petroleum Co.)

Three possible methods presented themselves:

(a) Use of directional apparatus in a ship to determine the direction of signals sent from the shore.

(b) Use of directional apparatus at one or more shore stations to take bearings of a transmission from a ship, the results being then passed to her.

(c) Use of a wireless beam rotating at a known speed. As it passed through north a distinctive signal was made and thereafter a steady transmission. The recipient measured with a stop-watch the time between the signal for north and the instant when the main signal was at minimum strength, and the proportion borne by this interval to the time for a complete revolution gave the bearing from the station.

The Germans had been experimenting with the rotating beam when the war came to an end and by 1922 plans were afoot in the United Kingdom to set up one or more experimental transmitters. From a military point of view the scheme had much to recommend it, since the ship wishing to fix her position did not need to break wireless silence and no additional gear was required. The Admiralty erected a station near Gosport in 1926 and three years later another at Orfordness. Trials were made with both, especially the latter, where over 160 merchant vessels reported the results of their experiences within a year of its having become operational. In 1931 there were plans to erect another station at Rangoon.

The use of directional apparatus fitted in a ship and needing no communication with the shore was also attractive for ships of war but it was at first thought that the apparatus would be too expensive to justify its fitting in merchant vessels. This fear was soon dissipated. One of the first vessels to be fitted was the *Olympic*, about 1924. Her master found the set to be of the greatest value when entering the Channel in fog and even used it for obtaining the bearings of other ships of the same line who being outward bound knew their own positions with considerable accuracy.

Early experiments made before 1922 showed that its accuracy depended to a great extent on the configuration of the ship and on the skill of her operator, and indeed it was at one time thought that there were some types of ship in which it would be useless. This fear was groundless, however, but it was necessary to calibrate the set by an operation analagous to the swinging of a ship to adjust her compasses. The maximum error was found to occur when the bearing was on bow or quarter, the sign changing in successive quadrants.

Another possible cause for error was, of course, that depending upon the gyro-compass, for as the bearing taken was one relative to the heading of the ship at the instant of observation this had to be applied to a reading of the ship's head to obtain the true bearing.

By the outbreak of the Second World War the use of shore wireless stations to take bearings of ships had become well established, but since the introduction of radar it has been little used. Stations were usually grouped so that they could give a fix by cross bearings. It had been found that accuracy was greatest when the station was near the coast and when the bearing did not cut the coast line at an oblique angle.

While the use of directional wireless was confined to about twenty-five miles from the coast it was possible to treat the bearing as one would a compass bearing and to plot it direct upon a mercator chart. With the increase of range this was no longer possible, for the bearing observed is along a great circle and so the bearing has to be corrected by half the convergency of the meridians before it can be plotted.

Another source of error is due to the signal being received either by ground ray which is reasonably accurate or by atmospheric ray which is less so and has its effect at closer distances during the period from one hour before sunset to one hour after sunrise. The accuracy of bearings can therefore be assumed to be within 2° at distances up to 300 miles by day but only up to twenty-five miles at night. By night, errors of up to 4° are to be expected at between 100 and 500 miles.

The direction finder is most useful in the landfall section of a passage and is used to fix the ship's approximate position whilst still well off shore (over twenty-five nautical miles). When visual and radar fixes are obtained, with their superior accuracy and speed of plotting, the WTDF is not used. Navigating officers in modern merchant ships gain very little experience in the use of the instrument, as landfall areas are critical points in the voyage and there are many other duties which need attention, particularly collision avoidance in the heavier traffic of coastal regions. As the usefulness of aural WTDF depends very much on the acquired skill of the operator, and this skill was not widely available, there were many ships in which the WTDF was seldom used except for statutory tests. Cathode ray tube displays and automatic reading WTDF sets have been considered and evaluated since 1946. A major step was made in 1960 when a commercial automatic WTDF was fitted in the *Scottish Monarch* and since that time the number of automatic sets has increased considerably.

In some ships with aural WTDF, the master required the radio officer to take the bearings, because he was familiar with WT signals and listening to morse code. With the introduction of visual indication of signal strength on a meter, and with fully automatic bearings, the aural skill is no longer required, bearings can be taken more quickly, and the new sets are more widely used by navigating officers.

RADAR: Collision Avoidance

Radar had a greater impact on marine navigation than any other device developed during and after World War II. The introduction has not always been uneventful, and accidents have been caused by misuse of radar information, particularly in collision cases.

The early P.P.I. (plan position indicator) displays were used in "ship's head up" orientation, with the bearing scale giving angles to port and starboard. This enabled easy correlation of the radar 'picture' with the view from the wheelhouse window, but made it difficult to· take bearings. An early improvement was the incorporation of a gyro repeater in the radar, so that true bearings could be read off at any time even if the ship's head was changing. This speeded up the reading of bearings needed for anti-collision plotting (Fig. 97).

Relative motion radar, showing the resultant movement of other vessels and "own ship", calls for careful plotting and construction to determine the true course and speed of other ships (Fig. 98). When traffic became congested and there was little time to construct a plot, a few navigators abandoned this method and developed a "rule of thumb" which seemed to work. If, in poor visibility, a vessel looked as if it were going to pass close they altered course a few degrees "to give her a bit more room" (Fig. 99).

If one or both vessels on reciprocal courses took this action, the manoeuvre was successful, but if the courses were slightly crossing the effect was very different.

There have been many collisions attributed to the cumulative turn (Fig. 100) where one or both of the vessels concerned made this type of alteration, notably the collision in the English channel in September 1961 between the *Crystal Jewel* and *British Aviator,* and within a few hours in the same area, the *Niceto de Larrinaga* and *Sitala.*

There was a genuine dilemma amongst mariners as to whether the collision regulations, which contained rules designed for manoeuvring

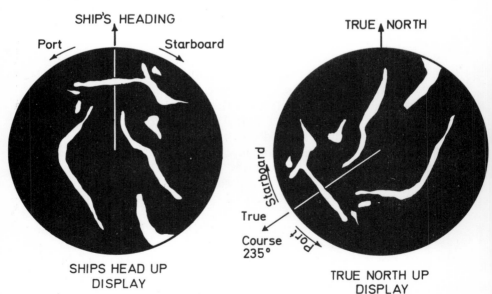

Figure 97   Two ways of displaying radar bearings of the view shown above to give *left* relative bearings and *right* true bearings.

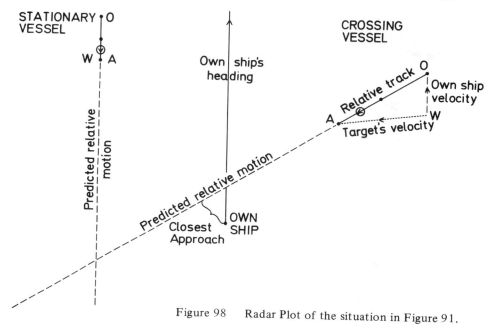

Figure 98   Radar Plot of the situation in Figure 91.

in clear weather, still applied to vessels in radar contact. The International Conference on Safety of Life at Sea, held in 1960, partly resolved the problem by stating that the Rules (numbers 17 to 24) applied only to vessels in sight of one another. There was an annex to the Rules added, but the advice it gave was rather sketchy and there is still a great deal of debate on the desirability of introducing far more rigid rules which will state suitable manoeuvres for all weather.

The successful navigator in poor visibility must proceed at a speed which allows information from the radar to be assimilated, and must be alert to the danger of meeting different types of vessel, for example those without radar, vessels fishing or vessels otherwise restricted in their ability to manoeuvre. He must pay attention to other vessels which may become a threat as well as to those at close quarters. To help provide the data in an easy form several plotting devices are available. A very basic one is the anti-parallax reflection plotter which allows plotting with a wax pencil, over the tube face (Fig. 101).

The Decca ARP (Automatic Relative Plotter) introduced in 1962

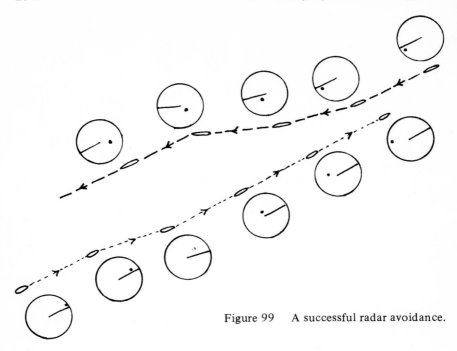

Figure 99   A successful radar avoidance.

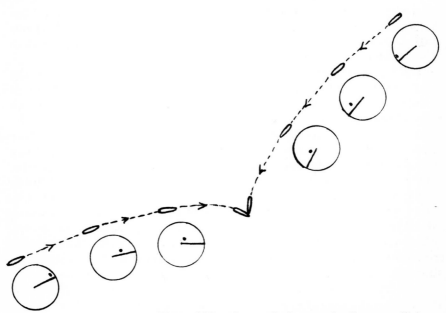

Figure 100   A cumulative turn leading to collision.

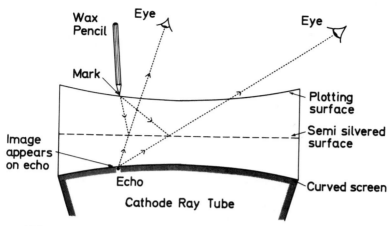

Figure 101   The Anti-Parallax Reflection Plotter for radar displays. The plot appears to be superimposed on the screen.

went further; a true motion radar was connected to a relative plotter, and plots were made simply by operating a switch at the display (Fig. 102).

Another radar introduced in 1962 was the Kelvin Hughes photoplot which used time exposed film of a small P.P.I. and extremely fast processing to produce a twenty-four inch diameter plot. Developing, fixing and washing the exposed film takes less than four seconds.

The increasing expense and complexity of modern radar has often been questioned by ships' officers, who would prefer two simple, yet reliable, radars to one very sophisticated set. Most large vessels are now fitted with at least two radars. In pursuance of simplicity, the Decca ARP has been superseded by the Decca AC66, which is a true motion radar with a simple but effective method of assessing collision risk by using markers produced electronically on the screen.

The search for more rapid processing of radar data has continued, and 1968 brought two new radars onto the commercial market. The AEI A4 Computer Predicting and Automatic Course Tracking (COMPACT) Radar (Fig. 103), which has a built-in electronic computer, will track selected targets and draw on the screen a green line indicating the target's course and distance in a selected time interval. By varying the Track Ahead time control it is possible to assess the nearest approach to the ship on this radar. It is also possible to display the effect of altering the ship's course and/or speed, before any action is taken.

Figure 102 Decca True Motion Radar and Automatic Relative Plotter. Selected targets are plotted by operating a switch at the radar position. (Courtesy: Decca Radar Limited).

The Marconi Predictor radar uses video tape techniques to store information from the radar and it can be recalled in any of three ways: True Tracks mode giving the true course and speeds of vessels over the last 1½, 3 or 6 minutes, which allows the navigator to assess the heading of other vessels (Fig. 104); Relative Tracks mode to allow an assessment of nearest approach and collision dangers; and Predicted Relative Tracks mode to assess the effect of own ship altering before action is taken.

These very advanced radars have speeded up the display of other ships' manoeuvres, but there are still many vessels with no radars,

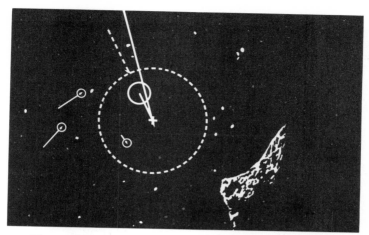

Figure 103   A.E.I. 'Compact' Radar/Computer Display.
(Courtesy: G.E.C.-A.E.I. (Electronics) Ltd)

yachts and barges for example. There are also vessels with very simple installations, like many tugs and coasters. In poor visibility the limitation of accidents finally rests on the skill, experience and diligence of the navigating officers and masters of all the vessels at sea.

Radar for position fixing

The greatest value of radar for position fixing lies in the accuracy of range measurement, and the ability to use it in all weathers and at night in areas where navigation marks are sparse. The problems associated with its use are, however, that some objects give poor response and may not show at all on the screen, and that others may show on the screen in such a way that they are difficult to identify.

The D-Day landings in 1944 saw a major advance in radar position fixing. Earlier radars had shown only large land masses, poorly defined, and they tended to be regarded as clutter or unwanted echoes. It is possible to predict mathematically which hills and features should show in the radar, and the results obtained by a radar survey craft show a remarkable correlation. The radar used in this case was an adaption of an aircraft navigation set, using 9 cm. wavelength. Later in 1944 3 cm. wavelength equipment was available, which further improved the definition of the 'picture'.

Figure 104   Marconi Predictor Radar in True Tracks Mode. (Courtesy: Marconi
Company Ltd)

Radar navigation took another step forward when transparencies
made up from photographs of actual radar pictures were used, rather
than theoretical predictions. These transparencies could be pieced
together into mosaics which could be correlated with the normal
navigational chart. These techniques were used in the Scheldt trials
of November 1944, when the importance of keeping supplies moving
in spite of frequent fog, led to a concentration of effort. On 19th
February 1945 a passage was made from Antwerp to Flushing in
conditions of dense fog, radar navigation being used throughout.

The British Admiralty began a project in the Thames estuary in
1945 which was to add to the knowledge of blind pilotage
techniques. Navigational buoys were introduced long before radar
and because the shape and size of them is such that not much radar
energy strikes them, and much of this is not returned, the radar
detection range is poor. When there is sea clutter or rain clutter they
may not be detected at all. ("Clutter" refers to unwanted echoes
from these sources.)

To improve the response of buoys, and give them a better chance
of detection, reflectors were fitted (Fig. 105). However, the echo of
a buoy with a reflector looks similar to that of a tug, coaster, fishing

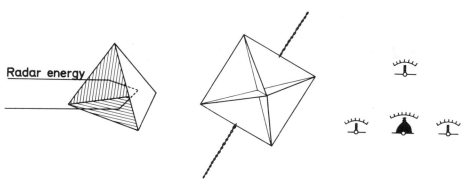

Figure 105   A single corner reflector.
An octahedral array.
A pattern of buoys with radar reflectors.

boat or other target, so the fitting of reflectors does not solve the problem of identification. This applies particularly to isolated landfall buoys, where ships may anchor nearby to await a tide or an improvement in visibility. Trinity House fitted reflectors to buoys and laid them in clearly defined geometrical patterns in the Thames Estuary as part of the project and these patterns were immediately recognisable on the radar screen. Unfortunately, in clear weather, some mariners tend to pass close to seamarks and the patterns lose their distinction in fog when one or more of the buoys has been run down and is missing. The expense of laying and maintaining these patterns has not proved justifiable in the long term. However, there are many places in which patterns of buoys or beacons occur fortuitously, and pilots and officers of regular trading vessels make good use of them.

The normal charts used by ships in 1945 were drawn for pre-radar times, when visual recognition was all important. The consideration of adapting them to show radar conspicuous features, or providing separate charts, received much attention. The Hydrographic Department of the Admiralty produced special charts for the Thames project, which had special distinctively coloured land height contours, making them easy to use in the dim lighting needed for radar observation. The problem of compromise between this and normal usage of the charts took a long time to resolve; from 1949

* Satow, Patrick Graham (1950) *Admiralty Chart 2649* – a Chart Adapted for use with Radar. Journal of Inst. of Navigation, (3, 22)

the Institute of Navigation assisted the Admiralty in evaluating a special version of the English Channel chart* which had been revised to include features to assist the radar user. The detailed colouring was not included but land contours were shown. Since 1955 the revision of charts has included the most useful features of this experiment. The charts still resemble the pre-radar charts rather than the radar mosaics which created such interest in earlier years.

In the winter of 1945-6 trials in blind pilotage were carried out in the Solent and in the Thames Estuary, in FLEETWOOD and POLLUX. From these trials the Royal Navy developed blind pilotage techniques, and discussions took place at the Institute of Navigation* concerning merchant ship applications. Individual master mariners, such as the late Captain Ellis Milne Robb, took a great interest in radar and developed their own techniques. Captain Robb, of the Blue Funnel Line, used radar fixes of shore objects to clear off-shore shoals.†

Many pilots and shipmasters took an interest in the potential of radar for pilotage, but few were in such a fortunate position to make use of it as the officers in the short sea trade. The pilot who boards a vessel at a pilot station is usually taking over conning in congested waters on an unfamiliar bridge, and with a radar set which has been 'set up' by the ship's officers. The radar controls may be labelled in a foreign language and will probably be arranged in an unfamiliar way, as there is no standardisation in the layout of switches. The pilot has, therefore, to cope with an unfamiliar ship in his familiar waters. The master, or officer, of a short voyage vessel, who cons his own ship into port has the advantage of a familiar radar set as well as familiar surrounding land and seamarks. Hence, the techniques of radar pilotage have been developed to the greatest extent in these specialised vessels, where radar is also used in clear weather as a primary navigational aid, and is used in the approach to the berth as well as in the estuarial phase of the voyages. In normal pilotage work, the radar is used to advantage in restricted visibility and at night, but the visible marks, lights and transits are more widely used.

The widely held opinion in 1946 was that some means would have to be provided for correlating the radar P.P.I. and the chart, if useful coastal pilotage was to be achieved with radar. There are two methods of correlating the information, the easier of the two being to project the chart image onto the P.P.I.. The U.S. Navy had used this technique in 1946, but the Royal Navy demonstrated a device in the FLEETWOOD which would project the P.P.I. 'picture' onto the

---

* *Blind Estuary Pilotage* – A discussion (1949) Institute of Navigation Journal (2, 57)
‡ Robb, E. M. (1961), *Precise Radar Conning* – Ibid. (14, 202)

Figure 106   Navigational Chart Comparison Unit, for viewing the radar and navigational chart simultaneously. (Courtesy: Barr and Stroud Ltd)

chart. This chart comparison unit (Fig. 106) was developed commercially, but has never reached the widespread usage which was originally envisaged.

Another interesting device is the radar beacon. In fact, the 1½ metre wavelength radars of the early war years were used for navigational fixing, despite their very poor bearing resolution, by taking bearings of coastal radar beacons which had been established for aircraft.

The two beacons considered by the 1946 I.M.R.A.M.N. were the U.S. Type AN/CPN–6 and the British Admiralty Type 952. Both these beacons were of the responder type which could be triggered by 3cm. wavelength marine radar. They also had a common feature which made them unlikely to be accepted for general use – they required modification of existing radar sets, and additional circuits.

The 'ramark' radar beacons tested at St. Catherine's Point and Portland Bill by the British Admiralty Signal and Radar Establishment in 1949 provided bearing information, and indentification of navigational marks, but did not provide range information. The range still had to be measured from normal coastal echoes. These beacons are not triggered by the user and produce a continuous line on the P.P.I. which may mask other nearby echoes.

The racon responder beacons were established in the *Tongue* lightvessel and *Bar* lightvessel. These beacons "sweep" the 3cm. marine radar band (9,320-9,500 MHz) and so can be received without additional equipment. They are seen as a series of dots and/or dashes starting just beyond the echo of the racon fitted vessel (Fig. 107). The beacon provides a very clear identification of the lightvessel, enhances the range of detection very slightly (although still limited by the radar horizon) and will provide range and bearing information.

The success of the racon, and development of small reliable transistorised transponders, led a working party (1962-1964) to recommend that racons should be fitted at fifteen sites, with further sites to follow. Thus, the racon has proved itself superior to the ramark and is likely to be in much wider use in the future. It is particularly useful in wide estuaries, near low sandy coastlines and in similar areas where the land echoes are poorly defined and the ships, buoys and off-shore structures may produce situations in which recognition of navigational marks is difficult.

Responders have long been used in the air to identify friendly aircraft (I.F.F.), and there have been many suggestions for identifying special classes of ship by fitting them with a responder beacon. For example, deep draught vessels which are restricted in their manoeuvres might show a coded flash. There seems little likelihood in the present structure of international discussion and conference that this will come into use, however, particularly as its usefulness is debatable. As with any recognition sign, if it is too widely used, the eventual effect can be confusion.

Problems of recognition are also likely to occur in the use of shore-based radar to assist in pilotage. Port radar service was established in Liverpool in 1948, to aid in the safe passage of ships in the River Mersey in poor visibility, and also to assist in estuary conservancy work. It is possible to identify buoys on the radar and to check their positions at regular intervals and rapidly report any that are out of position.

In Liverpool, as with most other shore-based radar stations, onus of identification is upon a vessel which requests radar advice and is usually effected by referring to a buoy or beacon, for example "This is British Ship *Georia,* I am two cables west of the *Bar* Lightvessel, heading 120°." This reference to geographical position is used

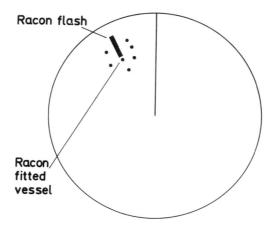

Figure 107   (a) A RACON identifies a light vessel amongst anchored craft.

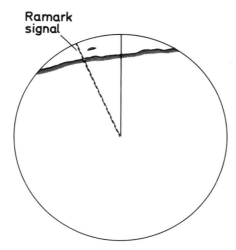

Figure 107   (b) A RAMARK beacon gives
bearing information on a featureless coast.

extensively in port radar services but does not work well when the
ships are well clear of land or seamarks. If the identity of a vessel is
established by the shore radar operator, he is then able to plot the
subsequent track of the ship and keep a note of the ship's name on
the plot.

The role of port radar services has never been clearly defined, and there was a great problem in early installations, in that the radar information was available ashore, but communications were inadequate to make full use of it. Increased fitting of VHF radiotelephone in merchant ships has helped pilots who would otherwise have been required to carry portable radio telephones to receive shore advice.

In the early stages, port radar services offered advice to vessels in fog which had no radar, or whose radar was broken down. This could be advice on where to anchor safely until the weather cleared, or could be adequate for a complete approach to locks or berth from the port entrance. The use of shore-based radar for conning a ship is analagous to Ground Controlled Approach for aircraft, and requires a measure of mutual understanding which is difficult to achieve in practice. Much depends on information which is available to the shore operator only, such as the track of the vessel, or to the pilot on board only, such as the rate of swing of the ship's head, whereas what is really required is a combination of information.

The next method of using the port radar service and one which is much more frequently applied, is for the shore operator to keep a general eye on a ship and give the pilot details of hazards in the channel ahead, such as ships at anchor, or approaching on reciprocal courses, whilst the pilot uses the ship's radar on very short range scale (say ½ nautical mile range) to con the ship. Situation reports on obstructions in the channel, vessels manoeuvring, etc. are usually provided in all visibilities by the harbour advisory service, and not just in fog.

The evolution of port services has taken another move forward with the use of computers to provide an overall traffic flow pattern for the benefit of all harbour users. In the programming of traffic flow it seems likely that port radar will in future be used for surveillance to supply information, along with other navigational aids, to a central control which will endeavour to make sure that the traffic flows freely. Some moves in this direction have already been made by the authorities in the Panama Canal who have installed a location and computation system, and in the New Waterway in Holland where traffic flow is partly regulated from a shore-based control.

Recent Improvements in Navigation by Reckoning

Most navigation consists of taking fixes at intervals and relying on navigation by reckoning between fixes. If the position fixing system in use is one in which fixes cannot be obtained at any required time, and if the interval between fixes is extended, then the errors in reckoning become very important.

Most vessels still estimate positions from course steered, speed through the water, and an allowance for current and weather effects. Whilst the course can be steered more accurately by improvements in the automatic steering, and the speed through the water can be assessed more accurately by improved logs, the allowance for current and weather is limited by the navigator's knowledge of his ship and his environment.

The meteorological services of maritime countries are continually amassing and analysing data on annual patterns and short term variations in current as sent in by observing ships. Improved accuracy in position fixing systems will improve the quality of this information, and electronic data processing methods will facilitate sorting, analysis and storing of the information, but it is a vast problem, and perfect prediction of current and weather effects will never be achieved.

In some vessels the errors have proved totally unacceptable and a new solution has had to be sought. The problems of the nuclear submarine have already been mentioned. With long intervals between fixes and uncertainty of sub-surface currents, and poor performance of compasses in high latitudes, the problem was critical.

The increase in off-shore exploration for oil has involved use of the satellite navigation system, in order to survey, mark and re-locate sites outside the coverage of shore based aids. The satellite system is capable of very great accuracy in fixing, errors being less than one tenth of a nautical mile in a moving vessel, and considerably better on a fixed platform. However, in a moving vessel, the drift in the period of about 1½ hours between fixes downgrades this accuracy to an unacceptable level.

Two possible means are now available to improve on traditional deduced reckoning techniques. One is the inertial system, the other the application of doppler techniques.

Beamed sound waves to detect underwater obstructions, submarines etc., had been used in World War II — the much lauded ASDIC system. The application of pulse-time techniques to measure

range is the principle of the echo sounder, but the comparison of
transmitted signal frequency with the frequency of the returning
echoes, to measure velocity, is a comparatively recent development.
In the doppler applications, either radio waves or sound waves are
compared in frequency with a standard and any change in frequency
is a measure of velocity.

The sound waves must be beamed from a transducer in the
underwater hull of the ship. They are likely to be reflected from air
bubbles, thermal layers, or suspended particles in the water. There
must be sufficient reflection from the sea bed to detect the returning
echo at the receiver; it is not normally possible to detect signals from
more than one hundred fathoms, but a 'water-referenced' return can
be used at greater depths. As the ship rolls or pitches, the projected
angle of the beam will change, so the transducers are fitted in pairs
facing in opposite directions. The mean of the frequency shifts from
the two transducers is used to assess velocity.

Application of these techniques (Fig. 108) to submarines was
obvious, but the extension of the system to merchant ships has been
envisaged and trials were held in the tanker *Esso Austria* in 1969.
The system tried here not only acted as a monitor for velocity along
the desired track and velocity across the track, but also served as a
berthing aid by displaying very small velocities in the approach to the
berth, and would analyse the swing of the ship's head and sideways
movement of the vessel, which is difficult to assess visually on very
large and slow-reacting vessels.

The use of doppler techniques underwater was concurrent with
the development of the same technique above water, but using radio
waves instead of sound.

In 1968 the Royal Radar Establishment initiated trials for the
Esso Petroleum Company, using two shore-based doppler radars to
measure the rate of approach of tankers to the berths at Milford

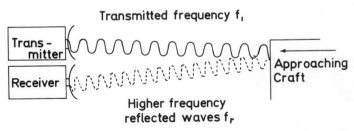

Figure 108   Principle of Doppler radar and Doppler sonar. Frequency
difference ($f_r - f_1$) is proportional to rate of approach.

Haven. These radars are similar in principle to the police radar "traps" used for measuring vehicle speeds. One radar measures the approach rate as the ship makes its approach down the last few miles of the channel (Fig. 109). The reading is relayed by VHF radiotelephone to the pilot. As the final approach phase is reached, two radars are required, one at the bow and the other at the stern so that any change of the vessel's heading can be detected. This equipment is now commercially produced and is being supplied to tanker berths in many countries, including the Persian Gulf states and Japan.

The doppler radar as described is a berthing aid (Fig. 110), but these techniques are likely to be applied in the future to integrated navigation systems. If a stable signal, such as an Omega transmission, can be detected and compared in phase with a very stable oscillator on board, then the phase-shift or doppler-shift can be used to determine the velocity of the vessel. Two such readings could determine the movement of the ship for a short period with great accuracy, and allied to the accuracy of a system such as the Navy

Figure 109 Doppler speed of approach measurement indicator (SAMI) measuring the rate of approach of a tanker to Texaco's Milford Haven oil terminal. (Courtesy: Marconi Marine)

Figure 110   Doppler Speed of Approach Measurement Indicator (SAMI) turned 90° to measure the approach velocity of the tanker's stern. (Courtesy: Marconi Marine)

Navigation Satellite System, could provide continuous accurate positions.

Doppler navigation involves the integration of velocities to find change of position, and uses transmitted sound waves or radar waves which can be detected by the enemy if they are used in naval vessels. They also are limited to the maximum range at which a returned echo is detectable, unless the 'local oscillator/stable transmission' technique is employed.

Hence the need to revert to an even more basic measurement, that of acceleration, to provide position through double integration, first to find speed, then distance. This inertial navigation (Fig. 111) is completely free from outside detection, not even requiring receiving aerials. The precision required to obtain and maintain the extremely high accuracy required in engineering and electronics in this system makes it very expensive, though some have suggested that a less accurate inertial navigator, backed up by an error analysis and correction computer might be acceptable to a wider range of vessels.*

* Videlo, D. A., Wright, D. L. *Inertial Navigation for the merchant marine*. Inst. Navigation Journal (23, 221).

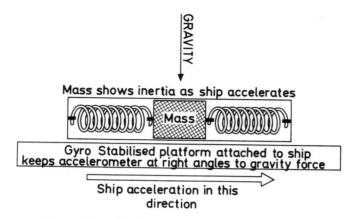

Figure 111   The Principle of Inertial Navigation.

Hyperbolic Position Fixing Systems

As an alternative to an accurate navigation by reckoning system, it is possible to navigate very accurately by fixing the ship's position so often that 'DR' errors are never allowed to accumulate. Ideally the fixing should be continuous and the plotting instantaneous. Whilst this can be achieved in some systems, and is almost imperative in aircraft where track-plotting flight logs are used, some delay is tolerable in most situations at sea.

The hyperbolic systems which are available include Consol, Decca Navigator, Loran and Omega.

Consol

The accuracy obtainable with Consol is not sufficient for coastal navigation, and the coverage is limited to parts of the north Atlantic. The accuracy also depends greatly on the skill of the operator, and this is directly related to his experience of the system. There are few vessels which can make use of the system, as the Consol fix is likely to be less accurate than the estimated position, and the coverage coincides with Decca Navigator coverage, the latter being far more accurate.

Small craft navigators are the major users. They have difficulty in maintaining a steady course even in moderate seas, many have no Decca Navigator or radar, so make frequent use of Consol. On ocean-going liners the system, which is primarily designed for aircraft, merely serves as a check.

The Norwegian authorities in 1961 appointed a committee to investigate the demands for electronic navigational aids, with particular reference to fisheries. It is significant that their decision was to install two systems, Decca Navigator for accurate coastal navigation, and Consol for ocean coverage. Three new Consol stations are being built at Andøya, Bear Island and Jan Mayen. Previous impetus for the extension of Consol coverage had come from a plan proposed by the International Civil Aviation Organisation technical committee in 1956.

Consol differs from the other hyperbolic systems in that the baseline is very short (about two to three nautical miles) and the position lines approximate to great circle bearings of the station. Overprinted lattice charts or tables can be used with the system, but craft within 25 nautical miles of the station are advised not to use Consol. In common with other hyperbolic systems the useful coverage is limited to two sectors on each side of the baseline, the areas 'behind' the aerials (the baseline extensions) being liable to ambiguous and erroneous readings.

The range of Consol is said to be 1200 nautical miles, but at that range the usefulness of the system is limited by the magnitude of errors.

Decca Navigator

The Decca Navigator system is based on proposals by W. J. O'Brien and was first used under the code name 'QM' in the Normandy landings of 1944. The principle of phase comparison of continuous wave radio signals is used, with four stations laid out in a star formation; the master at the centre and the slaves at 120° intervals (Fig. 112).

The slaves are designated red, green and purple; each combines with the master to provide one position line which is appropriately coloured on the chart. The coverage extends nominally to 240 nautical miles from the master station, and at any position within the area two position lines will normally be available. The coverage is limited by interference from skywaves which make the signals erratic at long range, especially at night and in high latitudes in winter. This range, however, can be considerably exceeded particularly in summer and with the latest equipment.

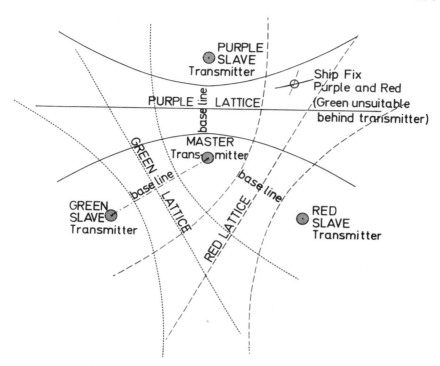

Figure 112   Decca Chain: normal layout with four stations.

Accuracy within the groundwave coverage area is better than ¼ nautical mile and the system is used for landfall, coastal navigation and in certain cases, for estuarial pilotage. Continuous wave phase comparison systems all have the tendency to "lane-slip" under certain conditions, that is, to read the correct lane fraction but to be one complete lane in error. This tendency means that the Decca Navigator must be carefully set up and checked at frequent intervals. With the wartime 'QM' and the post-war commercial Mark IV equipment the checks had to be made by other navigational aids. This restricted the Decca Navigator to the role of an improved "DR" aid over short periods of a few hours. The introduction in 1948 of the Mark V receiver with lane identification was a major advance, as additional signals provided a course pattern by which the lane number could be checked without reference to other methods of navigation. The Decca Navigator was thus self-contained and use could be extended beyond immediate coastal areas. The Mark V lane identification signal tended to be more liable to skywave distortion than the basic decometer signals, making long range night-time signals erratic, but this problem was resolved in 1962 by the introduction of the Mark 12 receivers with 'multipulse' lane identification (Fig. 113).

The Mark 12 receiver which provided rapid tuning and quicker lane identification sequences, also allows the use of inter-chain fixing techniques at long range, using the best position lines from two or more chains and thereby again extending the useful coverage.

Decca Navigator has become a must for most coasting vessels in coverage areas, and for fishing vessels even down to those less than thirty feet in length. The provision of the equipment in ocean-going vessels is carefully considered, in the light of the likely length of time that the vessel will spend within the coverage area, the hazards of navigating without this all-weather aid, and the economics of the

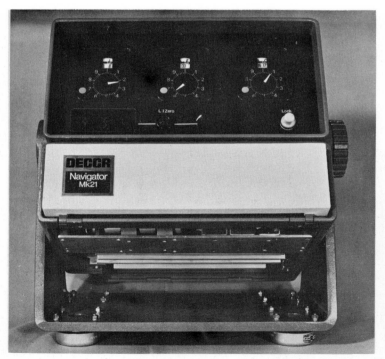

Figure 113   Decca Navigator Mark 21 Display. (Courtesy: Decca Navigator Company Ltd)

ship's operation. A vessel which visits northern Europe once or twice a year and spends most of its time outside the coverage is unlikely to be fitted, but with extension of Decca coverage to South Africa and Japan and the increasing importance of maintaining schedules, the number of vessels fitted is continually increasing.

Fishing vessels are able to return to the same Decca co-ordinates to fish in prolific 'holes', and some fishing vessels make use of track plotters driven by two Decca readouts. The charts are constructed so that the hyperbolic lattices are represented by rectilinear axes, thus distorting the land and geographical features. Owing to this distortion, the charts are only suitable for use in particular work such as hydrographic surveying, under sea oil exploration, cable laying, buoy maintenance and dredging, or for fishing where marks can be plotted and tracks planned in advance and followed accurately on the track plotter (Fig. 114).

Figure 114   Decca Track Plotter. (Courtesy: Decca Navigator Company Ltd)

Short sea trading vessels, ferries and naval craft frequently make use of homing techniques using Decca Navigator, where the vessel is conned on a course which coincides with a Decca position line or cuts it at a predetermined angle. This practice is not altogether desirable if it leads to a concentration of traffic on reciprocal courses near to focal points in traffic lanes, as may happen if a Decca lane passes approximately along a much frequented route.* Deliberate use of homing techniques has been made in the entrance to the New Waterway, to keep deep draught vessels in the long dredged channel leading in from seaward towards Europoort. The stations were set up ashore so that the hyperbolae coincide with the two main legs of the approach course.

Homing techniques remain fairly specialised, however, and the normal use of the Decca Navigator is to plot the position in coastal areas by reading the co-ordinates and plotting them on a lattice chart. Early Decca charts were simply used for plotting and the fix transferred to a normal corrected navigational chart. Current practice is to keep the Decca charts corrected for normal navigational warnings and to dispense with the re-plotting.

With cheaper digital computers available and the requirement to have accurate and instantaneous knowledge of the vessel's position, particularly for deep draught tankers in narrow waters, it is inevitable that a track plotter will be produced which presents fixes derived from Decca Navigator on a standard undistorted chart. Already this technique has been applied to hovercraft navigation in the Sealane project initiated by the Ministry of Technology to enter service in 1971.

Loran and Gee

Gee was proposed in 1937 by R. J. Dippy, in the United Kingdom, and was developed in 1940 to meet the needs of the British bomber force. Loran (Fig. 115) used a lower radio frequency at which the groundwave coverage was better than Gee, especially over sea areas. Loran is a long range navigational aid as its name implies; it was proposed, developed and brought into operation in the U.S.A. between 1940 and 1943.

Both systems use pulsed transmissions from master and slave stations and by measuring the time interval between the arrival of

---

* Warning in Board of Trade Merchant Shipping Notice No. M.594

master and slave pulses at the ship it is possible to determine a line of position and plot it on a lattice chart. A second reading from another pair of stations will give a fix. To read and plot a fix takes about one to two minutes for a skilled operator, which is considerably longer than plotting a Decca fix. A major advantage is that the groundwave pulse arrives before the skywave pulse and can be differentiated from it on the cathode ray tube display. This enables the system to operate up to ranges of 700 nautical miles by day. It was found that the skywave reflections from the E-layer of the ionosphere were stable enough to use and, by applying skywave corrections, extended coverage up to about 1400 nautical miles may be obtained at night, albeit with slightly less accuracy.

Coverage areas are mainly in the Pacific, and the Atlantic coast of the U.S.A.; hence few European vessels on the major trade routes to South America, South Africa or the Far East, would find it beneficial because they are seldom in the coverage areas. The system has been fitted to most American vessels on North Atlantic or Pacific routes and to many vessels of all nationalities in the U.S. coastal trade. It is also widely used by fishing vessels in northern waters. The sets can be bought outright and the stations are maintained by government agencies (mainly the U.S. Coastguard). This differs from the Decca

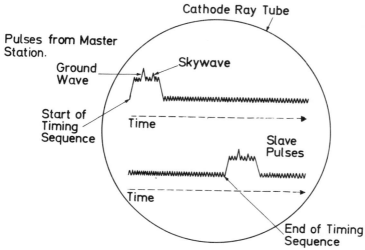

Figure 115   Loran Display: the skywave pulses arrive after ground waves, so they are shown to the right.

system, in which the sets can only be hired as the revenue is used to maintain the transmitting stations.

In 1944 experiments in the U.S.A. attempted to produce a Loran system in a still lower frequency band to extend groundwave coverage still further. These were interrupted after the war, but revived in 1955 leading to the establishment of the first Loran — C chain in the eastern U.S.A. in 1957. This system is widely used for military purposes, and by using phase comparison techniques plus pulsing, gives high accuracy, unambiguous lane identification, continuous readouts suitable for driving track plotters; in fact it combines the advantages of Decca Navigator and the older Loran — A. The main disadvantage is the high cost of receiver equipment which will take full advantage of the range and accuracy of the system and the limited number of established chains, so that its use is mainly confined to military vessels, survey and oceanographic vessels and a few trading and fishing vessels which spend long periods within the coverage and can justify the high cost, or can make do with less accurate receivers which are cheaper.

Gee was used around the United Kingdom during the Second World War but was never widely used in merchant vessels. The system was very limited in range (about 200 nautical miles over sea, less over land) and was never likely to be extensively used for ships in peacetime, though it proved very valuable to naval vessels in wartime, despite enemy attempts to jam it. The resistance to jamming of Gee and Loran pulsed signals as opposed to continuous wave transmission offers a military advantage.

Omega

The further extension of Loran coverage is likely to be curtailed because the Omega system should provide worldwide coverage with fewer stations (eight instead of hundreds) (Fig. 116).

In 1946 proposals were in hand for very low frequency Decca, to take advantage of the extended groundwave coverage of the VLF band transmissions. Subsequent proposals were made by the Decca Navigator Company under the title DELRAC (Decca Long Range Area Coverage) in 1954, and field trials were carried out, but the system was not commercially viable.

The Omega system which is very similar in principle, was developed in the U.S.A. by the U.S. Navy Electronics Laboratory and came into limited use in 1966. This system uses phase

Figure 116   Omega receiver with two 'line of position' recorders alongside.
(Courtesy: Marconi Marine)

comparison techniques similar to Decca Navigator and is thus
susceptible to the same lane slipping and requires accurate fixes to
set it up in the correct lane. The lanes are about eight nautical miles
wide on the baseline between stations.

The eight stations will not be arrranged in chains but will all be
synchronised to a single time standard, so that any two stations can
be phase-compared. The lane readings will be plotted on a lattice
chart as with Decca Navigator, with one difference, Decca readings
need only to be corrected for minor errors introduced through
assuming ideal conditions in calculating the lattice. With Omega, the
skywave interference causes phase shifts in a diurnal cycle, which are
predictable and are published in several volumes of tables. The errors
are large and must be corrected if the published accuracy of one
nautical mile by day and two nautical miles by night are to be
achieved.

A lane identification system is provided for in Omega by using
frequences other than the basic 10.2 KHz. The effective lane widths
are twenty-four nautical miles and seventy-two nautical miles. The
additional cost of lane identification may discourage some ship
operators, but some problems have been experienced in early

single frequency equipment through losing 'lock' on the signals and experiencing difficulty in 're-acquiring' them. It is premature in 1971 to assess the usefulness of Omega to shipping as the system is not fully established and the signals are not up to full power.

One possible use of Omega is in differential mode, in which a receiver at a fixed shore station monitors the errors of the signals, and the corrections are broadcast to ships in the vicinity. In this mode, the tabulated errors are not used, and the closer to the monitoring station the ship approaches, the more accurate become the fixes. With automatic correction using this method errors may be as low as one hundred metres.

Changes in Route Planning

The Ocean Phase

Methods of forecasting sea wave systems were developed during World War II to predict conditions during beach assaults. After the war the methods used were adapted to predict the optimum track for vessels on ocean routes. The route selected could be chosen for minimum time on passage or for the most favourable sea state. The efficiency of this weather routing depends on the accuracy of forecasting the sea conditions, and the skill in predicting the effect of those conditions on ship performance. There was some scepticism about its viability, but in 1956 the U.S. Hydrographic Office initiated a ship routing programme,* and tests were carried out using vessels of the U.S. Military Sea Transportation Service which had an ideal fleet for such experiments, including many ships of the same class. The success of these experiments and the results obtained by commercial weather bureaux showed that the method was efficient.

There is some divergence of opinion as to whether the route planning should be ashore, in the forecasting centre, or on board where local conditions can be assessed. Following experimental voyages in 1967 the British Meteorological Office established a shore-based routing advisory service and about the same time several ships were being routed by the masters and officers on board with the aid of weather chart facsimile receivers. These instruments are similar to the recorders used to receive newspaper photographs by

---

* Hanssen, George L. and James, Richard W. (1960) *Optimum ship routing.* Journal of Inst Nav (13,253).

radio or wire, and had been intended for transferring information between meteorological centres (Fig. 117). However, the demand was such that regular broadcasts of weather and wave conditions are now supplied for ships. There are good services in well frequented waters such as the North Atlantic, but in the southern hemisphere there are large areas where little data exists and the service is poor.

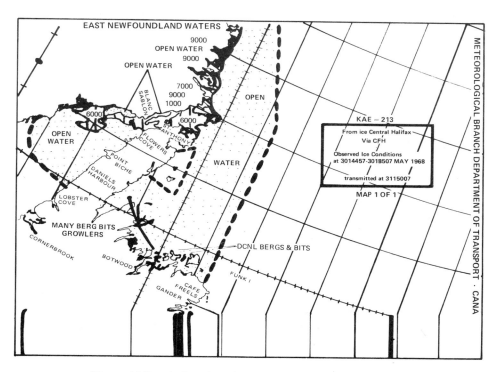

Figure 117   A drawing of an Ice Chart received by radio.

Ideally the routing is based on the shore advice tempered with a knowledge of local conditions assessed by the master who should be in possession of facsimile charts. Many ships still use climatological routes which take account of time of year rather than weather forecasts for a few days ahead. This method works quite well in predictable monsoon conditions but is less effective if conditions vary as they do in depressions.

The Coastal Phase

The concentration of traffic in focal areas of sea lanes, the higher speeds possible in restricted visibility by using radar, and a rising awareness of the dangers of pollution from oil spills, led to a critical situation off some coasts. In September 1960 the Institute of Navigation set up a working group to discuss the organisation of traffic in the Dover Strait and co-operation between Britain, Germany, France, Belgium and Holland, and consultation with other users of the Strait through I.M.C.O. (Intergovernmental Maritime Consultative Organisation), has led to the establishment of a traffic separation scheme. Inward bound vessels for the North Sea ports use the French side of the Channel, outward bound ships use the English side. Coastal zones are set aside for inshore traffic. By cutting down the number of end-on encounters these routes have reduced collision hazards, and the scheme has been extended to many other focal areas (Fig. 118).

The Future of Marine Navigation

The philosophy of automation is to make machines perform simple routine tasks and release men to tasks which are more productive and require initiative. The use of automation involves changes in education, training and social patterns, and its effects are being experienced at sea.

A typical example of automated navigation is the almost universal use of automatic pilots on ocean passages. There are many ships which use autopilots on coastal routes and are only steered manually in the final port-approach phase. The helmsman or quartermaster, who acted as an extra pair of eyes to keep lookout, has been made redundant, crews are smaller, and the officer on watch has added responsibility. Attempts to automate the lookout function using radar-actuated alarms, are not yet perfected.

The Russians in 1963 devised a remotely controlled vessel with no crew on the bridge or in the engine room, with machines working out the route. It is perhaps significant that this tanker was operating on the Caspian Sea where international laws and agreements are not involved. The likelihood of complete automation of navigation in normal vessels is still remote, and we shall depend for many years to come on the foresight, skill, alertness and judgement of navigating officers. Automation will, however, assist the navigator by removing

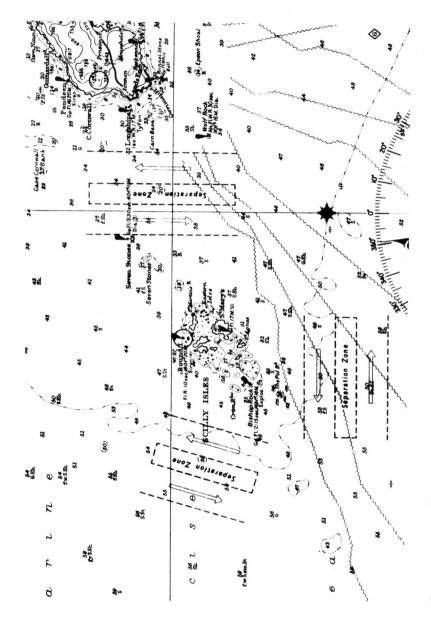

Figure 118   Traffic Separation Zones off Lands End and the Scilly Isles. (Reproduced from British Admiralty Chart No. 2649 with the sanction of the Controller H.M. Stationery Office and of the Hydrographer of the Navy).

the routine tasks and providing information to assist his decisions. The comparison of the gyro and magnetic headings is usually carried out by a device which actuates an alarm if they differ by more than, say five degrees, from the expected values. When the alarm goes, the navigator must assess the cause and take the necessary action. This automatic checking can be extended to position fixing, and a digital computer will receive information from various navigational aids and warn the navigator if there are discrepancies between them.

More accurate position fixing gives the mariner far better statistical information on ship performance and this can be analysed by electronic data processing methods. More accurate logs give better assessment of speed through the water, and more accurate weather forecasts give predicted conditions.

The high capital cost of ships, many of which are for specialised scheduled trades, and the cost of terminal facilities which must be used to full advantage, make the efficiency of the ship vital to a transport system.

The development of electronic navigational aids gives a challenge to the mariner to adapt his art to make use of them in much the same way as the change from sail to steam changed the routing and pilotage techniques in earlier years. The navigator who regards the changes from 'navigational art' to 'navigational science' as a curb to initiative can still set out in a small craft to follow Sir Francis Chichester or Thor Heyerdahl in pursuit of adventure.

Bibliography

Some Historical Works

AZUNI, D. A.   *Disertation sur l'origine de la Boussole*, 1st French ed. 1805.

BENJAMIN, Park   *The Intellectual Rise in Electricity*, 1894.

COSTA, A. Fontoura Da   *A Marinharia dos Descobrimentos*, 1938.

COTTER, Charles H.   *Brief History of Nautical Logs to A.D. 1800*. (Journal of the Institute of Navigation, Vol. 23 (1970) pp. 187-195.)

COTTER, Charles H.   *A History of Nautical Astronomy*, 1968.

FRANCO, Salvador Garcia   *Historia del Arte y Ciencia de Navegar*, 1947.

GOULD, Rupert T.   *The Marine Chronometer*, 1923.

HEWSON, J. B.   *A History of the Practice of Navigation*, 1951.

KLAPROTH, M. J.   *Lettre sur l'Invention de la Boussole*, 1834.

MARGUET, F. P.   *Histoire Generale de la Navigation du XV au XX Siecle*, 1931.

MAY, W. E.   *The Double Altitude Problem*. (Journal of the Institute of Navigation, Vol. 3 (1950) pp. 416-421.)

MITCHELL, A. Crichton   *Chapters in the History of Terrestrial Magnetism*, I. (Terrestrial Magnetism and Atmospheric Electricity, (1932) pp. 105-146.)

MOTTELAY, Paul Fleury   *Bibliographical History of Electricity and Magnetism*, 1922.

NEEDHAM, Joseph   *Science and Civilisation in China*, Vol. 4, Part 1, 1962.

NORDENSKIOLD, A. E.   *Periplus*, 1897.

QUILL, H.   *John Harrison, The Man who found Longitude*, 1966.

RITCHIE, G. S.   *The Admiralty Chart*, 1967.

ROBINSON, A. H. W.   *Marine Cartography in Britain*, 1962.

TAYLOR, E. G. R.   *The Haven-finding Art*, 1956.

WATERS, David W.   *The Development of the English and the Dutchman's Log* (Journal of the Institute of Navigation, Vol. 9 (1956) pp. 70-104.) 1956.

WATERS, David W.   *The Art of Navigation in England in Elizabethan and Early Stuart Times*, 1958.

267

Treatises on navigation

Some of these are referred to in the text by the name of the author. The dates given are those of first editions.

ATKINSON, James   *Epitome of the Art of Navigation*, 1686.

BEZOUT, Etienne   *Traité de Navigation*, 1769.

BLUNDEVILE, Thomas   *His Exercises*, 1597.

BOND, Henry   *Seaman's Kalendar*, 1648.

BOND, Henry   *The Longitude Found*, 1676.

BOUGUER, Pierre   *Traité de Navigation*, 1753.

BOURNE, William   *Regiment of the Sea*, 1574.

BOWDITCH, Nathaniel   *The New American Practical Navigator*, 1802.

COIGNET, Michiel   *Instructions Nouvelle des Poincts plus Excellents et Nouvelles, touchant l'Art de Navigeur*, 1581.

CORTES, Martin   *Breve Compendio de la Sphera*, 1551.

DAVIS, John   *The Sea-mans Secrets*, 1594.

DECHALES, Claude F. M.   *L'Art de Naviger*, 1677.

DUDLEY, Robert   *Arcano del Mare*, 1546.

FOURNIER, Georges   *Hydrographie*, 1643.

GRANT, Charles, Viscount de Vaux   *The Means of finding the Longitude at Sea*, 1808.

HARRIS, Joseph   *Treatise of Navigation*, 1730.

HARRISON, Edward   *Idea Longitudinis*, 1696.

LECKY, Squire T. S.   *Wrinkles in Practical Navigation*, 1881.

MACKAY, Andrew   *The Complete Navigator*, 1804.

MACKAY, Andrew   *The Theory and Practice of Longitude*, 1793.

MARTIN, William Robert   *A Treatise on Navigation and Nautical Astronomy*, 1888.

MAURY, Matthew Fontaine   *A New Theoretical and Practical Treatise on Navigation*, 1845.

MEDINA, Pedro de   *Arte de Navegar*, 1545.

MOORE, John Hamilton   *The Practical Navigator and Seaman's New Daily Assistant*, 1772. From the 9th edition, 1793, this work was called *The New Practical Navigator*.

NEWHOUSE, Daniel   *The Whole Art of Navigation*, 1685.

NEWTON, Samuel   *The Art of Navigation*, 1715.

NORIE, John William   *A New and Complete Epitome of Practical Navigation*, 1805.

NORWOOD, Matthew   *System of Navigation*, 1685.

NORWOOD, Matthew   *The Sea-mans Practice*, 1637.

POLTER, Richard   *The Pathway to Perfect Sayling*, 1605.

RADOUAY   *Remarques sur le Navigation*, 1727.

RAPER, Henry   *The Practice of Navigation*, 1840.

ROBERTSON, John   *The Elements of Navigation*, 1755.

SELLER, John   *Practical Navigation*, 1669.

STURMY, Samuel   *The Mariner's Magazine*, 1669.

VAUX, *see* GRANT.

WRIGHT, Edward   *Certaine Errors in Navigation*, 1599.

Index

The names of all vessels have been collected together under the heading 'Ships'.

Where such prefixes as le, de, della, van, von, &c. occur in the names of individuals these have been ignored and they appear under the initial letter of the main word of the name. The prefix has however been retained in geographical names where by long usage it is always used.

Ranks and titles have been omitted.

In the case of the more common expressions of navigation only the more important references are listed.

270